ONE HUNDRED GREAT LIVES

ONE HUNDRED GREAT LIVES

by

NORMAN J. BULL, M.A., Ph.D.

Illustrations by Graham Humphreys

HULTON EDUCATIONAL PUBLICATIONS

© 1972
Norman J. Bull
ISBN 0 7175 0582 0

First published 1972 by Hulton Education Publications Ltd.,
Raans Road, Amersham, Bucks.
Reprinted 1977, 1980
Reproduced and printed by photolithography and bound in
Great Britain at The Pitman Press, Bath

Contents

Contents *continued*   *Page*

Contents *continued* | | *Page*

John Mark, the First Gospel Writer

JOHN MARK lived in Jerusalem in the time of Jesus. His parents had a fine house with a guest chamber built on the flat roof. He was only a young man when Jesus, the famous Prophet from Nazareth, came to Jerusalem to preach the Kingdom of God. Mark's mother became a follower of Jesus, and sometimes Jesus and his friends met in the guest chamber. Then they went away from Jerusalem and Mark wondered if they would ever come again. For he had heard that the Priests and Pharisees hated Jesus and wanted to get rid of him. It would be dangerous for him to come back.

Every year Mark looked forward to the Feast of the Passover, for it was an exciting time. Jerusalem was crowded with Jews from all over the world, and the city buzzed with news. That year it was more exciting than ever. Jesus had come back! Mark heard the strange story of how he had ridden into Jerusalem on an ass, and turned the tradesmen out of the Temple courts. How brave Jesus must be, and how Mark longed to see him again. At last the great day of the Feast came. In the afternoon two men came secretly and he heard them preparing the room overhead. When it was dark, he heard the tramp of feet on the outside stairs. Jesus had come to eat the Passover meal with his disciples in the guest chamber. Mark listened to the murmur of voices. He had to go to bed but he couldn't sleep. About midnight he heard them singing a psalm, and soon they were coming down the steps. Still in his night garment, Mark followed them down the quiet street, out through the city gate, over the brook Kedron, and up the slope to the Mount of Olives. They went into a Garden. Mark could just see them through the trees in the pale moonlight. He watched them there. Jesus went on alone and seemed to be kneeling in prayer. The group of disciples looked as if they were asleep. Suddenly he heard voices, footsteps, and the clink of armour. Lights twinkled among the trees. Mark crept nearer and hid behind a tree close by Jesus and his disciples. The soldiers burst into the Garden, led by a man who came up to Jesus and kissed him. Then tumult broke out. Mark was frightened and turned to run away. One of the soldiers saw the white of his garment and seized him. Mark struggled in terror, wriggled out of his linen shirt and fled naked. He did not stop till he got back to the safety of his home.

Mark heard the terrible news the next day. Jesus had been arrested, tried, and put to death on the cross. How sad it was. But the first day of the week came wonderful tidings. Jesus had risen from the dead and shown himself to his disciples! Seven weeks later they had a wonderful experience in the guest chamber. The Spirit of Jesus came to them. Now they were new men and they began to preach boldly in the name of Jesus. Mark's house was their headquarters and soon John Mark was helping their leader, Simon Peter. He became a Christian and Peter baptised him. For a long time Mark was his faithful helper. Then his uncle, Barnabas, took Mark with him to Antioch. He went with Barnabas and Paul on their journey to Cyprus and Asia Minor. For some years he travelled as a missionary. Then Paul sent for him to come to Rome. Paul was a prisoner there, waiting for his trial, and Mark gladly went to minister to him. But Peter was in Rome, too, and Mark was remembered most of all as the disciple of Peter. They had known each other ever since those days when Mark was a boy in Jerusalem, and in one of his letters Peter spoke of him dearly as "Mark, my son".

It was in Rome that Mark did his greatest work. The wicked Emperor Nero attacked the Christians there in A.D. 64. Both Paul and Peter were put to death. No longer could Peter tell his precious memories of the life and teaching of Jesus. Mark decided to write them down so that they would never be lost. He wrote his Gospel in Rome about A.D. 65. When he came to Peter's account of the arrest of Jesus, Mark added his own story of how he had fled from the Garden.

His Gospel was the first to be written, and it was used by the writers of St. Matthew and St. Luke. So the Gospel of John Mark is the most precious book in the world to Christians.

2 Peter the Leader

How happy those first Christians were, with their new faith in Jesus! They still went to the Temple at the hours of prayer, like other Jews. But they lived in fellowship together, visiting each other's houses. Eagerly they listened to stories of Jesus, of his life and teaching and rising from the dead. They met together for prayer. Above all, they broke bread and shared the cup of wine together as Jesus had bidden them at the Last Supper. To show their love for each other, they shared all they had. The Church grew as more Jews were baptised. For the apostles preached boldly in the name of Jesus.

One day Peter and John were going to the Temple for the three o'clock service. A lame man lay on his mattress at the gate, where his friends brought him every day so that he could beg for money. He asked Peter and John. Peter said, "Look at us!" The man looked up eagerly, expecting a rich gift. "I have no money to give you," Peter said. "I can give you something much more precious. In the name of Jesus Christ of Nazareth, rise up and walk!" Taking him by the hand, Peter lifted him up. The man stood on his feet, amazed, and began leaping and dancing for joy. He went with them into the Temple to thank God. Everyone knew him, and an excited crowd gathered round them. Peter spoke to the people, bidding them believe in Jesus and begin a new life.

The Chief Priests heard of this tumult. They came with the guard and took Peter and John to prison. The next day they were brought before the Council to be tried, just as Jesus had been a few weeks before. Peter, filled with the Spirit, spoke boldly of Jesus and his rising from the dead. "It is in the name and power of Jesus that this lame man has been healed," he said. The Council ordered Peter and John not to speak again in the name of Jesus. "Are we to obey God or you?" Peter replied. "We must be witnesses of what we have seen and heard".

Peter and John were set free and went back to their preaching. Again they were put in prison, tried, beaten, and their lives threatened. Nothing could stop them, for they had no fear. So the Church grew in Jerusalem, with Peter the fisherman as a brave leader. He went to preach at the cities of Samaria, Lydda, and Joppa, too.

While Peter was staying at Joppa, by the sea, he had a vision. It showed him that God loves men of all nations. Now the Jews were taught by their Law to have nothing to do with people of other races, the 'Gentiles' as they called them. They believed themselves to be God's special people. Would it be right for Peter to baptise Gentiles who believed in Jesus?

At Cæsarea there lived a Roman officer, Cornelius, who loved God. He sent servants to ask Peter to come to his house. Peter came and preached to Cornelius and his friends about Jesus. They believed in him, and the Spirit of God came upon them. They were baptised and so became Christians.

When Peter went back to Jerusalem, the other apostles and all the disciples argued with him. They said, "You should not have gone to the house of a Gentile. You have broken the Law, sitting and eating with Gentiles!" Then Peter told them everything that had happened. He ended, "God gave his Spirit to them just as he has to us, for they too believe in Jesus. This is God's doing, not mine. Can I go against God?" Then the others argued with him no more. Instead, they praised God. "God welcomes Gentiles as well as Jews in his Church," they agreed.

About this time Herod the king began to persecute the Church. Many Jews were pleased. They hated the Christians because they mixed with Gentiles. When Herod saw how glad they were, he persecuted the Christians even more. The apostle James was put to

13

death. Peter was thrown into prison and chained up between two soldiers. He was to be killed, too. But wonderfully he was delivered out of prison. He had to flee from Jerusalem. He went to Cæsarea and stayed there with his Christian friend Cornelius, the Roman centurion.

Peter must have taken a ship from Cæsarea to Italy. For he went to Rome, the capital of the Roman world. He was a brave leader of the Church there, too.

Then the Roman Emperor, Nero, began to persecute the Church. The Christians had to meet in the underground passages at Rome, called 'catacombs'. Some ran away. There is a legend which tells how Peter was fleeing from Rome when he had a vision of Jesus coming into the city. "Lord, where are you going?" he asked. Jesus said, "I go to Rome to be crucified." "Lord, are you being crucified again?" "Yes," said Jesus, "I am being crucified again." Then Peter was ashamed, and with new courage went back to Rome, back to certain death. He was crucified by Nero about A.D. 65.

The mighty cathedral of St. Peter was built over the tomb of this brave 'fisher of men'. He is remembered every year on June 29th as a great Christian leader.

Paul, Apostle of the Gentiles

1. Saul the Pharisee

As the Church grew in Jerusalem, there were many tasks to be done. The apostles had to care for the sick and the poor, widows and orphans. But their most important work was to preach and teach about Jesus.

The twelve apostles and many of the first Christians were Jews of Palestine. They spoke Aramaic, the language of Jesus. But some were Jews who had been brought up in other lands and spoke Greek. They began to grumble. "Our widows are not being cared for," they said. Peter called a meeting of the whole Church. "The work is growing too much for us," he said. "We twelve must devote ourselves to preaching and worship. We need helpers. Choose seven men, full of the Spirit of God, to look after these tasks." The people were very pleased and chose seven helpers, or 'deacons', to assist the apostles. They were all Jews from other lands who spoke Greek. One of them was called Stephen, a man who loved God very much and was full of his Spirit. As he went about the city many came to know him. For he was a fine Christian and he spoke of Jesus with great courage and sincerity.

The Jews began to hate Stephen. They argued with him, but his wisdom and power were too much for them. False witnesses were hired to accuse him. He was seized and brought before the Great

15

Council. The accusers said, "This man has blasphemed against Moses and against God! He never stops speaking against the holy Temple and attacking the Law! He says that this Jesus of Nazareth will destroy them both!" The members of the Council—Scribes, Priests, and Pharisees—were horrified. For they lived by the Law and the Temple. If these went, their power would go, too. Stephen stood there, alone and fearless, his face shining like an angel. He began to speak. "You believe that God can be worshipped only in this Temple. But our forefathers worshipped him in many different ways and places. God is the Lord of both heaven and earth. He does not dwell in buildings made by men. He made everything! He can be worshipped anywhere! He sent messengers, filled with his Spirit, to speak for him and to prepare the way for the coming of his Son. But your forefathers were hard-hearted men. They persecuted these prophets of God and would not hear them. You are the same! Your hearts are hardened with pride! You murdered the Holy One of God! You ignore the Spirit of God and break the Law!"

The Council was in an uproar. Everyone was shouting with anger and fury, shaking their fists at Stephen. But he looked upwards and cried, "I see the heavens open, and Jesus standing at the right hand of God!" They rushed at him and dragged him out into the street and through the city gate. They found a pit and cast him into it. They took off their heavy cloaks so that their arms were free. Then they picked up stones to hurl at Stephen until he died.

A young Pharisee stood there watching them. His name was Saul of Tarsus. He had been brought up a strict Jew. He hated the Christians, too, for they spoke against the Law. He had argued with Stephen before and thought he was a blasphemer. The penalty for blasphemy in the Law of Moses was death by stoning. Stephen must be punished for his wickedness as the Law commanded. So Saul watched.

The Jews laid their cloaks at his feet and began to cast their stones. He heard Stephen cry out, "Lord Jesus, receive my spirit!" Then he saw him kneel down and say his last words, "Lord, forgive them". And so Stephen died.

December 26th every year is the day set aside to the memory of this first Christian martyr.

2. Paul the Christian

SAUL strode back to the city. He had watched the Christian preacher stoned to death. Stephen had deserved it, for he had blasphemed against the Law of Moses and the Temple of God. Never again would he preach in the synagogues. But there were others. They must be stopped as well. Persecution must go on against these Christians and their false teaching. As a good Jew, Saul must do his part.

No one attacked the Christians more fiercely than Saul. Like a madman, he hunted them down. He had spies and the Temple police to help him. He would creep into their houses and catch them meeting together to worship Jesus of Nazareth. They were dragged off to jail, beaten and imprisoned. Because of this savage persecution, some of the Christians left Jerusalem and went to other towns. Many went to the city of Damascus in the north, just over the border. But Saul was determined they should not escape so easily. He went to the High Priest. "Some of the Christians are escaping to Damascus," he said. "Will you give me the authority of the Great Council to go after them?" Gladly the High Priest gave him written orders to show his authority, and arranged for a guard of the Temple police to go with him and bring back the prisoners.

It was about 140 miles to Damascus, a long walk along the hot, dusty road. It would take about six days. Saul hurried along, the soldiers following him. For it was not right that an important Pharisee should make friends with common soldiers. He was impatient to get to Damascus and hunt out the Christians. How he hated them! How sure he was that he was right to persecute them! Yet the picture of Stephen dying kept coming into his mind. It was strange. Stephen had not been afraid. He had seemed quite happy to think he was going to be with his Jesus. How obstinate these Christians were! They were all like that—happy, unafraid, and full of faith. There must be some secret to explain it.

Saul was so impatient that he would not even stop for the midday rest. It was foolish to travel in the heat of the day. But he went on, madly, as if he could not rest. Suddenly, when he was nearing Damascus, something happened. The blazing sun burned all around him. He fell to the ground, terrified. Then he heard a voice inside him, saying, "Saul, Saul, why do you persecute me?" Saul whispered,

17

"Who are you, Lord?" The voice replied, "I am Jesus whom you attack so bitterly. It is hard for you to kick against me." Saul trembled with fear and amazement. Then he said, "Lord, what do you want me to do?" The voice answered him, "Rise up now and go into Damascus. You will be told there what you must do."

The soldiers came running up and lifted Saul from the ground. He opened his eyes, but he could see nothing. The soldiers took his arms and led him into Damascus, a helpless blind man instead of a powerful enemy. They took him to the house of his friend, a man called Judas, where he was going to stay. Saul lay there on his bed for three days, blind, wanting neither to eat nor drink, wondering at what had happened to him.

Now there lived at Damascus a Christian called Ananias. He had a dream in which Jesus spoke to him, and told him to go to the house of Judas in Straight Street and find Saul the Pharisee. Ananias was terrified. All the Christians in Damascus had heard of this man and of his fierce persecution of the Christians at Jerusalem. But Ananias knew he must go.

He found Saul lying on his bed. He put his hands on him and said, "Brother Saul, Jesus has sent me to lay my hands on you so that you may see again and be filled with his Spirit". Saul arose and opened his eyes. He could see again. Humbly he asked Ananias to baptise him. So Saul the persecutor became Paul the Christian.

Paul went out into the desert of Arabia, just as Jesus went into the wilderness before he began his ministry. He, too, had to think out what he must do. Then he came back to Damascus and went into the synagogues, preaching that Jesus is the Son of God. The Jews were astonished at the change in him, and soon they became angry. They plotted to kill him, and kept watch on the city gates so that he could not escape. But his Christian friends let him down over the city wall in a basket by night. So he escaped and travelled back to Jerusalem to visit the apostles of Jesus. At first they were afraid of him and suspicious. Then they came to realise that he was a new man. Soon he was preaching with them.

The Jews at Jerusalem came to hate him, too. Again he had to escape. He was smuggled out of Jerusalem and went to the city of Cæsarea on the coast. He took ship there and sailed back to his native city called Tarsus in Cilicia. There he stayed for nine years, preparing himself for his life's work.

Christians remember St. Paul every year on January 25th. There are many things about him to thank God for on this day. But the most important is the wonderful change that happened to him on the road to Damascus. For without that we should never have heard of him at all.

3. Paul goes to the Gentiles

BECAUSE of the persecution which Paul had led, many followers of Jesus left Jerusalem. Wherever they went they took the Good News of Jesus. Some went to the island of Cyprus and started a church there. From Cyprus they went to the great city of Antioch in Syria. Here for the first time Christians preached to the Gentiles.

Antioch was a mixed city of Syrians, Greeks, Jews, and Romans. It was just the place in which to begin missionary work. It was an evil city, too, where the goddess Daphne was worshipped. Here the followers of Jesus of Nazareth were first nicknamed 'Christians', a word used for them ever since. When the apostles at Jerusalem heard about the church in Antioch, they sent Barnabas to lead it. Barnabas, who came from Cyprus, was a good man and full of the Spirit of God. He knew just the man to help him, for he had been a friend of Paul in Jerusalem. He went first to Tarsus, found Paul, and brought him to Antioch. There they preached to both Jews and Gentiles.

The church at Antioch grew fast. Many Gentiles believed, and the Spirit of God came upon them as well as upon Jews. Soon the Christians felt they must take the Good News of Jesus to other Gentiles, too. They chose Paul and Barnabas as their first missionaries, and sent them forth.

They went first to Cyprus. No doubt Barnabas wanted to preach to his own people, just as Paul had done at Tarsus. They landed at Salamis and preached in the synagogue. Then they went right across the island to the city of Paphos, where the Roman Governor of the island lived. He asked to hear them and himself became a Christian. After this preaching in Cyprus, Paul and Barnabas took ship back to

Asia Minor. They came to another city called Antioch in Pisidia. Here Paul was invited to speak in the synagogue on the Sabbath day. He told the Jews how all their history was preparing the way for the coming of Jesus. When the time was ready, he had come and the Jews had killed him. But that was not the end. God had raised him from the dead to show he really was the Messiah, the Son of God. "The Law cannot save you, but he can," Paul said. "These are the glad tidings I bring you. Believe in him and be forgiven! Believe in him and overcome this evil world just as he did!"

There were some Gentiles listening in the synagogue. When the Jews had gone angrily away, they asked Paul to speak again the next Sabbath. A great crowd of Gentiles came to hear him. The Jews were jealous and became even more angry. They accused Paul of blasphemy. He said to them, "It was right to bring the Good News to you Jews first. But since you will not listen, we must turn to the Gentiles. For, as the prophets foretold, Jesus is a light to the Gentiles. The Gospel is for men of every nation." The Gentiles were glad when they heard this, and many believed. But the Jews plotted against Paul and Barnabas. They made a riot and had them cast out of the city.

The same thing happened in other places, too. Many Gentiles became Christians, but the Jews hunted Paul and Barnabas from city to city. Finally, they came back to Antioch and told the Church all that had happened. The Christians there were filled with joy that so many Gentiles believed. But some Christian Jews came from Jerusalem to Antioch. They said, "If Gentiles want to enter the Church, they must first accept the Law of Moses". Now Paul and many others did not believe this. The matter must be decided once and for all. So Paul and Barnabas and some others were sent to Jerusalem to talk with the Apostles.

There was much discussion at Jerusalem. First, Peter told how he had learnt that God has no favourites and welcomes believers of every race. Then Paul told of his work, and how many Gentiles believed and received the Spirit of God. At last they all agreed. There was no need for Gentiles to accept the Law of Moses in order to become Christians. This was written in a letter which Paul and Barnabas took back to Antioch. The letter was read to the church there. Everyone was delighted that the matter had been decided.

Now they could preach to the Gentiles freely. The door of the Church was open to men of all nations.

4. Paul goes to Europe

PAUL did not stay long at Antioch. He was too eager to be off again, to preach to other Gentiles. This time he took with him a man called Silas. They set off to the north. Paul wanted to visit again the churches he had set up on his first journey, and to read to them the letter from the council in Jerusalem. They came at length to a busy town by the sea called Troas, the ancient city of Troy. It was the nearest port to Europe, for across the water called the Hellespont was Greece. Troas had a Greek theatre and a gymnasium where Paul may have seen the athletes at their sports, for he wrote about them in one of his letters. Most important of all, Paul was ill at Troas. A Greek doctor called Luke came to make him better. He was a man of Macedonia. He listened to Paul speaking about Jesus, and he believed and was baptised. From that time he travelled with Paul, and it was Luke who wrote the rest of the story of Paul in the book of Acts, as well as his Gospel. He pleaded with Paul to cross over to Greece and to preach Jesus there. Paul had other plans, but he knew that this must be God's way of calling him. So they took ship together and crossed over into Europe.

Paul went straight to Philippi, the chief city of that part of Greece, and an important Roman town. He found a few Jews there, meeting by the river, as they had no synagogue. Some Gentiles were with them. A wealthy Greek lady called Lydia believed and was baptised. Paul and Silas stayed at her house during their visit.

Trouble soon arose. A poor girl, half mad, followed them about everywhere, crying out that they were men of God. Then Paul commanded the evil spirit to come out of her and she was cured. Her masters were very angry, for they had made much money out of her. People believed that the spirit in her was a god, and they paid to hear her. For they thought she could tell them the future in her ravings. Now her masters would make no more money. They dragged Paul and Silas before the magistrates, accused them of troubling the city and said they taught customs against the law of Rome. Paul

and Silas were at once stripped of their clothes, beaten, and thrown into prison. They were given no chance to defend themselves.

The jail was a damp and dirty cell. Paul and Silas had their feet fixed in the stocks and were left in darkness, their backs sore and bleeding. Yet they sang praises to God. About midnight, an earthquake shook the prison. The building rocked, the doors burst open, and the prisoners' chains came out of the walls. The jailor rushed in. Seeing the doors opened, he pulled out his sword to kill himself, for he thought the prisoners had escaped. "Stop!" said Paul, "we are all here!" The jailor fell before Paul and Silas on his knees in gratitude. Then he took them both into his house, bathed their wounds, and gave them food. That same night he was baptised as a Christian, he and all his family.

The next morning the magistrates sent men with orders to release Paul and Silas. "No," said Paul. "We are both Roman citizens, yet

23

they beat us, without even a trial." The magistrates were terrified when they heard this. They came to the prison themselves and pleaded with Paul and Silas to forgive them and to leave the city. So they said good-bye to Lydia and departed. They went on the main road to other towns, preaching Jesus. They came to the city of Thessalonica. Paul preached in the synagogue, saying, "The Scriptures tell how the Messiah must suffer and die. Jesus of Nazareth is the Messiah." The Jews hated this. They paid some ruffians to cause a riot, and brought Paul and Silas before the rulers of the city. "These men speak against Cæsar and cause trouble," they said. "They say there is another king called Jesus." Paul and Silas had to leave the city so that their friends there should not suffer. They went on to another town called Berea, where the same thing happened. Leaving his friends Silas and Timothy there, Paul went on to Athens.

The wise thinkers of Athens were long since dead, but its glory remained in its great buildings. Everywhere Paul saw temples and shrines and statues to gods and goddesses. He even found a statue to 'The unknown god'! The men there loved hearing anything strange and new. Paul spoke to them. "There is only one God," he said. "He made everything. He gives us life and breath and all things. He made all nations of one blood. He is not far from each one of us. For in him we live and move and have our being." He went on to tell them of Jesus and of his rising from the dead. Some of them mocked and called him a babbler. Others said, "Come back to-morrow and we'll talk with you again." But Paul left Athens. The last thing he saw on the horizon was the Parthenon, the great temple of Athene, goddess of wisdom. He was sad, for he felt he had failed. He could not know that one day the Parthenon itself would become a Christian church.

From Athens Paul went on to Corinth, a great city and an important seaport. People of all nations lived in this rich and evil city. He kept himself by working as a tent-maker, preaching in the synagogues on the Sabbath. The Jews hated him for teaching that Jesus was the Messiah. "Then I will preach to the Gentiles," he said.

After spending over a year at Corinth, Paul set out on the voyage back, and came at length to Antioch. His second great missionary journey was ended.

5. Paul builds Churches

PAUL was like a wise builder. When he first visited a new place he preached and won people to faith in Jesus. He stayed there, or left other missionaries there, until the church was well settled. So he laid firm foundations. But he did not forget his new churches. He went back again, as we have seen, to make sure that all was well. As he travelled, he also wrote many letters to the churches. Some of them are in our New Testament.

It was like that on the last journey of which we know. He began by visiting again the churches he had founded in Asia Minor. Then he went on, with two young disciples Timothy and Titus, to Ephesus. This was an important city of the Roman Empire, and rich in trade. It was a pagan city, and its goddess was Diana. Her great temple was one of the wonders of the ancient world.

At Ephesus Paul found some men who had been baptised by John Baptist, but they knew nothing of Jesus or of the Holy Spirit. So Paul told them of Jesus. Then eagerly they were baptised in the name of Jesus, and when Paul blessed them the Holy Spirit came upon them.

For two years Paul taught at Ephesus in a hall, for the Jews would not have him in their synagogue. Many pagans believed in Jesus, and made a great bonfire of their books of spells, charms, and magic. Many of them gave up worshipping Diana and no longer bought the little silver statues of the goddess which were supposed to bring good luck. This made the silversmiths angry, for they lost their trade. They stirred up a riot and filled the amphitheatre with a huge crowd of people, chanting, "Great is Diana of the Ephesians!" Paul wanted to face the mob, but his friends would not let him. It would be too dangerous. The town clerk of Ephesus made the crowd quiet and spoke sternly to them. "These men have done no wrong. They are not robbers or blasphemers of your goddess. If the silversmiths wish to accuse them, let them do it in the law-courts, not raise a riot. If the Romans hear of this tumult, there will be trouble for all of us. Go to your homes in peace!"

From Ephesus Paul went on to visit the churches in Greece again. He wrote letters on the way. Some were to the church at Corinth, and we have them in our Bible. One was to the Christians at Rome, saying that he hoped before long to visit them too. But first he must

25

go to Jerusalem. So he began the journey back, hoping to be at Jerusalem in time for the Feast of Pentecost. He stayed for a few days at Troas, and then sailed on to the port of Miletus. As he was in a hurry, he did not go inland to Ephesus but sent for the leaders of the church to come to him. When they met, Paul spoke his last words to them. He bade them be good shepherds to the flock of Christ, and commended them to God. Sad at parting, they watched his ship sail out of harbour. So Paul came to Jerusalem.

6. Paul the Martyr

JERUSALEM was crowded for the Feast of Pentecost. Jewish pilgrims had come from all over the world to keep the feast in the Temple. Some of them knew Paul already. For he had been to their cities on his journeys, preaching the Gospel. He taught that Jesus of Nazareth was the Messiah of God, and that if they believed this they could give up the Law of Moses. He mixed with Gentiles, and both Jews and Gentiles lived together in his churches. All this was breaking the sacred Law. So they hated Paul bitterly and wanted to kill him. They soon found an excuse to stir up a mob against him.

Paul went each day to the Temple to show he was a good Jew. One day they saw him near it with a Greek from Ephesus who was a Christian. His enemies saw their chance. "Help!" they shouted, seizing Paul. "This man has taken a Gentile into the sacred Temple!" This was a dreadful sin, and the penalty was death. Soon a crowd gathered and dragged Paul outside the gate to kill him. The captain of the guard heard the din and hurried up with soldiers. They pushed through the mob and made a circle of shields around Paul, saving his life. The captain said to Paul, "Are you another of these rebels against Rome?" Paul replied, "I am a Jew of Tarsus, a citizen of no mean city. Let me speak to them." The captain was amazed. This little old man with grey hair, bent shoulders, and scarred body, was certainly brave. He let Paul speak. They were standing on the steps leading up to the castle, the crowd yelling below. Paul cried out to them in the language of the Jews of Palestine. At first they listened, angrily. Paul told them how he had been brought up a strict Jew, how Jesus had spoken to him on the road to Damascus,

26

and how he had been called to preach to the Gentiles. He got no further. "Away with him! Kill him!" the people cried. The captain took Paul into the castle to examine him. He ordered him to be tied up and beaten. "Is it lawful to whip a Roman citizen without a trial?" Paul said to the centurion. The captain was told and hurried out. "Are you a Roman citizen?" "I am," Paul replied. "I paid a lot of money to become a citizen," said the captain. "I was born a Roman citizen," Paul replied, proudly. Then Paul was untied and put in a cell.

The next day the captain ordered the Great Council of the Jews to gather, and brought Paul before them, guarded by soldiers. Again there was a riot, and again the captain had to save Paul and bring him back to the castle. That night Jesus spoke to Paul in a dream. "Be of good courage," he said. "You have been my witness in Jerusalem. Soon you shall be my witness in Rome."

Now a band of forty Jews plotted against Paul. They vowed they would not eat till they had killed him. They said, "Let's ask the captain to bring him before the Council again to-morrow. That will be our chance." Paul's little nephew overheard them and came and told his uncle. Paul sent him with a soldier to the captain. The captain took him by the hand and said, "What have you to tell me?" The boy told him everything. Then the captain thanked him and said, "Tell no one about this". That night an armed guard of nearly 500 soldiers took Paul to Cæsarea where he would be safe.

The Roman Governor at Cæsarea was called Felix. He waited till Paul's accusers came from Jerusalem and then heard the case. But he gave no judgement. Paul was given a room in the Roman fortress, guarded by an officer. Felix hoped Paul would give him a bribe, for he was a greedy man. But Paul waited for fair trial. For two years he was kept there under guard.

A new Governor came to Cæsarea. His name was Festus. Eagerly Paul awaited a new trial, sure of his innocence. But Festus, anxious to please the Jews, asked Paul if he would like to be tried at Jerusalem. Paul realised that he would not get justice. "I am a Roman citizen," he said. "I have the right to be tried at Rome by the Emperor. I appeal unto Cæsar!" "Very well," said Festus. "You shall go to Cæsar."

Paul was given into the charge of a centurion for the voyage to Rome. It was autumn and they must hurry to reach Italy before the winter storms. They embarked in a small boat which sailed along the coast up to Myra. Here they changed to a ship carrying grain to Rome, and sailed southwards to Crete. They put in for shelter at the harbour called Fair Havens. It was dangerous to go on, but the centurion insisted. Soon the winter storms caught the ship. For two weeks it was driven by the gales till at last it ran aground off the island of Malta. Everyone escaped from the wreck on broken timbers, and so came ashore.

After three months, the bad weather was over, and a ship took them safely on to Rome. Paul was allowed to live in his own hired house, though chained to a Roman soldier. For two years he awaited trial. But he was not idle. Every day he had visitors. Messengers came from the churches all over the east, and took back with them precious letters from Paul himself.

Many people believe that Paul was set free after this time. One story says that he went as far as Spain in the west. He may have visited the churches in the East again, too. One thing is certain. He came back to Rome again to be tried by the wicked Emperor, Nero. He was taken just outside the city and beheaded. An old man of nearly seventy, this great soldier of Jesus had fought a good fight and kept faith with his Master.

Andrew, the Patron Saint of Scotland

ON the north shore of the Sea of Galilee lay the town of Bethsaida, a name which means 'place of fishers'. It was an important fishing town. Two brothers lived there called Andrew and Simon, and both were fishermen. Andrew was not often at home. He had become a disciple of the great new prophet, John the Baptist. John preached and baptised by the river Jordan, and Andrew was one of his helpers. One day Jesus of Nazareth came to be baptised. John said, "Behold the Lamb of God!" Andrew heard him, and he turned and followed Jesus. He was so excited that he hurried to find his brother and said to him, "We have found the Messiah!" Simon came with him to Jesus. When Jesus saw Simon, he said to him, "Your name is Simon. I am going to give you a new name, Peter, which means 'a rock'." They both went back with Jesus to Galilee. They were still fishermen, and each day went out in their boats. But not long after, Jesus came and stood by the shore. He called out to them both, and they brought their boat to shore. "Come," Jesus said. "You are fishermen. I will make you fishers of men." They left their boat at once and followed him.

So Andrew was the first of the twelve apostles. He believed in Jesus ever since he first saw him, and followed him faithfully. Andrew was a sensible man, and was always helpful. One day a great crowd had followed Jesus out into the desert, and he taught them. Then they needed food. Philip, one of the disciples, said, "Wherever can

29

we get food for all these people?" Andrew found a boy who had brought some lunch with him. It was only five little loaves and two small fishes. But Andrew trusted Jesus and took the lad to Jesus with his gift. So Jesus was able to feed them all.

On Palm Sunday, when Jesus rode into Jerusalem, there were some Greeks in the city. They had heard of Jesus, the great Prophet of Nazareth; and they wanted to meet him. They came to Philip and said, "Sir, we would like to see Jesus". Philip was not sure whether Jesus would want to talk with them, so he told Andrew about it. Andrew had no doubt, and he took them straight to Jesus.

Andrew was with Jesus all through his ministry. He saw Jesus when he had risen from the dead. He was in the upper room on the Day of Pentecost, the birthday of the Church. He became one of its leaders, and a great missionary.

Andrew is a Greek name and perhaps he came from a Greek family. When the Christians at Jerusalem were persecuted, he travelled away to the East. He was a missionary in Scythia and in Achaia, a part of Greece. It was here that he met his death as a martyr about A.D. 70. He was crucified at Patras, a Greek town by the sea. It is said that the cross was shaped like the letter X. That is why the flag of St. Andrew is a white X cross.

How did St. Andrew become the patron Saint of Scotland? It was probably through St. Augustine, who came from Rome as a missionary. Augustine had been Prior of a monastery at Rome named after St. Andrew. So he was glad to have churches in England named after Andrew, too. One of these was at Hexham in Northumbria, and some relics of the saint were placed in it. Not long after, Angus, King of the Picts, founded a church of St. Andrew in Scotland. It was built in one of his settlements in Fifeshire. The relics were taken there from Hexham. A great cathedral was built many years after, and there grew up the town which is called St. Andrews to this day.

Often the Scots believed that St. Andrew was helping them in their battles. Legends grew up about him. He became famous throughout the whole of Scotland, and so he was made its patron Saint. Every year he is remembered on his day, November 30th, as one of the first great missionaries of the Christian Church.

30

Alban, the First British Martyr

A LEGEND says that Christianity was brought to Britain by Joseph of Arimathea, who was a secret disciple of Jesus and had laid the body of Jesus in the tomb in his garden. It told how he was driven out by the Jews and went as an exile to Britain, where he settled at Glastonbury in Somerset. It became the most sacred place of the ancient Britons and a famous abbey was built there in later times.

When the Romans conquered Britain, many soldiers and merchants went there. Some of them were Christians, and of course they took their faith with them. The Britons lived in huts. But the Romans built fine cities of brick and stone. One of them was called Verulamium, and it stood on Watling Street, a great Roman road which ran from London to the border of Wales. Verulamium had fine Roman houses, or villas, a forum or market-square, and a big open-air theatre. In one of its finest houses lived a young man called Alban. His family were Roman citizens, rich and important. He had been sent to a school in Rome, and then had been a Roman soldier. Now he had come back to his home.

Alban was a pagan. He worshipped the gods of Rome and made sacrifice to the statue of the Emperor. But he was kind and generous. One day an old man came to his house for food and shelter. His name was Amphibalus, and he was a Christian priest. The Christians were being persecuted, and the aged priest came to Alban, for he knew of his kindness. Alban took him into his house and cared for him. He soon came to like the old man. He often saw Amphibalus at prayer, and asked him about his God. The priest told him about the life and teaching of Jesus, how he was the Son of God, had suffered, and died, but is alive for evermore. Here, thought Alban, is a God far greater than all the gods of Rome. It was not long before he asked the priest to baptise him. So Alban became a Christian and promised his loyalty to Jesus.

In a few days the rumour spread that Alban was hiding a Christian priest in his house. The pagan Governor heard it, and he sent soldiers to search the house and seize him. Alban's faithful servant saw the soldiers coming and rushed in to tell his master. Quickly Alban took the priest's cloak and put it on himself, and the hood over his head. He told his servant to hurry out through the back gate with the priest and hide him in the woods.

When the soldiers burst in they saw the priest kneeling at prayer. They seized him and dragged him away. When he came before the Governor, he threw back his hood. It was Alban, the Roman citizen. The Governor was furious with him. "You are a traitor to Rome!" he shouted. "But you are a citizen, and I will pardon you if you worship the gods of Rome."

"I cannot," said Alban. "I am a Christian, too." The Governor ordered him to be tortured to make him give in. But still Alban would not sacrifice. So the order was given to put him to death.

The soldiers led Alban out of the town. There was hardly room for them to cross the bridge over the river. For the story had spread quickly, and many of the people had come to show their love for Alban. They climbed a wooded hill and came to the place of execution. The officer gave the order for Alban to be beheaded. But the soldier who carried the sword threw it down. "I cannot kill so good a man," he cried. Seizing the sword, the officer killed Alban, and then the soldier.

Alban died on June 22nd in the year A.D. 304, and is remembered every year on this day. On the place where he died a church was built, and then, 500 years later, a great abbey. Alban was made a saint, and soon people forgot the Roman name of the town and called it St. Albans. To-day the old Roman city lies under the fields. But the city of St. Albans and a great church live on in memory of the first British martyr.

6 George, the Patron Saint of England

ST GEORGE, the patron saint of England, lived far away from our country. Yet in many ways he was like St. Alban. He was born in Cappadocia, near Palestine, in the east of the Roman Empire. Like Alban, he came from a rich and noble family. Like Alban, too, he served in the Roman army. The Emperor came to hear of him. He was so pleased with him that he made George an officer in his own Imperial Guard. One story says that he was a friend of Constantine, another officer, who was to become the first Christian Emperor. We know that Constantine served in Britain. The legend says that George came with him and visited such holy places as Glastonbury.

George returned to his own country, a Roman soldier, but a soldier of Christ too. Now the Emperor, whose name was Diocletian, had ordered that Christians should be persecuted throughout the Eastern Empire. The edict was put up in every town. Churches were to be destroyed, and the sacred books of Christians burnt. George, with great courage, tore down the Emperor's order. He was at once arrested and tortured. When he refused to worship the gods of Rome, he was put to death. At about the same time, another young nobleman, St. Alban, was put to death in far-away Britain. The body of George was buried by the sea at Lydda. But his fame quickly spread. Soon he was called a saint. Churches were built in his name and prayers were offered up for him. When Constantine became Emperor, he said that all Christian men should strive to be like George, and he ordered a church to be built over the grave on the seashore.

Legends grew up about the saint. The most famous is of his fight with the dragon. George was stationed with the army in Libya, North Africa. The dragon lived in a lake outside a town called Salone. So many of the country people had been eaten by it that the rest fled into the town. The dragon, like a huge crocodile with scaled wings, came up to the gates seeking food. Even people inside died from its poisonous breath. Sheep were tied up outside the walls to feed it and keep it away. But soon there were no sheep left. Then the people in the town decided to give the beast one child each day. One day the daughter of the king was chosen to be sacrificed. Her name was Sabra. In her finest clothes, the poor girl was taken and left outside the city wall. George came riding that way on his white horse. He rode up to the

weeping maiden and she told him of her dreadful fate. "Do not fear," George told her. "I will help you in the name of Jesus Christ." Soon after, the dragon came up out of the lake for its daily food. George attacked it with his lance and, after a terrible struggle, pierced it through. Then he told Sabra to tie her belt round its neck. They dragged it back into the town and, amid the cheers of the people, George struck off its head. Then he spoke to the people in the name of Jesus and, soon after, the king and all his people were baptised as Christians.

This legend may have arisen from a fight George did have with a crocodile. It became very popular. It was told in many Christian books, with lovely pictures by fine artists.

In the Middle Ages many Englishmen went to Palestine to win back the Holy Land from the Saracens. George soon became their favourite Saint. Some said they saw him in the sky, helping them in their battles. King Richard the Lion-heart of England rebuilt the church over George's grave at Lydda, to show his thankfulness. The flag of St. George, the red cross on a white background, became popular in the English army. When the Crusaders came back to England, they spread the fame of St. George. April 23rd, the day on which St. George was martyred, was made a holiday in England in 1222. It became a great day for services in church and processions through the towns, for tournaments and sports, feasts and plays. Ever since then England has kept it as St. George's Day.

There are many other ways in which St. George is remembered in England. The famous Order of the Garter is named after him, and its badge shows St. George killing the dragon. Many churches are named after him, such as the Royal Chapel at Windsor. The Order of St. Michael and St. George is an honour which links him with the angel leader of the hosts of heaven. Because of his burial by the sea, he became the patron saint of dangerous waters. So the rough channel between Ireland and Wales was named after him. His flag is part of the Union Jack.

St. George is remembered by Christians all over the world. In Greece he is called 'The Great Martyr'. So, all through the years and all over the world, he has inspired men to be true soldiers of Christ.

Ulfilas, Apostle of the Goths

CONSTANTINE the Great, the first Christian Emperor, decided to build a new capital city. Rome was too far west to be a centre for the vast Roman Empire. He chose a place called Byzantium between the East and the West. There in A.D. 330 he built a wonderful new city, four times bigger than the old. It had great stone walls, fine streets, beautiful houses and churches, libraries and shops. Ships from all over the world could sail into the deep waters of its natural harbour called the Golden Horn. The new imperial city was given a new name—Constantinople.

It needed strong walls for all round it lived fierce, warlike tribes called the Goths. They had come long ago from Scandinavia in the north. Some settled in the East in what is now Russia, and are known as the 'East Goths' or 'OstroGoths'. Others settled in the West, in Europe, and are called the 'West Goths' or 'VisiGoths'. These VisiGoths lived by the River Danube. Constantine had to fight their king Alaric. The Roman legions defeated the fierce but undisciplined Goths and Constantine made peace with them. Some Gothic boys were taken as hostages to Constantinople to make sure that the Goths kept the peace treaty. One of them was a boy named Ulfilas.

Ulfilas had been born in A.D. 311. His name in Gothic was really 'Wulfila' which means 'Little Wolf', for his parents hoped that he would become a great warrior. He grew up in his home in the woods where life was simple and savage. He loved best the evenings round the camp fire when warriors celebrated their victories in songs of battle and of war. There too he heard songs and stories of the gods of his people—Tiw the god of war, Woden the chief of the gods, Thor the god of thunder, and Balder the gentle sun god. Suddenly he was taken away from his home and sent to Constantinople.

Ulfilas had never seen a town before, let alone a wonderful city like this. We can imagine how amazed he must have been at this strange new life and how homesick he must have felt for his own home and his own people. But he soon found lots of things to interest and excite him, especially at school where he learnt to read and to write. There he learnt not only the Latin tongue of the Romans but also the Greek language. So he read books written in Greek. Homer's stories of the heroes of old would remind him of his own people and the Gothic warriors. But he also read something he had never heard of before—the story of Jesus Christ and his teaching. Here was a new kind of hero and it was not long before Ulfilas knew that he wanted to be a warrior of Jesus Christ.

Life in Constantinople was full of interest and comfort and Ulfilas could have stayed there in wealth and ease. But he had never forgotten his own people. He wanted to go back to them and to give them what Constantinople had given to him. In A.D. 341, when he was thirty years old, Ulfilas was made a bishop and set off back to his people.

The Goths welcomed him warmly and many listened gladly to the message of Jesus which Ulfilas brought them. But some of them would not hear of giving up the old gods and began to attack Ulfilas and his followers. He asked the Emperor if he might take them westwards over the River Danube so that they could settle there under the rule of Rome. They made their homes there in 348 A.D., in the country now called Rumania, living by their cattle and trade and no longer by war.

For over forty years Ulfilas worked as a missionary among his people. But he did more than preach. He soon realised that the Goths must have the Bible to read if they were to remain Christians. But there were great difficulties. The Goths could not read or write. There was no Bible in Gothic. There was not even a Gothic language! All they had was a few crude letters called 'runes' for marking their possessions. Ulfilas started from the beginning. First, with his knowledge of Latin and Greek, he made a new Gothic alphabet. Then bit by bit he turned the Greek Bible into his new Gothic language. It took him years and years to do his great work. At last it was finished. The Bible was written in Gothic for his people to read. But it was not quite the whole Bible. Ulfilas deliberately left out of his Bible the Old Testament books of Kings, for they are full of stories of war and Ulfilas did not want to encourage his warlike people to start fighting again!

Today the Bible is printed in over a thousand different languages. For missionaries in modern times have done what Ulfilas was the very first missionary to do: translate the Bible into a language which no one knew how to write. Christian missionaries, trained by Ulfilas, travelled among the Goths, taking the Bible with them. At camp fires, instead of savage stories of the old gods being told, the story of Jesus was read instead. Through the work of one man the fierce Goths and the tribes of Teutons around them were turned from paganism to the Christian faith.

Ulfilas died in A.D. 383. Some years later his people revolted against the Roman Emperor. Under their king Alaric they invaded Italy. In A.D. 410 they entered Rome itself and sacked the great city. But the churches were spared and Christians who sheltered in them were unharmed. For, through the great work of Ulfilas, even these fierce warriors had been tamed by the Gospel of Jesus Christ.

The Gothic Bible of Ulfilas

The Lord's Prayer

Atta (Father) unsar (our)

Thu in himinam,

Weihnai (hallowed be) namo thein.

Qimai (come) thiudinassus (kingdom) theins.

Wairthai (be done) wiljo theins,

Swe (as) in himina

Jah (also) ana airthai.

Hlaif (loaf) unsarana (our) thana (the) sinteinan
    (daily)

Gif uns himma daga (on this day).

Jah (and) aflet (let-off, forgive) uns

Thatei skulans sijaima (what owing we are)

Swaswe jah (as also)

Weis afletam thaim skulam (the debtors) unsaraim
    (our).

Jah ni briggais uns in fraistubnjai (temptation),

Ak (but) lausei uns af thamma ubilin;

Unte (for) theina ist thiudangardi (kingdom)

Jah mahts (might)

Jah wulthus (glory)

In aiwins (eternity).

Amen.

St. Matthew 6. vv. 9 - 13.

Telemachus, the Martyr Monk

8

CHRISTIANS were persecuted for three hundred years. Sometimes the Roman Emperor made an order against them. Sometimes priests of the pagan religions led riots against them. They were jealous because people no longer brought sacrifices to the temples of the ancient gods. But all this time the Church went on growing. The faith and courage of Christians, even when they suffered, made pagans admire them. So by A.D. 300 the Church had spread all over the Roman world. Then another Emperor made a bitter attack on Christians and many were put to death. St. George and St. Alban became martyrs at this time. But it was impossible to destroy the Church. In A.D. 312 Constantine became Emperor and one of the first things he did was to forbid attacks on Christians. "Christians and all other people must be free to worship as they wish," he ordered.

Now Christianity became the religion of the Roman Empire. Constantine made Sunday a public holiday so that Christians could go to church freely, and beautiful new churches were built. He made new laws to end cruelty to children and slaves and prisoners. Animals were to be treated kindly by drivers and carriers. The public Games, in which hundreds of men as well as animals were put to a cruel death, were to be stopped.

For a long time the Romans had enjoyed these Games. Every Roman city had its arena where the people gathered on holidays and

41

festivals. It was shaped like a circle, covered with sand, and there were stone seats all round it. Just as we go to watch sports today, the Romans loved to go to watch the Games. But theirs were cruel and bloodthirsty. Sometimes animals fought against each other or even against men. Sometimes gladiators fought each other. These were specially-trained men, paid to fight each other with armour and swords or with nets and tridents. When one was beaten and the other was.about to kill him, he would put his hand up to show he was defeated. If the crowd wanted him to be spared they waved hand-kerchiefs. But if they wanted him to die they all turned their thumbs outwards. Then the victor would kill him.

No wonder Constantine, the first Christian Emperor, wanted to end these cruel Games. For a long time Christians had spoken against them and would never go near them. At last the law forbade them all over the Empire. But the Romans loved them too much to give them up all at once, and it seems that they were still held in some places.

About A.D. 390 an Emperor named Honorius ruled over the Empire in the West. He was troubled because savage tribes were attacking the Empire. The fierce Goths invaded Italy but the Roman army managed to defeat them and drive them back. Honorius was so delighted that he ordered public Games at Rome to celebrate his triumph. They were to be held in the great Colosseum which still stands today. This huge arena had tiers of seats round it for nearly 90,000 people. At last the great day came and the Colosseum was packed to the doors with an excited crowd eagerly waiting for the fighting to begin. It was January 1st in the year A.D. 391.

A certain monk named Telemachus was in Rome at that time. He came from the East where he lived alone as a hermit, devoting his life to prayer. He was not in Rome by chance. It seems he had heard of these terrible Games and was horrified by them. How could a Christian Emperor and Christian people find sport and pleasure in watching men kill each other? He must end this cruel bloodshed and murder, he decided. So he had made the long journey to Rome to speak for God.

Telemachus was in the crowd at the Colosseum that day. He watched the strong, young gladiators march into the arena and up to

42

the royal box where the Emperor sat in state. "Hail, Cæsar!" they cried. "We, about to die, salute thee!" The huge crowd roared with pleasure and excitement. Suddenly they stopped. Telemachus had climbed over the stone wall round the arena and this strange figure was running towards the gladiators, shouting. What was it he was crying out? They could just hear: "Stop! In the name of Jesus Christ who died for men—stop!" Telemachus had thrust himself between the gladiators, separating them from each other. "The Games! The Games! Kill him! Kill him!" shouted the mob. One of the heartless gladiators pierced Telemachus with his sword and the holy man of the East fell dead upon the blood-stained sand.

A sudden silence filled the vast arena. The people there were not pagans as they had been in the old days. They called themselves Christians. They realised what they had done and they were ashamed. A monk, a holy man of God, had been murdered for their sport. Even the Emperor Honorius hung his head. Slowly the people began to make their way to the exits and silently they went back home. Before long the Colosseum was empty.

Never again were the Games held. The Emperor made a law banning them throughout the Empire. Everywhere people were so shocked by the murder of Telemachus that they never again clamoured for the blood sports of the arena. Christians never forgot how he had given his life to shame them into giving up their evil ways. Every year the anniversary of that day, January 1st, is set aside by many Christians to the memory of Telemachus the monk. His sacrifice had done what laws could not do. It had made Christians realise that every living person is sacred and precious to God.

9 Martin of Tours

MARTIN the soldier-saint was born in the year A.D. 335 in Eastern Europe. His father, a Roman soldier, was stationed there in the country now called Hungary. Both his mother and father worshipped the pagan gods but it seems that Martin heard of Jesus Christ when he was still a boy. For one story says that when he was ten years old he ran away from home to become a monk. Of course he was much too young, and both his parents were angry. Martin's father wanted him to become a soldier too, and when he was fifteen he had to join the Roman army. But while he did his duties well, Martin knew in his heart that he would never be content with soldiering. A friend of Martin's wrote the story of his life which we can still read. He says that Martin was a kind officer, good to his men, and spending little of his pay so that he always had money to give away.

Martin moved from one garrison to another with his troops. When he was eighteen years old his regiment was posted to Amiens, a city of France, in the Roman province of Gaul. It was a hard winter that year and the troops were glad to be protected by their thick uniform. One morning they marched out of barracks into the crisp, frosty day. Martin was riding with his men, wearing his fine, warm military cloak. Suddenly he noticed a beggar, sitting by the city gate, blue with cold. He sat shivering, waiting for alms. Martin was full of pity for the old man and reached for his purse. But it was empty. He had given away his last coin. What could he do to save the beggar from freezing to death? A sudden idea came to him and he leapt off his horse. He quickly drew out his sword and, snatching off his thick cloak, he sliced it in two. Gently he wrapped one part round the half-frozen beggar and then, remounting his horse, galloped after his men. Martin forgot all about the incident but that night it came back to him while he slept. In his dream he saw Jesus, surrounded by the angels, telling them how Martin had given him his cloak. When he woke, Martin knew what he wanted to do with his life. Soon after, he was baptised into the Christian Church and obtained his release from the army. Now he would be a soldier of Jesus Christ for the rest of his life.

Martin knew that, if he was to be a good Christian soldier, his life must be just as stern and disciplined as it had been in the Roman army. He read the life of a famous monk named Antony and learnt from it how to fight the evil temptations inside himself. He knew he had to battle against pagan gods and evil ways, too, so he must be strong in spirit. He decided to become a hermit. He lived far from men but close to God. He slept on the ground, lived on roots and herbs, and spent his time in prayer. It was during this time that he became a friend of beasts and birds for he was kind and tender, sharing his scanty food with them. That is why old paintings of Martin show him with a hare at his feet.

After spending some years as a hermit, Martin went to the city of Poitiers in France where the saintly Hilary was Bishop. Martin loved him dearly and wanted to be near him. There he founded the very first monastery in France. Later he moved to the banks of the River Loire, just outside the city of Tours, and founded a new monastery. He and his monks lived in caves cut in the cliffs. Their life was hard and simple for, like Martin, they were to be Christian soldiers. When they were trained, the monks went out in bands of twelve with a leader, like Jesus and his apostles, and each band founded a new monastery. These monasteries were to be Christian 'garrisons' in enemy territory, for the people of Gaul were pagans. Martin's monks were to be missionaries, taking the light of the Gospel into the darkness.

Martin's fame spread and the people of Tours grew to love this holy monk. In A.D. 371 their bishop died and they had to choose another. There was no doubt whom they wanted but would the humble monk be willing to become a bishop? One story says that Martin was tricked. A citizen of Tours went to the monastery and pleaded with Martin to come to his sick wife. Martin left his cave at once and when he reached the city was seized by the people and forced to become their Bishop.

For nearly thirty years Martin worked as Bishop of Tours. He still lived a hard life but no longer in his monastery. He travelled ceaselessly through the countryside, preaching and teaching, caring for the poor and needy. He had simple food and little sleep and at night lay on the bare ground, wrapped only in his simple cloak. His goodness and love helped Christians to follow Jesus more faithfully. His self-sacrifice and his fearless teaching won pagans to the faith he preached and lived.

Martin hated cruelty of any kind and when false teachers were arrested by the Emperor he pleaded for them. He was very angry when he heard that the Emperor had put them to death and fearlessly said so. They were savage and cruel times and Martin's Christ-like character brought him the love of his people. He died in A.D. 397 but he was never forgotten. He was made patron saint of his own country, France, but his fame spread to other lands. In England many churches were named after him. The oldest was at Canterbury where there has been a Christian church dedicated to him for over 1,400 years. In London the famous church of St. Martin-in-the-Fields is named after him. November 11th was set aside in each year as the day dedicated to the memory of Martin, the great soldier of Christ and loving shepherd of his flock.

Ambrose of Milan | 10

AMBROSE was born in the year A.D. 339 at a place called Trier in France, for his father was the Governor of France, or Gaul as the Romans called it. He was rich and important and Ambrose grew up in a happy and wealthy home. He had a brother and sister whom he loved dearly all his life. When he was ten years old his father died and his mother went back to live in her old home near Rome. There Ambrose grew up into a fine young man. He studied law and soon showed himself to be wise as well as clever and a fine speaker. When he had finished his studies, he was appointed to a government post like his father before him. So great was his ability that in A.D. 370 he was made Governor of Northern Italy. His residence was at the city of Milan which had become even as important as Rome itself. For Milan was much nearer to the northern frontiers of the Empire where fierce tribes were always threatening. The Emperor often lived at Milan instead of Rome so Ambrose held a very important post. He ruled wisely and firmly and the people of Milan soon came to love him for he was always just.

Four years later the Bishop of Milan died and the people had to choose someone to succeed him. There was a sad quarrel in the church at the time, and there were two different parties. One group taught that Jesus was a very fine man but that he was not truly God. They were called 'Arians' after their leader, Arius. Other Christians opposed them, for they saw how dangerous and untrue this teaching was. They were called the 'orthodox', or 'right believing' party. For they taught the true faith of the whole Church. The old Bishop of Milan had been an Arian and his followers hoped to choose another Arian for bishop. The other party of course wanted an orthodox bishop.

When the day came for the election the cathedral at Milan was packed to the doors. Ambrose the Governor was there, for a quarrel might break out between the two parties and turn into a riot. He stood up to address the people and to bid them choose their bishop peacefully. As he waited for silence a child cried out—"Ambrose, Bishop!" Suddenly everyone took up the cry—"Ambrose for Bishop!" The Governor tried to silence them but they went on shouting, "Ambrose for Bishop!" Finally he had to give in. At that time he was undergoing the long preparation for baptism. But the people would not wait and within a week he was baptised and made Bishop of Milan.

Ambrose ruled over the Church wisely. His fine character and his Roman training in government made him a great leader of the church in Italy. He lived a simple and strict life and set a splendid example to others. He gave all his money to his brother to use for charity. He did all he could to help the building of monasteries where men lived together in poverty, devoting themselves to the service of God and men. His sister became a nun.

Because he feared God, Ambrose feared no one else and stood up even to rulers when they did wrong. The Roman Empire was now divided into two parts, East and West. In the West the Empress Justina ruled for her young son. She was an Arian and soon hated Ambrose who taught the true orthodox faith of the Church. She had many Goths serving as soldiers in her army and they were Arian Christians too. She demanded a church in Milan for their use but Ambrose refused. She sent her soldiers to surround the church she wanted but Ambrose filled it with his followers and taught them new hymns which he himself had written. Even the Empress dare not send her soldiers to attack the congregation and she had to give in. The next year she ordered Ambrose to argue against an Arian bishop in her own court but again he refused. "The Empress is a member of the Church, not lord over it," he said. Justina died not long after, and the false Arian teaching about Jesus soon died out. Ambrose saved the true Christian faith by his courage.

A HYMN OF PRAISE
(Written by Ambrose)

Infinite God, to Thee we raise
Our hearts in solemn songs of praise;
By all Thy works on earth adored,
We worship Thee, the common Lord;
The everlasting Father own,
And bow our souls before Thy throne.

Thee all the choir of angels sings,
The Lord of hosts, the King of Kings;
Cherubs proclaim Thy praise aloud,
And seraphs shout the Triune God;
And 'Holy, Holy, Holy' cry,
Thy glory fills both earth and sky.

Father of endless majesty,
All might and love they render Thee;
Thy true and only Son adore,
The same in dignity and power;
And God the Holy Ghost declare,
Thy saints' eternal Comforter.

Translated by Charles Wesley

Cherubs, seraphs—angels
Triune—three in one, the Holy Trinity
Comforter—Strengthener

It was like that, too, with the Emperor of the East named Theo-dosius. He was a sincere Christian but his fiery temper sometimes made him do terrible things. Once when he was in Milan he came to the cathedral for the service of the bread and wine. He came up to the altar to make his offering. But instead of returning to his seat he stayed there in the sanctuary, the holiest part of the church. Ambrose sent him a message telling him to go back to his place in the con-gregation. The Emperor had to obey. "Now I know the difference between a Bishop and an Emperor!" he said afterwards.

Some time later Theodosius did a dreadful deed. His officer in the city of Thessalonica in the East arrested a famous charioteer for a crime he had committed. The people were very angry for they were looking forward to the Games. There was a riot and the officer was killed. The Emperor was furious. "They shall have their Games," he said, grimly. The great day came, the arena was packed and the doors were locked. The Emperor had sent his soldiers in among the crowd. At the signal they drew out their swords. Seven thousand people died in a horrible massacre. A few months later the Emperor came to Milan and on Christmas Day went to the Cathedral for Holy Communion. Ambrose met him at the door. "You cannot receive the bread and wine till you have done penance for your awful deed," he said. Theodosius realised then how great was his sin. Only after penance was he admitted to the church.

Ambrose was a great teacher and preacher. In his sermons and hymns and books he proclaimed the true faith. When he died in A.D. 397 he was never forgotten. April 4th was set aside each year for Christians to remember and to thank God for Ambrose of Milan, a great leader of the Church.

Jerome of Bethlehem

JEROME was born in A.D. 342 near the town of Aquileia in the far north of Italy. His parents were well-to-do Christians and when Jerome was seventeen years old he went to Rome to study. The Church was strong in Rome and its Bishop was becoming important. But many of the people of Rome were still pagans and they lived for wealth and comfort. The Church was no longer persecuted and so it was easy to be a Christian. Some members of the Church began to live like the pagans in luxury and gaiety. Jerome was shocked by their easy ways for he believed that a Christian should live a strict, disciplined life. While he was in Rome he was baptised and then he travelled for a time in Gaul. He returned to Italy and settled near his home with some friends. They planned to live strictly and to study the Bible. But Jerome was a quarrelsome person and they soon parted.

Jerome set off to visit Palestine and on the way stopped at Antioch in Syria. Here he had a dream which changed his whole life. He dreamed that he was being judged by God for preferring other books to the Bible. When he awoke he determined to study nothing but the Bible. He left the city and went off into the desert alone. There he lived as a hermit for several years, devoting himself to prayer and study. His life was terribly hard and strict. He went without food and denied himself sleep. Under the glaring sun his body became as

51

black as an African's, he said. All through his life Jerome treated his body like this. Perhaps it was this that helped to make him so quarrelsome and ill-tempered.

While Jerome lived near Antioch he met a Jew who had become a Christian. From him Jerome learnt the Hebrew language. This was to make him an even better scholar of the Bible. For of course the Old Testament had been written in Hebrew. After nearly five years in the desert Jerome went back to Antioch and then on to Constantinople where there were fine Christian scholars and manuscripts. Then he returned to Rome.

The Bishop of Rome at that time was named Damasus. He soon realised what an excellent scholar Jerome was and made him his secretary. Even in Rome, with all its wealth and gaiety, Jerome lived a stern life and wore the rough garment he used in the desert. In his sermons he bitterly attacked Christians who wore fine clothes and lived in luxury. Bishop Damasus encouraged him to go on with his Bible studies. But when Damasus died, Jerome had made so many enemies in Rome that he determined to leave. In A.D. 386 he finally settled at Bethlehem where he lived for the rest of his life.

Jerome founded a monastery at Bethlehem and some ladies from Rome set up a nunnery nearby. Here Jerome devoted himself to the two things he loved best—a strict life and study. For thirty-four years he worked in his cell on a new Latin Bible. There was already a Latin Bible used throughout the Church but Jerome had discovered how bad it was. The Old Testament had been first written in Hebrew and the New Testament in Greek. Jerome knew both these languages and he wanted to make a Latin Bible that was a true one, not full of mistakes like the one people used. He was never satisfied with his work and he went over it again and again. At last in A.D. 404 it was finished. He had translated the whole Bible into Latin. Though it was a new Bible it was really the oldest, for it was translated from the very earliest manuscripts. Latin was the Roman language and now everyone could read the Bible.

At first many people did not like Jerome's Bible. It was often different from the one they were used to. Jerome expected this and he wrote in the preface of his Bible—"Both clever and ignorant people will call me a forger and a blasphemer for daring to change and to correct the Bible they know." But what mattered was the truth of his Bible. Scholars like Augustine of Hippo saw at once what a wonderful Bible it was and slowly others began to get used to it. In time it grew so popular that it became the Bible of the whole Church in the West.

Jerome's Bible is known as the 'Vulgate'. The Latin word *vulgatus* means 'made known to the people', and the Vulgate was the people's Bible of Europe all through the Middle Ages. Then people began to want the Bible in English. The Roman Catholic Church had always used the Vulgate as their Bible and in 1609 it was turned into English. It was used in making other English Bibles, too, for it was the best Latin Bible, going back to the earliest manuscripts. We can see then how great Jerome's work was.

In his little cell at Bethlehem Jerome wrote many other books on the Bible. He was the greatest scholar of the Church and his books helped Christians to understand and to teach the Scriptures. He wrote many letters, too, for his advice and help were wanted on the problems of the Church. He wrote bitter letters against false teachers who disturbed the Church, for he was still very quarrelsome. But we can understand that, because his life was so hard and strict. He always denied himself and he tried to persuade others to live as he did.

Jerome died in A.D. 420 and was made a 'Doctor' or 'Teacher' of the Church. Artists always pictured him with a lion, for it was said that when he was a hermit a lion was his friend and companion. September 30th was set aside to his memory. But the Bible is the best memorial we have of Jerome of Bethlehem, the great Christian monk and scholar.

12 Augustine of Hippo

WHEN Bishop Ambrose spoke to the people in Milan Cathedral, a young man sat listening to him eagerly. His name was Augustine and he came from Tagaste in North Africa where he had been born in A.D. 354. His father was a pagan but his mother, Monica, was a Christian and she had great hopes for her son. He began the preparation for baptism, but when he went to university, in the city of Carthage nearby, he gave up his Christian training. Many years later he wrote the story of his life and in it he tells about his childhood and youth. He remembered how he and his gang had raided the orchard of a neighbour and stolen his pears. They were not even ripe and the lads only took nibbles before throwing them to the pigs. It was such a stupid thing to do but Augustine could see later that many things he had done had been silly and sometimes evil. He was very clever at the university and studied to become a lawyer. But he wasted much of his time in idleness and folly. He followed strange religions but his mother went on praying that one day he would find real truth and wisdom in Jesus Christ.

Augustine went to live and teach in Rome and then became a professor at Milan. Here he listened to the sermons of Ambrose and was very attracted by the wisdom and by the pure life of the great Christian leader. Ambrose seemed to have the answers to the problems that had always troubled Augustine. Could Christianity be the truth? One day Augustine sat in a garden at Milan thinking. Two words kept running through his mind, "Tolle, lege"—"take up, read". He looked around him and saw on a bench a scroll. It was part of the New Testament. He began to read it and suddenly felt that his long struggle was over. Here was the truth and he gave himself to it with a full heart.

How happy Monica was that day before Easter in the year A.D. 387 as she watched Bishop Ambrose baptising her son. She died soon after but she had lived long enough to see all her prayers answered. Augustine went back to North Africa and lived with some Christian friends in a monastery at his home town of Tagaste, studying and writing. He became a priest and, though he still lived in his monastery, his influence spread. In 395 A.D. he was made Bishop of the town of Hippo and lived there for over thirty years, a great shepherd of the flock of Christ.

Augustine lived in troubled times. Fierce pagan tribes were battering at the frontiers of the Roman Empire and breaking them down. In A.D. 410 the warlike Goths invaded Italy and sacked the great city of Rome. It seemed like the end of the world. "Why does God allow this to happen?" Christians lamented. Augustine answered them in his greatest book of all called 'The City of God'. Empires rise and fall, he said, because they are made by greed and conquest. But the Church of God is an eternal city and his kingdom can never fall. Even as Augustine lay dying at his home in Hippo, other fierce barbarians, the Vandals, were hammering at the gates of his city. But Augustine's great faith comforted many Christians and helped the Church to go out and win these barbarians to Jesus Christ.

There were enemies within the Church as well. When Christians had been persecuted, many years before, some of them had been so afraid that they had denied Jesus and worshipped the pagan gods. When persecution ended they wanted to come back to the Church again. Wise bishops welcomed them back, if they were truly sorry. But some proud members of the Church would not agree and they went off and started a separate church of their own. They said that their church was the true one for there were no sinners in it who had denied Jesus. All their members were holy, they said proudly. Augustine was horrified. He knew that the Church is holy because

Jesus founded it. But that did not mean that everyone in it was holy. The Church is like a hospital. For a hospital is full of sick people who go there for healing. The Church is full of people who enter it to seek God's healing power for their souls. Augustine said that the Church is like an ark or a ship, a place of safety from the dangerous waters of the world. His teaching about the Church saved it from any more divisions.

Augustine found another enemy within the Church. His name was Pelagius and he came from Britain where he was a monk. Pelagius went to Rome and taught there. When Rome was taken by the Goths he went to North Africa. Augustine was shocked by his teaching. Pelagius taught that everyone is born good and is free to choose good or evil. It was easy for Pelagius to believe this. He had lived quietly in a monastery all his life and had never been really tempted to do wrong. But Augustine had never forgotten how he had stolen the useless pears when he was a boy, just out of sheer devilment. He had known many temptations all his life and he had done great wrong. It was God who had made him see the light and turn from his evil ways, not his own goodness. So Augustine began to speak against the teaching of Pelagius. He taught that it is only through the grace or power of God that we can live good lives. The Church realised that he was right and the teaching of Pelagius was condemned.

In such ways Augustine fought as a doughty champion of the Church. He died in A.D. 430 but he still spoke to Christians through his many great writings. He was made one of the four great 'Doctors' or 'Teachers' of the Church, for his teachings guided it for many centuries to come. August 28th was set aside as the day in each year on which Christians should remember Augustine of Hippo, a great leader and teacher of the Church of God.

A PRAYER OF AUGUSTINE

O Thou who art
The light of the minds that know Thee,
The life of the souls that love Thee,
The strength of the wills that serve Thee;
Help us
So to know Thee that we may truly love Thee,
So to love Thee that we may fully serve Thee,
Whom to serve is perfect freedom.
Through Jesus Christ our Lord.

Amen.

13 Ninian, Apostle of Scotland

THE Roman legions first landed in Britain in 55 B.C. under the great Julius Caesar. But it was not till 100 years later that they really conquered the island and made it part of the Roman Empire. Even then they could not defeat the fierce tribes who lived in Scotland or, as the Romans called it, Caledonia. These wild men tattooed their bodies so the Romans called them 'Picts' from the Roman word for 'painted'. When the Roman legions marched against them they hid in the hills. Then, when the Romans went back, they came down into the lowlands again to plunder. In A.D. 81 the Romans built a line of forts across Caledonia to keep the Picts out. It ran from the Firth of Clyde to the Firth of Forth. Later, a rampart of earth piled on stones was made along this line of forts and it was known as the Wall of Antonine. Even this did not stop the Picts. In A.D. 121 the Emperor Hadrian had a new line of fortifications built further south. It ran from the Solway Firth to the mouth of the River Tyne and later on it was made even stronger. This is called Hadrian's Wall and its ruins can still be seen to day. It was made of stone 15 feet high and was $73\frac{1}{2}$ miles in length. This great wall was guarded by thousands of soldiers who lived in its forts. So long as the Romans stayed in Britain to man it, Hadrian's wall did keep out the fierce and savage Picts.

In the year A.D. 360 a son was born to a chief who lived in Britain near Hadrian's Wall. He had become a Christian so his son was baptised and given the name of Ninian. When Ninian showed a great love for God, his father was glad and sent him to Rome so that he could have a good education. The Roman Emperors were Christian by that time and of course the wonderful Roman roads made travel easy. We can imagine how excited Ninian was to journey south, over the Channel and through Gaul, till he came to the greatest city in the world. At Rome there would be many things to interest him. But Ninian had one thought on his mind. Often as a boy he had heard stories of the savage Picts. Now he recognised that God was calling him to take the Good News of Jesus to them. So he studied hard in Rome to become a priest. In A.D. 394 he was made a bishop at Rome and set off to begin his great work for God.

Ninian sailed from Rome and landed in southern Gaul. On his journey northwards he stopped at Tours where the great St. Martin had his monastery. Ninian had heard of his fame and longed to meet him. They became great friends. Ninian saw how Martin trained his monks to go out in bands of twelve with a leader to start a new monastery. Each monastery became a Christian outpost, for from it the monks went out to teach pagans the Gospel of Jesus. Every monk was a missionary. Ninian thought this was a wonderful way for Christians to convert the heathen. He decided that he would copy Martin in his work among the Picts.

It was in the year A.D. 397 that Ninian crossed over Hadrian's Wall and settled in the lowlands of Scotland. He made his way to the south-west and there he lived in a cave which can still be seen today. He began first to build his church. One ancient writer says that Martin had sent some monks to accompany Ninian. They were masons to help him build. The natives of Britain lived in crude huts built of wood and wattle. Ninian wanted a fine church that would be strong and beautiful. It was made of white stones and so it was called 'The White House' or, in the Roman language, 'Candida Casa'. Later on, the Saxons came to Britain and in their language 'White House' was 'Whit hern'. So the town which grew up there came to be called Whithorn and you can find it on your map of Scotland in Wigtownshire.

When his church was finished, Ninian and his monks built their monastery around it. Here they lived together devoting their time to worship and study. Ninian trained his monks just as Martin had done so that they could go out as missionaries among the Picts. He never forgot Martin and when he heard of the saint's death, he gave his 'White House' a new name—St. Martin's Church. Like Martin, too, he loved to be alone with God. Often he went out to his cave in the cliffs, three miles away, just as Martin had done in his cave by the River Loire.

Soon the first monks were ready to go out and set up new monasteries among the Picts. Each one had its church and school for worship and study. Over the years these missions spread out over Scotland. But Ninian himself was not content to stay at the 'White House'. He led the way, going ever further North. It needed great courage to go alone and unarmed among the wild Picts, but Ninian never thought of himself. His goodness and love made him many friends and prepared the way for his monks. He worked among the Picts for thirty-five years till his death in A.D. 432. By then there were monasteries right up to the North and even across the sea in the Orkney and Shetland Islands.

So the 'White House' became the headquarters of a great missionary movement. Monks went out from it to the Picts in eastern Scotland; to the Scots in western Scotland and Ireland; to the Britons in England and in Wales. All this came from the work of Ninian and his name was revered far and wide. His body was buried in his own church and pilgrims came to Candida Casa to honour his memory. September 16th was set aside as his feast day so that Christians might never forget him. Later, Saint Columba came from Ireland and set up his monastery on the Island of Iona. His monks carried on the work of Ninian among the Picts, following in the footsteps of the great 'Apostle of Scotland'.

Patrick, the Patron Saint of Ireland

In A.D. 410 the Roman soldiers left England. For Rome itself was threatened by savage tribes. Then England was overrun by the pagan Angles and Saxons, and became heathen once more. Only in the far west of Cornwall, Wales, and Scotland, were any Christians left.

On a farm by the river Severn there lived a Roman called Calpurnius. He was a Christian, and he brought up his family to worship Jesus. But his son, Patrick, was a lazy boy and took little notice of what he was taught. One day, when Patrick was about sixteen years old, some fierce Irishmen landed on the coast. They killed Patrick's parents, and took him back to Ireland to be a slave. He was sold to a chieftain called Milchu. For six years he had to look after his master's pigs on the hills. He was very lonely and sad. Then he remembered what he had been taught about God. He began to say his prayers again. Slowly he came to love God and wanted to serve him. One night he had a dream. An angel told him to go to the coast, find a ship, and return home. Patrick ran away. After walking many days and nights, he came to the coast and found a ship. At first the captain would not take him. But he found Patrick was useful, for he had a lot of fierce Irish dogs on board to take to France. The sailors could not manage them, but Patrick soon made friends with them. So he was taken to France.

Patrick knew now what he wanted to do. God was calling him to go back to Ireland as a missionary to the heathen Irish. But first he must make up for his lazy childhood, and learn again. He studied hard for several years, and then became a priest. Soon he was ready to depart. He was made a Bishop and sent to be the missionary to Ireland. Fourteen years after he had run away, he landed there once again to begin his great work.

There were many kings in Ireland in those days. The greatest of them was called the High King. He had his palace at Tara, the chief town in all Ireland. It was the centre of the pagan religion of the Druids. Soon after he landed, Patrick went to Tara at Easter. It was the time when the Druids had their great festival of the spring. No light was allowed until the sacrifice was set ablaze in the palace of Tara. It was night, and everything was in darkness. Suddenly a great pillar of fire appeared on a hill outside the city. The pagans were angry and scared. What could it be? The High King and his soldiers drove furiously to the hill. They found Patrick and his monks there. It was he who had lit the fire. At first the King was very angry. For the Druids said that, if the fire were not put out, the whole of Ireland would be destroyed. But he found that Patrick was a man of courage, peace, and love. "I bring the true light to lighten this dark land!" Patrick cried. The King promised to hear what he had to say about his new God.

The next day was Easter Day, and Patrick preached in the hall of the High King's palace at Tara. Many of the chiefs became Christians, and some of the Druids too. The King gave Patrick freedom to preach throughout the land, and promised to protect him. Far and wide Patrick travelled, preaching and teaching, baptising and building churches. The Druids plotted against him, but no harm ever came to him. It was said that he wore invisible armour. Patrick himself said that it was Christ who protected him.

Patrick and his men travelled from place to place, holding services in the open air. They rang a bell, and sang hymns till a crowd gathered. Then Patrick would talk with them. One day a man said, "You tell us about God the Father. You tell us about God the Son. You tell us about God the Holy Spirit. That makes three Gods. But you say there is only one God. How can that be?" Patrick reached down, plucked a shamrock, and held it out to the man. "Look!" he said.

"Here are three leaves in one leaf. That is what God is like."

For thirty-six years Patrick worked for God. He was given a hill on which to build his own church at Armagh. The cathedral stands there to-day, and the Archbishop of Armagh is head of the Church of Ireland. On the hill of Tara stands a statue in memory of the great missionary of Ireland.

Patrick died on March 17th in the year A.D. 461. Every year that day is kept as St. Patrick's Day. Sometimes it is called 'Shamrock Day', and Irishmen wear a shamrock to honour their patron saint. You will know why.

Patrick's work went on after his death. Through all the land there were churches and monasteries. At one of these was a monk whose grandfather had been the High King to whom Patrick preached. He became St. Columba. He and his monks helped to bring back Christianity to heathen England. So the English, too, must thank God for the work of Patrick, the patron Saint of Ireland.

15 Benedict, Founder of the Monastery

BENEDICT was born in Italy in A.D. 480. His parents were rich and gave him a fine education. They expected him to lead an easy life of pleasure. But Benedict wanted to serve God, and when he was about twenty years old he left home. He went and lived in a cave in the hills, alone with God. In those days many monks lived alone as hermits. But Benedict came to realise that this was a selfish life. The hermit monks thought only of themselves and did no good in the world. Some monks lived together in monasteries, but they had no rules to guide them and became lazy.

After three years Benedict was invited by the monks in a monastery nearby to rule over them as their Abbot. He was stern with them and made strict rules, and soon they hated him. They tried to poison him and he went back to his cave. But the fame of the holy Benedict was spreading and good men came to him and pleaded with him to be their leader. They were troubled times. The Roman Empire had been broken down by fierce barbarian tribes. The savage Goths and Vandals had spread over Europe; even the city of Rome had been plundered. Men came to Benedict seeking the peace of God, and noblemen sent their sons to be trained by him in the good life. Soon he decided to found his own monastery in a quiet place, far from the noisy world. Near the city of Naples was a hill where there had once been a shrine of Apollo, one of the pagan gods of Rome. Here he decided to build his monastery. It became known as Monte Cassino, the most famous monastery in the world, and it is still there today.

Benedict insisted that the monks must live together, not alone. He ruled over them strictly but with kindness. "The Abbot must be merciful, ever preferring mercy to justice," he said. The monks were to be obedient and humble. They must own nothing, they must live together as brothers. No monk was allowed to be idle, each served the others as best he could. Benedict wrote all this down in his famous 'Rule'. It became the pattern for monks everywhere, for it gave them rules for every part of life in the monastery.

Benedict died in A.D. 543. Forty years afterwards his monastery was plundered by the barbarians and the monks fled to Rome. Here they were taken in by Gregory, the future Pope, who made his rich house into a monastery and became their Abbot. In A.D. 597 Pope Gregory sent some of the Benedictine monks to England to preach the Gospel to the heathen Angles. They were led by Augustine who built a monastery at Canterbury. Soon Benedictine monks were building monasteries throughout England. In every one the monks lived by the rule of Benedict.

A monastery was like a village, for it had everything needed for daily life. The buildings included the church, dining-room, bedroom, kitchen, hospital, meeting-room, workroom, and a room for visitors. Outside, there were the fields where the monks grew their food and kept their animals, vegetable gardens, barns, bakehouse, dairy, and craft-rooms. Every monk worked with his hands. The abbey church was the centre of the life of the monks. When they were not at worship the monks were busy on their various jobs. They set a fine example to people outside the monastery, and of course they helped them in many ways, especially in caring for the poor and the sick. But, above all, the monastery was a centre of education. Boys were trained there, and in the large study the monks were busy studying and writing out their beautiful books. It was the monasteries which kept the lamp of learning alight in dark and savage times. Above all, they kept the light of the Gospel burning bright. From them monks went out as missionaries to teach the pagan tribes till at last Europe was Christian once again.

Still today there are Benedictine monasteries where monks,

dressed in their black 'habit', live and work together by their Rule. On March 21st each year they specially remember their great founder and thank God for the life and work of Benedict the monk.

Columba, the Dove of the North

ST. PATRICK of Ireland had been dead about sixty years when a little boy was born in Donegal. His father was a chief and his mother a princess. Since he would one day be a king, his father decided that he must go to school. He was a gentle boy, and so he was given the name 'Columba', which means 'a dove'. Columba was sent away to a monastery school. He worked hard in the study, and in the fields as well. He learned quickly, and soon he could read and write. He loved drawing and painting. In those days there were no printed books. The monks wrote out the Bible on beautiful paper or 'parchment', with a quill pen. Some of the letters were painted in fine colours, red and blue, gold and silver. Columba loved this work best of all.

When he grew up, Columba knew that he could not be a king. He wanted to serve God as a priest. So his family gave him a hill on which he could build his church. The name of the hill meant 'an oak wood'. When the English conquered Ireland, long after, they changed its name to Londonderry. The hill was by the sea, which Columba loved. He was very happy there, ruling over his monastery. Its school became very famous, and many beautiful Bibles were made there.

Then Columba quarrelled with the High King of Ireland. He visited another monastery where they had a beautiful book of Psalms. He made a copy of it secretly by night. But the Abbot saw it

67

and said it must be his. Columba asked the High King to decide. "I made it," said Columba. "But it was my book you copied," said the Abbot. The High King said, "To every cow belongs her calf, to every book its copy". So he gave the copy to the Abbot and put Columba in prison. Columba escaped and went back to his home in Donegal. The men of his tribe were very angry with the High King. They fought against him, and many men were killed in battle. Columba was very sad, for it was all because of him. He went to a holy man. "What can I do to make amends?" he asked. The hermit said, "Leave Ireland. Go as a missionary to the heathen over the sea." So Columba, with twelve monks, sailed away across the sea.

They landed on a little island off the west coast of Scotland. It was called Iona. Here they made their monastery. They built a church of wood; wooden cells, with roofs made of twigs; a dining-room, where they could eat together; a hut for strangers; and a workroom for making books. The people were poor. The monks taught them how to grow better crops. They built a dairy and a bakehouse. Sick people and travellers were always welcome, and there were many visitors. Columba was a wise Abbot. He still loved to make Bibles. But he loved people, too. Sometimes he went out with the fishermen. He was a great friend of animals. Many legends were told of his love for the birds and how he would talk with them.

Before long, Columba knew he must start new work. "Pray for me," he said to the monks. "I am going to the Picts to tell them of God." Then he got into his little coracle and rowed away to the mainland of Scotland. The Picts were fierce warriors who worshipped pagan gods. Columba made his way to Inverness, where their king lived. His name was Buda. The gates of the town were bolted, for the people had heard that Columba was a magician. He waited outside the city wall. At last he was let in, for he seemed an ordinary man. He wore his simple monk's cassock and hood made of wool, and sandals on his feet. The King of the Picts liked him and Columba stayed with him a long time, telling him about Jesus. King Buda himself became a Christian. He sent an order to all his tribes to welcome Columba and his monks.

Columba hurried back to Iona with the good news. Soon the monks were going out in their little coracles to teach the heathen

Picts. Some went to the Orkney and Shetland Islands, others to the Faroes and the Hebrides. Some went as far north as Iceland. Others went south into Northumbria, in England. Everywhere they went they told the story of Jesus. They built churches and monasteries and schools. But they never forgot Iona, their home. It was only a little island. But it became the mother of many monasteries in Scotland and north-west England. From it the light of the Gospel shone far and wide.

Columba grew old and knew that his time had come. He went slowly round his monastery at Iona, blessing every part. He blessed his friends, the birds and animals. Then he went back to his cell to finish the psalm he was copying out till it was dark. At midnight he went into the church for the first morning service. The monks found him lying there and ran to pick him up. "Be at peace with each other," he whispered. "Be kind, and love one another." So he died.

St. Columba is remembered every year on June 9th. Iona was never forgotten. Many pilgrims went there through the years. Saints lived there and kings were buried there. The old ruins have been rebuilt, and to-day men live there as 'brothers', like Columba and his monks of old.

17 David, the Patron Saint of Wales

WHEN the Romans left Britain, fierce tribes invaded the land. The Angles and Saxons attacked the east, the Picts and Scots came down from the north, and Irish pirates plundered the west. The Angles and Saxons were pagans and very strong. They drove the ancient Britons to the west. England was heathen again. But the Britons were Christians. So Wales was still a Christian land.

Many monasteries were built in Wales. Christian missionaries would come to a new place and get permission from the chief to dwell there. They built a church of wood. Around it they made little huts or 'cells' to live in. They made them of 'wattle', as we make wicker baskets. Then they built a big hedge right round their church and houses. The whole place was called a 'Llan', which is still the Welsh word for a 'parish'. The most important work of the monks was to worship God. They studied too, and many were great scholars. They worked hard in the fields, tilling the ground and growing food, both for themselves and others. They kept bees, and gave the honey to the sick and poor. So they lived busy, useful lives. Above all, they taught the people about God. For the monks were missionaries.

In the vale of Glamorgan was a monastery called Llantwit Major. Its head was St. Paulinus. Many monks lived and studied there and then went out to make new monasteries. It was really a kind of 'university'. One of the monks was called Dewi or David. He was the son of a chief called Sandde. His mother, Nonna, was a good Christian woman who became a nun. When David had finished his studies, he went away with a few other monks. They settled in a lonely valley in Pembrokeshire at a place called Glyn Rhosyn. Here they built a monastery, with David as head.

David was a very holy man. He lived a strict life and worked hard as a monk and as a missionary. He made stern rules for his monks. They were to worship God regularly, to study and work hard, to teach and care for their people. They were to live on bread and water. They were to pull the plough themselves and not use oxen. David was strict with his monks because he knew idle people are soon in trouble. But he was very kind to the poor and needy.

David soon became famous. Men came to his monastery from all parts of Wales, from France and Ireland too. Ships could land at Porth Mawr, a good harbour nearby. The valley came to be called Menevia. When the old bishop died, the leaders of the Church met to choose a new one. They chose David. He was not at the council. So he was sent for and made Bishop of Llandaff and Caerleon. But he would not move to Caerleon where the bishop had lived. He kept his home at Menevia and his bishop's church was there.

David became famous throughout all Wales, and all the people loved him as their chief bishop. He travelled through the land, preaching and teaching, making new churches and new monasteries. Men came from abroad to seek his advice.

David died an old man, and was buried in his own monastery. So great was his fame that for hundreds of years pilgrims came to his tomb. Then he was made a Saint. The Pope said that two pilgrimages to David's tomb were as fine as one pilgrimage to Rome itself. It was not long before the place of David's tomb grew into a town. Still to-day it is called St. David's, and more than fifty churches in South Wales are named after him. March 1st was set aside as St. David's Day, and it is a time of great rejoicing for Welsh people everywhere. No country could have a finer or more popular patron Saint.

18 Gregory the Great

GREGORY was born in Rome in the year A.D. 540. His father was a ruler of the city for his family was rich and noble. Gregory had a happy and comfortable home and a good education. He studied law and when he was a man he, too, shared in the government of Rome. In A.D. 573 he was made the chief magistrate and had to judge between the citizens. He could be stern in seeing that justice was done but he won the love of many by his fairness and kindness. When his father died, soon after, he inherited great wealth and he could have lived in idleness and pleasure. But he was a sincere Christian and he wanted to serve his Master with all his heart. There were some monks in Rome who lived together by the Rule of the great St. Benedict. Gregory gave away all his wealth to the poor and joined them. Their simple life seemed to him very close to the life of Jesus and he followed it for the rest of his days.

When he was trained as a monk Gregory set up his own monastery in Rome named after St. Andrew, as well as six other monasteries on the island of Sicily. He lived happily at St. Andrew's, spending his time in prayer and study. But it was not long before the Bishop of Rome asked Gregory to help him in governing the Church. Gregory was sent to the great city of Constantinople, far away to the East. When he came back he was happy to enter his monastery again where he was made Abbot.

One day Abbot Gregory was going through the market-place where the merchants from near and far were selling their wares. One of them had some boys for sale as slaves. They had pleasant faces, fair hair and golden bodies, quite unlike the olive-skinned boys of Italy. Gregory stopped to admire them and asked where they came from. "They are pagans from Britain," replied the merchant. Gregory looked sad. "What are they called?" "Angles," answered the merchant. "Angles?" said Gregory. "They are indeed like angels. What part of the country do they come from?" "Deira," was the reply. "Good!" said the Abbot. "They must indeed be saved from 'Dei ira', the wrath of God, and brought to know their Saviour Christ. And who is their king?" "Aella," said the merchant. "Then Alleluia shall be sung to God in their land!" vowed Gregory.

He never forgot his promise. He longed to go to the land of the Angles and win them for Christ. As soon as he could, he set off on the long journey. But within three days messengers came from Rome and hustled him back. The Bishop had died from the plague and everyone wanted Gregory as their new Bishop. He gave in and accepted the great honour. But he never changed in any way during the fourteen years he was Bishop of Rome. Always he wore the simple rough garment or 'habit' of the monk. He chose for himself the title 'Servant of the servants of God'. For though he was the greatest man in Italy, Gregory was also the humblest.

He was a great leader both of the church and of his country. The Emperor lived far away in the East and had no real power in Italy. The fierce Lombards had invaded the land. There was fighting and lawlessness, plague and famine. By this time the Bishop of Rome owned large estates in the south of Italy and all the money from them. For emperors and rich men had given them over the years to the Church. Gregory used all this wealth for the good of the Church and people. He made a treaty with the Lombard invaders. He appointed governors for the cities. He provided for the sick and the poor. He was the ruler of Italy.

Gregory's influence spread all over Europe. By this time the Bishop of Rome, or the 'Pope' as he was known, had great power in the Church. Pope Gregory was greater than all those before him. He chose certain bishops in France and Spain and North Africa to be

his 'vicars', that is, his deputies. They acted for him and through them he ruled over the Church of the West.

Gregory never forgot the slave boys in the market-place. If he could not be a missionary himself then he would send others. He chose a certain Augustine, the Prior of his own monastery at Rome. Augustine set off with forty monks on the long and adventurous journey. While they were travelling through Gaul they heard dreadful stories of the cruel Angles and became frightened. The monks sent Augustine back to ask if they could return to Rome. Gregory gave him new hope and encouraged him to go on. So at last in A.D. 597 Augustine and his monks landed at Ebbsfleet in Kent and soon they had made a monastery at Canterbury. Gregory sent Augustine many letters, telling him what to do and giving him wise advice. So it was through this great Pope that Canterbury became the mother of the English Church.

Gregory never lost his love of learning and he wrote many books. One of them was a book to guide bishops in their work as shepherds of the flock of Christ. Later, King Alfred the Great translated it into the language of his people and Gregory's book was used by bishops for many centuries to come.

Gregory loved music best of all. He founded a 'School for Singers' in Rome. It was the very first 'Choir School' and through it the music of the church services became far more worthy. Gregory invented a new kind of singing for the services. It is called 'plain-song' or the 'Gregorian chant'. Though it was much simpler to sing, it was very beautiful and it was used in monasteries where it is still sung today.

Gregory died in A.D. 604 and was at once made a saint of the Church. March 12th was set aside as his memorial day each year. On that day Christians remember his work as Bishop and Pope, missionary and musician, and thank God for the life of Gregory the Great.

A MORNING HYMN OF ST. GREGORY

Father, we praise Thee, now the night is over,
Active and watchful, stand we all before Thee;
Singing we offer praise and meditation:
> *Thus we adore Thee.*

Monarch of all things, fit us for Thy mansions;
Banish our weakness, health and wholeness sending:
Bring us to heaven, where Thy saints united
> *Joy without ending.*

All-holy Father, Son and equal Spirit,
Trinity blessed, send us Thy salvation;
Thine is the glory, gleaming and resounding
> *Through all creation.*

19 Augustine of Canterbury

In A.D. 597 a missionary went to England from Rome to spread the Gospel of Jesus. It happened in this way.

There lived in the city of Rome a man called Gregory. His family was rich and powerful. Soon he became a very important man in Rome. But he was not happy. He heard the call of God to become a monk. He gave up his wealth and turned his palace into a monastery. Other monks joined him and he was their Abbot. One day Gregory was going through the market-place. Some slaves were standing there, waiting to be bought. They were English boys, with blue eyes and fair hair. Gregory thought how fine they looked. "Who are they?" he asked. "They are Angles, boys of England," the man said. "Angles? They are like angels," Gregory said. "What part of the country do they come from?" "They are from Deira," he was told. "They must be saved from the 'Dei ira'," Gregory replied. By this he meant 'the anger of God'. Then he vowed that he would go to England and teach the heathen people there. He went to the Pope, the Bishop of Rome, to ask if he might go. But the people of Rome loved Gregory so much that they would not let him go. When the Pope died soon afterwards, Gregory was made Bishop in his place. But he never forgot the slave boys.

Gregory could not go to England himself. But he could send someone else. He chose the Prior of a monastery in Rome, whose name was Augustine. Soon Augustine set out with forty monks to go to England. They crossed over the Alps and travelled through France. Here they were told terrible stories of the savage people of England. They were frightened. They sent Augustine back to Rome to ask Gregory if he would let them return home. But Gregory sent Augustine back again with letters to read to them all, giving them new courage, and they went on.

Augustine and his monks landed on the shore of Kent at a place called Ebbsfleet. The King of Kent was called Ethelbert. His wife, Queen Bertha, was a Christian. They came to hear St. Augustine. The King said they must meet out of doors. For he was afraid of magic, and he believed that Augustine's spells would not work in the open air. The monks came in a procession, singing hymns, a wooden cross and a picture of Jesus carried before them. The King heard Augustine speak about his God and could find no harm in his words. He gave the monks freedom to teach his people. He gave them a house in his city of Canterbury, and the old British Church of St. Martin for their worship. Now they began to go through Kent teaching the heathen Saxons about Jesus. The monks were good and holy men. Before long, King Ethelbert was baptised and many of his people too.

Augustine often wrote to Gregory for advice. Gregory made him Archbishop of England and said, "You will be head of the Church in the south of England, with twelve bishops to help you". Gregory sent other men from Rome. Augustine made one of them Bishop of Rochester and another Bishop of London. So the Church began to grow. Then Augustine asked Gregory, "What shall I do about the heathen temples?" Gregory wrote back in his letter, "Don't destroy them. Throw away the idols inside. Put in their place Christian altars and relics of the saints. Then use them as Christian churches." Augustine obeyed his wise advice. In Canterbury was a very old heathen temple in ruins. Augustine built a monastery there. It was called Christ Church. The monastery became great and famous. The church grew into the great Canterbury Cathedral which stands there to-day. "What about the pagan feasts?" Augustine asked. "Turn them into Christian feasts," said Gregory.

There was one thing that Augustine had to do by himself. He had to make friends with the British Church in Wales and western England. It was not easy. The British hated the Angles and Saxons who had conquered their land. Augustine came from another land and they were suspicious of him. They had different ways of worshipping God, too. They wanted to keep their own ways and be free. Augustine went to meet the British bishops. They met under a tree, ever afterwards called St. Augustine's Oak. It was probably near Cricklade in Wiltshire. The bishops were unfriendly because they were suspicious of St. Augustine. One story says that Augustine did not rise from his chair to greet them. They thought him a proud man. They could not agree, and Augustine went back to Canterbury. It was not till sixty years later that the two Churches joined together and made one Church in England.

Augustine was old when he came to England. He had lived here for only seven years when he died in A.D. 604. He was buried in the church of his monastery at Canterbury. He is remembered every year on May 26th. He had done a great work. Kent was now Christian, and missionaries would go out from there to other parts of England. Ever since that time Canterbury has been the centre of Christianity in England and the Archbishop of Canterbury head of the Church of England.

Aidan, the Apostle of Northumbria

Do you remember who founded the great monastery on the island of Iona? His monks travelled far and wide preaching the Gospel. One day a messenger came to Iona from King Oswald of Northumbria. Oswald was a Christian and he wanted to make his rough people Christians too. "Send me a holy man," he asked. "My people are savage. They need to learn the Christian way of peace and love." The monks chose Corman. He was hard and fearless. He would be just the man to deal with those fierce people. Corman set off, sure that he would succeed. Some months later he came back, cross and disappointed. "They are savages," he said. "No one could make them Christians." The monks listened to his story. He had been fierce with the people of Northumbria, warning them of God's anger. One of the monks was a gentle, quiet man called Aidan. He said to Corman, "Perhaps you have been too strict with them, brother. Babes must be fed with milk, not meat. These people are little children. They need to be told of the love of God, not his anger." Then all the monks cried out, "Aidan must go! They need him!" So it was decided, and Aidan set off in his coracle for the mainland.

After a long journey Aidan came at last to the fortress where King Oswald lived. It was a place called Bamborough, near the east coast of Northumberland. Oswald welcomed him warmly. At first Aidan could not speak the language of the people. But King Oswald taught

him, and soon Aidan could go about by himself. "Where would you like to build your monastery?" the King asked. "I come from Iona, an island," said Aidan. "I should like to live on the island of Lindisfarne." "Then you shall have it," Oswald replied. So Aidan and his monks built their monastery on the rocky island off the coast. There they could live in peace. But Aidan had not forgotten his task. When the tide is low, it is easy to walk from the island to the mainland across the sands. So he and his monks could travel about from Lindisfarne just as they used to from Iona. There they built their little church, their huts, and their school. It was the headquarters for their work.

Aidan became greatly loved, for he was a loving man. He travelled on foot all over the country, a friend to everyone he met. Many of the heathens became Christians and many churches were built. King Oswald was a great friend to Aidan and helped him all he could. Many of the chieftains were baptised. Aidan loved everyone, high or low, rich or poor. He taught men the love of God. But he taught it most of all by the way he lived. Many presents were given to him, but he never kept them for himself. He gave away all he had to the poor and needy. Always he lived simply, a holy man of God, loving and kind.

A sad day came when the country was attacked by Penda, the heathen King of Mercia. King Oswald was killed in battle, but Penda could not capture his fortress of Bamborough. The people fought hard and drove Penda back. Oswin, a nephew of Oswald, became King of Deira, the southern part of the land. He was a Christian and helped Aidan gladly in his work. One day he gave Aidan a very fine horse. He did not think it right for the holy man of God to walk everywhere in his rough sandals. Aidan met a beggar soon afterwards and gave him the horse. Oswin was angry when he heard about it. "Fancy giving that fine horse to a beggar! Any old horse would have done for him!" But Aidan said gently to the king, "Which do you think God loves most, the fine horse or the poor man?" The King saw at once how wrong he had been and asked Aidan to forgive him.

Soon there was fighting again. Oswin was killed, and Aidan mourned his good friend. He was old now. For sixteen years he had travelled through the land, doing his great work for God. Now it was ended, and a few days after the death of the King he died in the church at Bamborough.

Never again were there any idols in Northumbria. The monastery of Lindisfarne became great and famous, sending missionaries over all the land. The island itself was given a new name, the Holy Island. Still to-day Christian pilgrims walk over the sands at low tide to Lindisfarne, especially on August 31st. For that is the day in the year set aside to think of St. Aidan and to thank God for his life and work.

21 Hilda and Caedmon of Whitby

AIDAN often visited the King's fortress at Bamborough. Sometimes he talked to a little princess there. Her name was Hilda. She had many things to learn, for one day she would rule over her people. She was baptised when she was a girl, and as she grew up she was taught to be unselfish and honest and kind. Very few girls had lessons in those days. But she was going to be a queen, so she had lessons in reading and writing. As there were no books in her Anglo-Saxon language, she had to learn Latin. She worked hard, too, at sewing and embroidery, making pictures in wool which were hung on the walls of the palace.

But Hilda knew more and more that she could not be queen. God was calling her to serve him in a very special way. She told her mother and father that she wanted to be a nun. They were Christians too, so they knew she must answer God's call. One day she packed away her pretty gowns, her rich jewels and the golden tiara she wore to show she was a princess. She put on the long, rough robe which nuns wore and the black hood over her head. Then Aidan said to her, "I want you to be Abbess of the nunnery at Hartlepool, by the sea. I know you will rule over it wisely." Hilda loved Aidan, the man of God, and she gladly went. She wanted her nunnery to be just like Aidan's monastery on the island of Lindisfarne.

Nine years later some land was given to Hilda's nunnery. It was on the high green cliffs at Whitby by the North Sea. Here a great new monastery was built. It was for monks and nuns as well, and Hilda was to rule over both men and women. She was a good and wise Abbess, and before long her monastery became famous. Every day the monks and nuns sang praises to God in their chapel. They worked in the fields, growing their own food. They kept cows for their milk and their meat. From their sheep in the hills they got wool for their clothes. They cared for the sick and fed the poor. Many girls and boys lived in the monastery school. They were taught to read and write so that they could study the Bible. One of the girls was the daughter of the King of Northumbria. She, too, became a nun, and took Hilda's place when the Abbess died. Many of the boys became monks and went out to teach the pagan people. Some of them became bishops.

Hilda had a big family to rule over. But it was a very happy one. She taught them to be peaceful and loving. They shared everything at the monastery and everyone was treated fairly. Besides the monks and nuns, there were ordinary people working there. On winter evenings they would all meet together for supper in the hall. There were monks and nuns, shepherds and cowherds, ploughmen and farm-workers. A big fire of logs in the middle of the hall gave them light and warmth. After supper there would be poems and songs. They would pass round the harp and anyone who wanted could play and sing. One of the cowherds was called Caedmon. He could not sing a note, and always had to pass the harp on to his neighbour. This made him sad, and one night he went out feeling very miserable. He went to the cattle-shed and made his bed on the straw. That night he had a dream. A voice said, "Caedmon, sing to me." But Caedmon said sadly, "I cannot sing. That is why I came out of the hall." The voice answered him, "Caedmon, you shall sing." He was astonished and said, "What shall I sing?" "Sing about the beginning of all things," the voice told him. "Sing the story you heard from the monks of how God made the world." Then, in his dream, Caedmon sang of the stars and the sky, the sun and the moon, the birds and the flowers. It was all so easy, and so wonderful to be able to sing the praise of God. But when he awoke, behold, he could still sing! All that day he sang at his work.

The other herdsmen were amazed and said, "We must tell Mother Hilda of this wonder". Hilda sent for Caedmon and asked him to sing to her. Then she said, "Caedmon, this is God's gift and you must use it. You will have no time to care for the cattle now. God has called you to new work, to sing for him." So Caedmon came and lived at the monastery. The monks told him stories from the Bible and he turned them into sweet songs in the language of the people. He sang in the hall after supper, he sang in the church. He went round with the monks and sang to the people in town and village. The monks wrote down his Bible songs and soon they were sung throughout the land. Very few people could read the Latin Bible. Very few people had a Bible. But everyone could join in the lovely songs of Caedmon, and learn the Bible stories they told. So Caedmon the cowherd became the poet and singer of the famous monastery of Hilda.

When Hilda died in A.D. 689, she had ruled over her monastery for thirty years. She was known throughout the land and everyone called her 'Mother'. Many people came to visit her and to seek her advice. A great Council of the Church was held at her monastery so that she could join in it. She is still remembered on November 17th each year. A College of Oxford University is named after her. For she was one of the greatest women in the history of England.

Cuthbert of Lindisfarne  22

EVEN when he was a young boy Cuthbert knew that he wanted to be a monk. He went to the monastery at Melrose in Scotland, by the River Tweed, as a lad. The Abbot was a good and gentle man and Cuthbert himself grew in holiness. As soon as he was old enough he took the monk's vows of poverty, chastity and obedience. When the Prior of Melrose died, Cuthbert was chosen to fill his place. He trained the boys and young men there in the monastic life. He taught them with authority, but he taught them best by his own simple goodness.

Many monks stayed in the monastery all their lives. Cuthbert loved to go out and travel among the people in the towns and villages, preaching the Gospel of Jesus. Sometimes he rode on a horse but he mostly went on foot. The people of Northumbria had not long been Christians and they easily fell back into their pagan ways. This happened especially in time of plague. There were no doctors or hospitals, except in the monasteries. The simple folk tried to stop the plague by calling on the pagan gods. They used spells and charms and magic arts. Cuthbert went out into the countryside particularly at these times. He taught them to give up such foolish ways and to make their prayers to the one true God.

When Cuthbert came to a town, people quickly gathered together. They listened eagerly to his preaching and gladly tried to live as he taught them. There was something different from other monks about

85

Cuthbert. When he spoke, his face shone like an angel. So great was his love that his hearers felt ashamed. They had to own up to him any wrong they had done. Nothing could be hidden from the saintly Prior. Then he gently told them how they should show God they were sorry.

Cuthbert did not often go to the towns. He loved best to go to the lonely villages tucked among the mountains, where the people never saw a stranger, for visitors feared to go there. The people were rough and poor and there were dangers on all sides. Sometimes Cuthbert was away in the mountains for a month at a time, teaching the lonely villagers the ways of God by his words and his example of love and kindness.

In the year A.D. 664 Cuthbert went with his Abbot to the monastery at Lindisfarne to be Prior there. His work was to train the monks and to teach the boys in the famous school of Lindisfarne. But after some years on the island, Cuthbert felt called by God to live alone. He loved his fellow monks but that was because he loved God most of all. He longed to be alone with God. He chose another island nearby named the Isle of Farne. No one dared to live there for it was believed to be the abode of evil spirits. Nor was there any water or trees. First Cuthbert drove out the evil spirits in the name of God. Then the monks willingly came to help him build a little hut for his new home. He bade them dig for water where he directed and there they found a clear flowing spring. He sowed barley and his good crop gave him food to support himself. Round the hut Cuthbert built a high wall of earth so that he could see nothing but the heavens. For eight years he lived the life of a hermit on his tiny island of Farne.

The fame of the holy Cuthbert spread throughout the kingdom of Northumbria. In A.D. 685 a council of bishops elected him to be Bishop of Northumbria. Messengers were sent to the island to fetch Cuthbert but he would not come. Then the King himself, with leaders of the church and the monks of Lindisfarne, went by boat to the island. They knelt before the saint and pleaded with him to become their bishop. At last the humble Cuthbert gave in to their entreaties and on Easter Day he was made Bishop in the Minster at York.

Bishop Cuthbert lived like the Apostles of Jesus. He was simple in his ways, fasting and denying himself. He was always humble and saw no difference between high and low, rich and poor, noble and peasant. He spent much of his time in prayer for the people given to his charge. His teaching won them to love God and each other. He was, as Bede says in his history book, the finest kind of teacher for he himself practised what he taught. His love and patience and kindness showed men what Jesus must have been like and they longed to be like him. He was never too busy to help anyone and he loved best to help those who had gone astray and needed him most. He was only a Bishop for two years. But during that time he did wonderful work for the Church in Northumbria.

Cuthbert was growing old and, when he knew the end of his life was near, he went back to his little island home to spend his last days with God. Some of the monks accompanied their beloved bishop. He wanted to be buried on the island he had loved best of all. But the monks pleaded with him to let them bury him on the Holy Island of Lindisfarne, within their own church. Cuthbert died on March 20th in the year A.D. 687 and was buried at Lindisfarne. In the years to come the Danes invaded England and Lindisfarne knew no peace. When at last England was united and fighting ended, the body of Cuthbert was taken to the Cathedral at Durham where it rests to this day.

Some of the Christians whose stories are told in this book served God as leaders of the Church, others as missionaries, and others as builders of churches. Cuthbert served God best of all by the simple goodness of his life. The day of his death, March 20th, was set aside in the Christian year as his festival day. On it Christians have always remembered him and given thanks to God for the holiness of his life and for the example he gives us of Christian love.

23 Bede, the Father of English History

MANY of the stories you have read in this book come from the very first English history-book. It was written by a monk and we call him the 'Father of English History'.

Thirty years after the death of St. Aidan a little boy was sent to one of his monastery schools in Northumbria. His name was Bede and he was seven years old. The monastery was at Wearmouth by the sea in the north-east of England. When he was ten years old, Bede was moved to a new monastery. It was at Jarrow, not far away. In this monastery he spent almost all his life. He never went farther than the seven miles to Wearmouth. Yet he worked so hard in his monastery that he is one of the greatest Englishmen in history.

Bede was taught by the monks to read and to write. It was not easy, for in those days all the books were written in Latin, the language of the Romans. But he loved to learn and became a fine scholar. He learned Greek as well. He was in the choir in the monastery church. There were several services each day. Bede was taught music and enjoyed singing the praises of God. Of course he took his share in the other work—cooking, cleaning, helping in the field and on the farm. It was a large school and the boys slept together in one big bedroom called 'the dormitory'. They went to bed at sunset and got up at sunrise. It was very peaceful in the monastery. But there was plenty of work to be done.

The Abbot of Jarrow sometimes made the long journey to Rome with his friend the Abbot of Wearmouth monastery. They brought precious things back with them. Bede loved best the beautiful books made by monks over the seas. The two monasteries each had a fine library, and Bede studied hard. When he was grown up, he was made a priest, and before long he was head of the monastery school. There were 600 boys in his school. Bede never learned just for his own sake. He studied so that he could teach others. In his history-book he says, "It has always been my delight to learn or teach or write".

You will remember that in those days all books had to be made by hand. Bede had to write out his own books. He wrote nearly fifty books altogether. They were always books to help others. Now in those days very few people could read Latin. So Bede said, "I must

turn the Bible into the language of the people". It was called Anglo-Saxon. If he did this, the monks would be able to read the Bible to the people. It was a long task, and took many years. He grew old, and the monks said, "Dear Father, you are too old to come to all the services. The walk to church is too much for you." But Bede said, "The angels are with us in church when we worship God. If I am not there, they will say, 'Where is Bede? Why has he not come with the brothers to pray?'."

But the day came when he could walk no longer. He had to stay in his bed, old and tired. His new Bible was not yet finished. The monks came and sat by his bed and wrote for him. He reached the Gospel of St. John and struggled on. He knew that his death was near. But he must finish so that the monks could read the story of Jesus to the people in the Anglo-Saxon they spoke. He had come to the very last chapter, when the old man lay back on his pillows. A young monk called Wilbert was writing. He became anxious. "Dear Master," he said, gently, "there is but one sentence more." "Then write quickly, my son." Soon Wilbert said, "Father, it is finished." "Yes," said Bede, "it is finished. Lift me up so that I may see the chapel." Wilbert held him, while Bede saw for the last time the church in which he had served God for sixty years. He cried out, "Glory be to the Father, and to the Son, and to the Holy Ghost". Then he sank back, and died.

Bede was buried in the chapel of his monastery. Many years later his tomb was moved to Durham Cathedral, and you may see it there to-day. His new Bible in Anglo-Saxon was written out by the monks, and copies of it went all over England. Soon he became known throughout the land. He came to be called 'The Venerable Bede', for he had been so good and holy a man of God. May 27th was set aside to remember him each year.

Many of his books have been lost. But we still have his famous history-book. He knew much history from all the books he had read. But he sent all over England, collecting stories of the past. His book tells the history of England from 55 B.C., when the Romans came, to A.D. 597, when Augustine landed in Kent. At the end he wrote his signature, "Bede the servant of God, and priest of the monastery of the blessed Apostles Peter and Paul at Wearmouth and Jarrow".

King Alfred the Great

Now that the Angles and Saxons had become Christians, England was a peaceful country. Then suddenly there was trouble again. Fierce warriors were landing on the east coast of England. They were sea-rovers, and they came from Denmark and Norway. We call them 'Vikings', which means 'warriors', or Danes. They came in long-ships with a hundred men in each one. They were tall, fair men and they fought with swords and battle-axes. No one could stop these savage pirates. They killed and plundered and brought terror to the land. At first they went back with their spoil. Then more came and stayed in England, driving out the Saxons from their homes. Before long they had conquered most of the east of the land. They worshipped pagan gods and they had no respect for churches and monasteries. Many were destroyed by them.

The King of the West Saxons was called Ethelwulf and his wife was Queen Osberga. They had four sons. The youngest was called Alfred. Sometimes the boys went to a monk at the abbey, who taught them. They learnt prayers and texts from the Bible and were told stories. But they did not learn how to read and write. One day Queen Osberga called her four sons. She showed them a beautiful book, written by monks, with lovely colours and fine letters. "Would you like to be able to read this book?" she said to them. "Oh no," said the three eldest. "We are too busy. Monks learn to read, not soldiers.

We must learn to fight so that we can help father against the Danes." The Queen said, "I will give this book to the first one who can read it to me". They all started reading lessons with the monk. The three eldest soon gave up. But Alfred worked hard at his letters. One day he came to the Queen. "Mother," he said, proudly, "I can read that book to you now. Listen." So Alfred won the beautiful book. It was his greatest treasure, for he loved books.

But he did not have much time to read. His father died fighting the Danes, and then two of his brothers. Alfred was eighteen now and he had to help his third brother fight the Danes. They fought many battles, often winning, but still more Danes came. Then his brother was killed and Alfred became King when he was twenty-three years old. Soon the Danes came with a great army and conquered the whole of Wessex. Alfred had to flee. He was a king without a kingdom.

Alfred fled to Somerset in the west. He found a hiding-place among the marshy swamps there. It was an island where he and his loyal men were quite safe. They called it Athelney, the 'Island of Nobles'. But Alfred was not beaten. He sent word round all the land. More and more Saxons came to their King, and soon he had a fine army. Now he was ready, but he wanted to be sure. He went to the camp of the Danes at Chippenham in Wiltshire. He was dressed up as a minstrel. He played the harp well and sang to the Danes. They took him to their King, Guthrum, who loved music and invited Alfred to stay. So Alfred learnt all the secrets of his enemies. Then he went back to Athelney and led his army out. He defeated the Danes at the battle of Ethandune, or Edington, in Wiltshire. They fled to their stronghold, but Alfred's army laid siege to it till the Danes had no food left and were forced to give in. Alfred did not kill them. That was not his way. He made Guthrum sign a treaty. The Danes were to have the eastern part of England, which was called the Danelaw, and never to attack Wessex again. Guthrum and his chiefs became Christians. So Alfred won back his Kingdom, and gave it peace. He made an army and a navy to keep Wessex safe, and built strong walls round his towns. He made Winchester his capital city.

Now there was peace, Alfred could turn to the things he loved best. Many monasteries and churches had to be rebuilt. He made new ones, too, like the abbey at Athelney. He invited monks to come to his kingdom from Ireland and France and even from far-off Rome. They were to set up new schools and to teach his people. One of them, a monk called Asser, was a famous scholar. He became Alfred's great friend. They worked together, turning the Latin books into the Anglo-Saxon language which the people spoke. Now the monks could read the Psalms and other parts of the Bible to the people in their own language. They turned the history-book of Bede into Anglo-Saxon and Alfred started a new history-book called the 'Anglo-Saxon Chronicle'. We can still read in it the story of those far-off days.

Alfred was a good Christian king. He was called 'Protector of the Poor', for he made many new laws so that there should be justice in his kingdom. Alfred loved God and he wanted most of all to make his people good Christians. At his court there was a school for the children and a church where every day Alfred worshipped God. Sometimes he went there secretly to ask God to help him be a good King.

Alfred died in A.D. 901. His body was buried at Winchester but his memory lived on. Of all the kings of England he is the only one we call Great. If you go to Winchester, you can see the statue of Alfred carrying his sword and shield. October 26th was the day in the year set aside to his memory. It is a day to thank God for this Christian king who saved England from becoming a pagan land, and left a fine example to all those who came after him.

25 Dunstan of Glastonbury

WHEN Alfred the Great died, his son Edward became King after him. Edward had three sons called Athelstan, Edmund, and Edred. Athelstan was the eldest, and when he was a little boy his grandfather was very fond of him. Alfred gave him a little sword, shining with jewels, and said he would become a great king. Athelstan was wise and good like his grandfather, but the Danes rebelled against him and he had to be a warrior. When he died, his brother Edmund became King. He was only eighteen years old and he, too, had to fight hard against the Danes. But not long after he was stabbed by a wicked man and his brother Edred had to take up the fight. Would there ever be peace with the Danes? Edred defeated them, but that was not enough. Saxons and Danes must learn to live together in peace. Edred chose a wise man to help him bring peace to England. His name was Dunstan.

Dunstan was born near Glastonbury in Somerset. He went to the school at the famous monastery there. He came from a noble family and he went to live at the royal court of King Athelstan at Winchester. He was a clever boy and worked hard. He soon learnt to read and write. He was fond of painting, too, and made his own books, like the monks did, with lovely colours. He made things with his hands out of wood and metal. Best of all, he loved music and never went anywhere without his harp. So he was clever at many things and became a great favourite of the King. But the other young nobles grew jealous and made up stories about him. So Dunstan was sent away from the royal court. Soon after, when he was very ill, he decided to become a monk. He lived all by himself, praying to God and doing the handiwork he loved so much.

When Edmund became King, he sent for Dunstan. "You are welcome to live with me here at court," he said. "But I know you want to be useful and to help others. I am going to make you Abbot of Glastonbury." Now Dunstan began his great work. He restored the Abbey at Glastonbury and made it very beautiful. He taught the monks to do crafts with their hands, making lovely furnishings for their church. He gave them new rules for their life together in the monastery. Some of the monks had become lazy. Dunstan made their life busy and useful. One part of the day was spent in the worship of God, one part in study, and one part in work. Some of the monks had married and lived outside the monastery. Dunstan knew this was bad. So he ordered that the monks must not marry and that they must live and work together. Soon the fame of Glastonbury spread through the land. Many of the monks became fine scholars, and the school at Glastonbury was like a university. Other monasteries began to copy Dunstan's ways.

Dunstan was very happy at Glastonbury, ruling over his monks. But there came a sad day when the body of the young King Edmund was brought to Glastonbury to be buried. The new King, his brother Edred, sent for Dunstan. "I need you," he said. "You must leave Glastonbury and live here at my court. You must help me rule over my kingdom and bring peace to England." So Dunstan lived at Winchester and helped the King all he could. Often Edred was ill, and then Dunstan had to look after everything. Always he tried to do what was right, both for his country and for his Church. Because of this he had enemies. They persuaded the new King to send Dunstan away, and he went to live in Belgium.

Not long after, Edgar the Peaceful came to the throne. At once he sent for Dunstan, and before long made him Archbishop of Canterbury. For twenty years Dunstan ruled over the Church, making wise rules for monks and priests. All over the land he made the monasteries like his own at Glastonbury, and he built many new ones too. Every one had its school, not only for reading and writing, but for art, and

craft, and music. Dunstan made the Church finer than it had ever been. He helped the King, too. On his advice, many Danes were given important work and began to feel they were no longer enemies. Edgar was called 'The Peaceful' because Danes and Saxons were learning to live together and there was no more fighting. For some time before this, the people had called themselves 'English'. Now the country was called 'Engealand', or 'England'. So Dunstan was one of the builders of England.

For the last nine years of his life Dunstan lived at Canterbury, worshipping God, working in his library and making harps and organs as he had always loved to do. He died in A.D. 988. He is remembered each year on May 19th.

There is one amusing legend about Dunstan. It tells how he was so busy doing good things that the devil became very worried. One day he poked his head through the window to find out what Dunstan was planning against him. Dunstan seized a pair of red-hot tongs from the fire and pinched his nose. The devil ran away and never dared come back. This legend was very popular in the olden days and artists often drew it. But Dunstan was remembered most of all as a great Christian leader of his Church and his country. He left England a far better country because of his life and work.

Queen Margaret of Scotland 26

THOUGH Princess Margaret was English she was born far away in the land of Hungary. Her grandfather had been the strong King of England. But when he died Prince Canute of Denmark seized the throne and Margaret's father was sent out of the land. He made his home in Hungary and there Margaret grew up with her sister Christina and her little brother Edgar.

Margaret was nine years old when King Canute died. Her uncle Edward became King of England, but he had no son to become King after him. He sent a royal messenger to Margaret's home in Hungary. "Bring Prince Edgar to England," he ordered. "Then he can grow up to be King after me." Margaret made the long journey to England with her sister and brother and they came safely to London. They lived in the royal Palace of Westminster and they had their lessons together. A wise priest named Lanfranc was their teacher and Margaret soon became his best scholar. She loved books and she worked hard at her studies. But best of all she loved God and she had her own precious prayer-books which she used every day.

When Margaret was 21 years old, those happy days came to a sudden end. It was the year A.D. 1066. Her uncle, King Edward, had died, but her brother, Prince Edgar, was too young to be king. William the Conqueror came across the sea from Normandy. He won the great Battle of Hastings and he became ruler of all England.

97

Margaret knew that her brother would be in danger now. She must take Christina and Edgar back to Hungary where they would be safe. They set sail across the English Channel but a terrible storm drove their little ship off its course. The fierce winds swept it up into the North Sea. At last they saw land through the storm-clouds. But it was the rocky coast of Scotland and their ship was cast ashore and nearly wrecked. Somehow it kept afloat and brought them into calm water. It was the Firth of Forth and where they landed was called ever afterwards St. Margaret's Hope. Wild warriors met them and took them to the royal Castle at Edinburgh. It stood five hundred feet high on the rock and it was the home of King Malcolm of Scotland. He welcomed them warmly to his castle. "I once had to flee from my own country," he said. "Your uncle, King Edward of England, was good to me and he gave me a home. Now I can repay his goodness and give you a home."

But it was not long before King Malcolm found that he wanted Margaret to rule over his castle home. He had fallen in love with the beautiful Princess, with her fair hair and blue eyes. He had never met anyone so kind and good and gentle. He asked her to marry him but Margaret refused. She had always wanted to be a nun, to live in a convent and to give her life to God. Besides, King Malcolm was so different from her. He was strong and brave and truthful but he did not know God; he could not read, and he spent most of his time fighting. Margaret prayed anxiously. At last she realised that she could serve God as a Queen and help the rough and savage people of Scotland to know him. So she and King Malcolm were married in the church at Dunfermline and went to live in Edinburgh Castle. At once Margaret wrote to her old teacher, Lanfranc. "Send me a good monk to teach my people," she asked. Lanfranc sent the good Prior of Durham monastery, named Turgot. He served Queen Margaret faithfully and when she died he wrote the story of her life. He says that the Queen went out alone every day to a cave by the castle. The King followed her to see what she did. He found her praying and reading from her book of Gospel stories. He had the cave made into a beautiful little chapel and soon he was kneeling beside her. Once the Gospel book disappeared and the Queen missed it dreadfully. A few days later the King gave it to her. Now it had a new cover made of gold and silver and precious stones. You can still see that book in the great Bodleian Library at Oxford. And you can still visit St. Margaret's Chapel in the castle at Edinburgh.

Margaret made the rough castle into a home. She taught her ladies to weave pictures in tapestry to cover the bare walls and to embroider curtains for the windows. She taught the rough chieftains to say Grace before meals in the hall. They had white linen on the table, fine plates to eat from, and they learnt to copy the Queen's good manners. Every day the castle doors were open to poor people, sick people, and especially boys and girls. The Queen taught her ladies never to turn anyone away.

King Malcolm soon found what presents would best please his Queen. She cared nothing for fine clothes and rich jewels. For her sake he built monasteries for monks and convents for nuns so that they could teach his people. Homes were built for orphan children and schools where the Queen taught herself. Inns were built near the rocky coasts for travellers and for pilgrims who came to St. Andrews. Soon people in other lands heard how the wild and fierce Scots were being changed. Merchants and traders and craftsmen came to live there and they brought with them the ways of peace.

Margaret had eight children of her own. She taught them to love God and to serve his people and three of her sons became wise Kings of Scotland. Her daughter Matilda became the wife of King Henry I and helped him to rule England wisely. But before that happened, there were often wars between England and Scotland. In 1093 King William II marched against Scotland. By trickery he trapped King Malcolm and his son and killed them both. Queen Margaret wept bitterly for her husband and her eldest son and she died soon afterwards. Her body was buried in the church at Dunfermline but her goodness lived on. In the year 1250 she was made a saint and June 10th was set aside every year to the memory of Margaret, the saintly Queen of Scotland.

27

Rahere, the Court Jester

IF you were ill, you would be taken to hospital and soon be made well again. There are hospitals in most lands today. They are bright and clean and comfortable. Kind doctors and nurses are there to look after you, and they have wonderful medicines to make you better. In the old days there were no hospitals at all. Many children died when they were young. Towns were dirty and plagues often came. There were no hospitals to care for men wounded in battle. But there was one place to which sick people could go. It was the monastery. There the monks never turned anyone away. For every monastery had its special house for people who were ill or old. It was called the 'hospice'. So you can see where our word 'hospital' comes from.

When Henry the First was King of England, his court was a very happy one. There was one man who made everybody laugh. His name was Rahere. He was the jester, full of jokes and witty sayings. He was probably a juggler too. He loved the jolly life at court. Then one day came a great tragedy. The King's only son, William, was coming back from France when his ship was wrecked. Everyone was drowned. The King was so heart-broken that he never smiled again. The court became sad and gloomy. It was no place for jolly Rahere. He decided to go on the long journey to Rome as a pilgrim. He would see lots of new places and make new friends. It would be an exciting trip to make.

So Rahere went to Rome to have a good time. But while he was there he became very ill. He had a fever called malaria. He would have died if no one had taken pity on him. But he was taken by some monks into their hospice. It was called the Hospice of The Three Fountains. The monks nursed him carefully during his long illness and were very kind. Rahere began slowly to get well and bit by bit his strength came back to him. He had a long time to think as he lay in bed. "How lucky I am to have my health back again!" he thought. "But it's only because of these kind monks. Why do they do this wonderful work? It must be because they are followers of Jesus. I wish I could do something like that instead of wasting my time at the King's court." Then Rahere had a wonderful idea. He thought about God more than ever he had done before. God had given him so much. What could he give to others to show how thankful he was? Why, he could build a hospice himself! He would become a monk and serve God by caring for the sick!

After many months, Rahere came back to England. His friends at court was astonished to see him in his black 'habit' instead of bright clothes. He did not waste time amusing them. He went straight to the King and told him his story. He told him how he had dreamed of St. Bartholomew, one of the twelve apostles of Jesus. Bartholomew had appeared to him. He bade him build a church and a hospital at at the Smooth Field, outside the gate of London town. Bartholomew had blessed him and said, "Build your church and hospital in my name".

The King was glad that Rahere wanted to do so much good for the people. He gave him the Smooth Field willingly and Rahere set to work with his own hands. Many people laughed at first, especially his friends, but he was not a bit dismayed. Then they began to help. The courtiers gave money and the poor people helped with their hands. It took a long time. At last it was finished. The church and the hospital of St. Bartholomew stood firm and strong outside the city wall. With them was a Priory for the monks and nuns who would look after the hospital. Now the sick had somewhere to go.

This first hospital was not like ours. In those days people did not understand sickness as we do. But there was shelter and beds and food. Most of all, there were kind men and women, doing their work

of love in the name of Jesus. Soon the hospital was full. Rahere
worked there for twenty years till he died in A.D. 1144. But the
hospital went on growing. It is still there to-day. Now it is a fine
modern hospital, but it is still called St. Bartholomew's. The name of
the place has changed from Smooth Field to Smithfield, but the
hospital is still on the land where Rahere began it. He was buried in
the Priory church. The ruins are still there and you can see his tomb.

Other Christian people followed Rahere. It is to them that we owe
our fine hospitals to-day. For, like Rahere, they followed in the steps
of Jesus who "went about doing good and healing all manner of
sickness among the people".

Bernard of Clairvaux

28

ONE day in the year A.D. 1090 there was great feasting in the castle of Fontaines in the land of France. For a son had been born to the lord of the castle. He already had five sons and a daughter and he loved them dearly. But little Bernard was the sweetest of all. Lady Elizabeth was a good Christian and she brought her children up to love God and to serve him faithfully. Her sons were going to be knights like their brave father. But Bernard was not very strong and he was sent to a school to become a scholar. He learnt the Latin language in which all books were written then. His favourite book was his fine Latin Bible. When he was nineteen years old he came back to his happy castle home. But soon after, his dear mother died and Bernard was very miserable. One day, as he wandered alone in the woods, he came to a little chapel. He went in and prayed, pouring out his heart to God. Suddenly he heard a voice within him, saying, "Come unto me and I will give you rest." Then Bernard felt at peace. He knew now that he would give his life to God.

Bernard had a fine voice and was a wonderful speaker. When he told his brothers that he was going to become a monk they all vowed to go with him. One day a band of thirty young nobles set out from the castle of Fontaines. Bernard was leading his brothers and friends to join a monastery. They went to the monastery at a place named Citeaux. The monks there were called Cistercians. It was a poor monastery with few monks. But Bernard and his friends brought new life to it. Bernard lived a strict and holy life. He loved God dearly and spent his time in prayer and in deeds of service. As his fame spread, other fine young men came to join the monastery. Soon there were too many and the Abbot said, "We must start new monasteries." Twelve monks went out with a leader, just like Jesus and his twelve disciples, and founded a new home. It was not long before Bernard was chosen as a leader and he set off with his twelve monks.

Monasteries had been started by the great Benedict many years before. His monasteries had grown so much that towns sprang up round them. They became rich and then the monks grew lazy. "We will live deep in the country," Bernard said. He found a lonely valley and decided to build his monastery there. Its French name meant "Valley of Bitterness", for it was poor soil and nothing would grow there. "I will call it 'Clairvaux', 'The Valley of Light'," Bernard said, "for from it the light of the Gospel will shine far and wide." Life was very hard at the monastery of Clairvaux. There was little food and the monks lived on nuts from the trees and soup made from leaves. They had to work very hard. Often they were hungry and wanted to give up. Then at last they had cleared the land and their own crops were growing. But they had strict rules about food and lived on rough, barley bread. Their day was divided between the worship of God, hard work on the land, and study.

Bernard lived the hardest life of them all. He was never strong and he treated his body strictly, going without food and sleep. But he was always kind and patient and full of love. The fame of his holy life and of his wonderful words spread far and wide. His monks went out into the towns and villages, founding new monasteries. They were called the "White Monks", for they wore a simple white 'habit' with a hood hanging at the back, a black girdle round their waists, and sandals on their feet. The Cistercian monks spread over Europe and before long they had built monasteries in England, always in lonely places and far from towns. The first was at Waverley in Surrey. Soon there were others at Rievaulx and Fountains in Yorkshire, and at Tintern in Monmouthshire. The monks set a wonderful example in prayer and holiness and in hard work as well. They grew good crops and kept splendid flocks of sheep and used their wool for making clothes.

Bernard became famous all over Europe. In the year 1128 he made the Rules for the Christian soldiers known as Knights Templars. Their round church or 'Temple' can still be seen in London. Two years later there was a great quarrel in the Church. The bishop of Rome had died and two men both claimed to be the true Pope after him. Bernard was asked to decide between the rivals and the whole Church gladly agreed. Now Bernard had great power and he was even more important than the Pope himself. Later on, one of his own monks became Pope. But Bernard never wanted to be great. He served God through his monasteries and through his own holy life and preaching.

Bernard was growing old but he still had a great work to do. The Pope commanded him to call for a new Crusade. Christian knights were wanted in the Holy Land to save it from the heathen Moslems. When Bernard was a boy, the first Crusaders had gone out to Palestine to win the land where Jesus had lived and died and risen again. They had captured Jerusalem and set up a Christian kingdom there. Now they were in danger from the Saracens, fierce Moslem warriors. Bernard used his wonderful gifts as a preacher to win Christian soldiers to this cause. "O brave knight! O warlike hero! Gird on your sword!" he cried. "Take the sign of the cross and fight

for the holy places!" A great company of knights rallied to his call and set out for the Holy Land in the year A.D. 1147. The crusade was a failure and Bernard was bitterly disappointed.

He died in A.D. 1152, worn out by his strict and busy life. The Church could never forget him. In A.D. 1174 he was made a saint, and August 20th in each year was set aside to his memory. He left 160 monasteries behind him to carry on his work. Still today Christians sing hymns which Bernard of Clairvaux wrote in praise of the God to whom he gave his life.

A HYMN OF ST. BERNARD

1. *Jesu, the very thought of Thee*
       With sweetness fills my breast;
   But sweeter far Thy face to see,
       And in Thy presence rest.

2. *Nor voice can sing, nor heart can frame,*
       Nor can the memory find,
   A sweeter sound than Thy blest name,
       O Saviour of mankind!

3. *O hope of every contrite heart,*
       O joy of all the meek,
   To those who ask, how kind Thou art!
       How good to those who seek!

4. *But what to those who find? Ah! this*
       Nor tongue nor pen can show;
   The love of Jesus! What it is,
       None but His loved ones know.

5. *Jesu, our only joy be Thou,*
       As Thou our prize wilt be;
   In Thee be all our glory now,
       And through eternity.

Translated by E. Caswall

Hugh of Lincoln  29

In the year A.D. 1140 a third son was born to the Lord of Avalon, a castle in France. Both his father and mother were good Christian people. Little Hugh was brought up strictly for they wanted him to be a monk and to give his life to God. When he was eight years old, his mother died. The Lord of Avalon was too sad to go on living in the castle. He shared all his possessions between his two elder sons. Then he took his youngest son with him to live in a little monastery nearby. The life there was strict and Hugh had to study hard as well. But he was very happy and he wanted to become a monk as soon as he could. At last, when he was nineteen years old, he was allowed to take his vows as a monk. Now he had to be obedient to the head of his monastery, to own nothing, and to give his life completely to God. How happy he was to be ordered to look after his father. For the Lord of Avalon was old and weak and Hugh was able to care for him tenderly until he died.

Now Hugh decided to join an even stricter company, or 'Order', of monks. They lived on a mountain slope in the Alps. The monastery was called the 'Grande. Chartreuse', and still has that name today. For it lies near the village of Cartusia. That is why its monks are called 'Carthusians'. They have always had very strict rules. They lived in tiny rooms called 'cells'; they ate very simple food and drank only water. They slept on the hard floor. They spent most of their time in loneliness and silence so that nothing could turn their minds away from God. They wore rough sheepskin for their dress or 'habit', a leather belt round their waists, and sandals on their feet. Hugh lived for fifteen years in the monastery of Cartusia. His life was strict and lonely and silent, but they were the happiest years of his life. For he lived close to God and he wanted nothing more. He loved men by praying for them. Some of his time was spent digging and some in making beautiful copies of the Bible. His best friends were the squirrels which he had tamed. He shared his scanty food with them and he loved them as creatures of God.

In the year 1175 Hugh had to leave his mountain home. Henry II was King of England as well as ruler of part of France. He was bringing peace to England by making good laws, by ruling the war-like barons, and by founding monasteries. One of these was at Witham near Frome in Somerset. But Henry was mean and would not pay for it. He took land and houses from the peasants for his monastery. No wonder they hated it and the Abbots gave up in despair. Then Henry heard of Hugh, the steward of the monastery at Cartusia. Messengers were sent from England but Hugh would not go. "I am not good enough," he said. But the Abbot said, "It is the call of God, brother Hugh. I order you to go." So Hugh sadly said goodbye to his squirrels and sailed to England.

Hugh soon found what was wrong at Witham. "You took the land and huts from the peasants," he said to the King. "Now you must pay them or else we must leave." The proud King was astonished. He had never met a man like Hugh. He did what the Abbot asked. Then Hugh and his monks built their own monastery, and for eleven years he ruled over them wisely and strictly. Though he was Abbot, he lived as simply as he had always done.

King Henry admired the brave Abbot. He needed a new Bishop of Lincoln to rule over much of England. Only Hugh would do for him, so the King ordered the churchmen of Lincoln to choose him. But Hugh refused! "You have chosen the man the King wants," he said to them. "You must choose the man God wants." They came back again and said, "The Church has chosen you." Still Hugh would not say "yes". He hated leaving his quiet monastery for the palace and power and rich robes of the greatest bishop in England. Again he

108

wrote to his old Abbot in the French mountains. "What should I do?" he asked. "You must go," the Abbot replied. "You can do a great work for God as Bishop of Lincoln." The churchmen came to fetch Hugh in their rich robes and in a gorgeous procession. Hugh rode on his mule with his bundle of rough sheepskins tied on the back. They were so ashamed that they cut off his poor bundle when he wasn't looking. He walked into Lincoln in his old monk's habit and with bare feet. The new Bishop was expected to give a grand feast for the rich noblemen. "Cook three hundred deer," Hugh said to the astonished steward. "That will feed all the poor people of Lincoln. Our feast shall be for the hard-working poor, not for the idle rich."

Hugh was always like that. As Bishop he had much money. He used it all to build hospitals for the sick and to care for the poor. He himself bandaged the sores of lepers. He carried heavy stones to help the masons rebuild the ruined cathedral. He loved children best of all and always stopped to bless them.

The new Bishop was strict in seeing that justice was done. The peasants loved him for this but the rich men hated him. England was covered with great forests. The nobles hunted in them but the cruel foresters kept out the hungry people. Hugh punished the foresters when they were unjust and the angry King sent for him. At the royal court Hugh was met by the chief forester named Galfrid, a proud tyrant. "You should stay in your church," he sneered at Hugh. "And you should see justice done in your forests," Hugh replied firmly. Then the King came in. "Why do you set yourself up as judge?" he cried angrily. "Because I knew your Majesty would want justice done." Hugh said calmly. The King had to agree and Galfrid was punished.

Whenever he could, Hugh went back to his old monastery in Somerset to spend a few weeks as a monk again. His simple and holy life ended in 1200 but it was never forgotten. November 16th every year was set aside to the memory of Hugh of Lincoln, a great man of God and a noble saint of the Church.

30 Francis of Assisi

JOHN, son of Bernadone, was born in the little town of Assisi in Italy in the year 1182. His father was a rich cloth merchant and the boy had everything he could want. He was always gay and fond of adventure. He did not bother much with his education and could never write very well. He was clever at making up songs and poems, and loved to play the lute. He thought of becoming one of the troubadours or wandering minstrels. They sang their songs in French, and because John was so good at singing he was nicknamed 'Il Francesco' ('The little Frenchman') or Francis. He led the young men of his town in their fun. He led them too on his fine horse when they went to war with other cities. He wondered whether to become a knight. But he was taken prisoner and spent a year in a dungeon with nothing to do but think. When he was set free he went back to Assisi and the old life, but it didn't seem so jolly now. Then he was ill for a long time and had more time to think. When he was better he went on a trip to Rome. Everywhere he saw beggars with no one to care for them. He was troubled when he got back home. What should he do with his life?

One day riding in the street he met a leper. He turned away from the ugly sight with disgust. Then suddenly he remembered how Jesus had cared for lepers and even touched them. He got off his horse and gave the poor man all he had. Then he bent and kissed his hand.

From that time onwards Francis spent his time with the lepers in their hovels and with the poor in their wretched huts. His father was furious and turned him out. Francis left his rich home and fine clothes and went off barefoot in the rough, grey woollen tunic of the peasant. He had never been so happy. "I am going to woo the most beautiful lady of all," he told his friends. "She is Lady Poverty. I am going to be God's troubadour and God's knight."

Francis lived among the sick and poor. He found a little chapel in the woods. He rebuilt it himself and made a little hut beside it to sleep in. Soon other young men gave up their wealth and came to join him. They went about among the poor, singing their 'canticles', or 'little songs', and preaching the Gospel of Jesus. They earned their meals by doing jobs and would never take money for their work. Most of the poor lived outside the city walls in their hovels, and there Francis and his followers lived with them.

Soon hundreds of men flocked to follow Francis. The Pope of Rome gave them his blessing. Francis said they were to be called 'Fratres Minores'—'Lesser Brothers', for he did not want anyone to think them important. He was not interested in making rules for them, nor were they to live in monasteries. They were to be God's merry men, bringing joy and peace and love wherever they went. They became known as 'Friars', or 'Grey Friars', from the rough woollen tunic they wore, with a rope round the middle. Soon they spread to other lands. In 1224 they first reached England, and before long friars were to be found living among the poor outside the walls of the big cities, London and York, Bristol and Norwich. Far and wide they travelled through the countries of Europe. Some went to lands in the East, and by A.D. 1294 they had even reached China. Everywhere they took with them the Gospel of love. For they followed Francis, the poor man of Assisi, who loved all God's creatures. Francis himself went to Egypt to preach to the leader of the heathen Saracens against whom the Christian Crusaders were fighting. "What is the use of fighting them?" he said. "We must win them by love."

One of the many lovely stories of Francis tells how he preached to the birds. "My little sisters the birds, you owe much to your Creator. He has given you feathers for dress, wings for flying, and freedom to

111

go where you will in the pure air. He gives you mountains and valleys for your refuge and tall trees for your nests. You cannot sow or reap, so he provides everything you need. He must love you greatly to give you so much. You must love and praise him in return." Then he finished, and the birds spread their wings and bowed their heads reverently to the ground.

When Francis knew the end of his life was near, he pleaded with his followers to bear him back to the little chapel near Assisi. There he died in A.D. 1226. This chapel of St. Mary is still there today with a lovely church built around it. On its walls are pictures of Francis painted by a great artist, and many people go there as pilgrims every year. Christians remember him specially every year on October 4th as a man who showed the love of Jesus in everything he did and inspired others to follow his holy and humble life. Still today Franciscan friars carry on the works of love and mercy which they learnt from Francis of Assisi.

John Wycliffe and the First English Bible

31

WHEN William the Conqueror went to England in 1066, he took with him the French language of the Normans. The people of England spoke the Anglo-Saxon tongue which you can read about in the stories of Bede and King Alfred. The Norman barons spoke their French. So the two tongues became mixed together into a strange new language. It was not till 300 years later that Geoffrey Chaucer wrote the first books in the new English tongue. All this time Latin was the language in which laws and the Bible were written. Church services were in Latin, too. Only scholars knew Latin. So the ordinary people still had no Bible. They learned about God from priests and monks. In their churches were paintings and lovely coloured windows to show them Bible stories. John Wycliffe was the first man to give the people the Bible in their own English tongue.

When he was young, John Wycliffe was sent to a new College at Oxford University. It was called Balliol College. He was such a fine scholar that he became Master of the College. Soon he became as famous throughout the land as Bede had been. He was a saintly man, very strict in his life. He loved best to study his Latin Bible. But more and more he thought, "How dreadful it is that people cannot read this great book in their own language". Then he decided, "I will translate it into English for them". He left Oxford and went to be a priest of the church at Lutterworth in Leicestershire.

113

It was a quiet village deep in the country. Here he could work hard
at his new English Bible. He had a friend to help him. He was a
scholar called Nicholas de Hereford. At last, after many years of
work, it was finished. But Wycliffe was never satisfied. He started
to go through it again and make it an even better Bible. He died
while he was doing it. Another priest named John Purvey finished

the work. Now, for the first time, there was a Bible in the English language.

Wycliffe wanted everyone to know the Bible. So he trained and sent out Poor Preachers. They were called Lollards. Wherever they went they took with them scrolls to read to the people. How excited English people were to hear the Bible in their own language! The scrolls were very precious. People bought them or copied them. Anyone who could read would gather his friends together and read to them the word of God. When the priests read the Latin Bible in church, no one could understand. Now the people of England could understand, and they learned many new things.

Life was very hard in those days for the poor people. A dreadful plague had swept through the land and half the people of England had died. There were fewer peasants to do the work, and they asked their masters for more money. The rich lords made harsh laws against them. The peasants revolted and many thousands of them were killed. Then the Poor Preachers began to go round the land, teaching the people and reading the Bible to them. The lords feared that they might encourage the peasants to revolt again. The leaders of the Church feared the Lollards, too, Some of the bishops were rich and idle and did not care for their people. Wycliffe and his Lollards said this openly. They accused the bishops of teaching things which were not found in the Bible. They even attacked the head of the Church, the Pope of Rome. So the lords and bishops made a cruel law against the Lollards. Men who said these things were to be burnt to death.

Wycliffe himself was accused. He was ordered to go to London to be tried, but at first he refused. In the end he did go to his trial. With great courage he attacked the bishops who accused him. He was saved by his friends, and allowed to return to his village. Then he was summoned to Rome to appear before the Pope himself. But he was too old and ill, and soon he died. Wycliffe had lit a fire in the hearts of the people of England. They wanted to be free to read the Bible themselves. They knew now that many things were wrong with the Church and wanted them put right. Other brave men came after Wycliffe and carried on his work. But we can never forget him as the man who gave us the very first Bible in the English language.

32 John Huss, the Reformer of Bohemia

In the year 1382 the lovely Princess Anne rode into the city of London. She had come to be the bride of the young King Richard II. No one knew her for she came from a country far away in Europe called Bohemia. But her goodness soon won the hearts of those who met her. People heard how she had brought her three precious Bibles with her. One was written in the German language, the second was in Latin, and the third was in her own Czech language. Some students came with her from Bohemia. They studied at Oxford University where they learnt much about England. When they went back to their own country they took with them English ideas and English books. Some of these books were written by the famous Englishman named John Wycliffe who lived near the city of Oxford.

John Wycliffe was a priest and a scholar. He thought that many things were wrong with the Church, and he determined to speak out about them. The Bible was written in Latin and few people could read it. Church services were in Latin too and few people could understand them. Some of the Bishops were rich and powerful men who did not care for their people. Many monks were lazy and greedy. Worst of all, he thought, was the Bishop of Rome. He was the Pope, the head of the Church, but he lived in wealth and luxury. Then came a time when there were two Popes, both claiming to be

116

the true Bishop of Rome. John Wycliffe believed that everyone—Pope, bishop, priest, monk—should be judged by the Bible. But how could people judge them if they could not read the Bible?

First John Wycliffe turned the Bible into English. Then he sent out Poor Preachers to teach the people in their own language. He wrote many books to spread his ideas. Soon the bishops and the rich nobles were angry. The Poor Preachers were persecuted and Wycliffe's books were burnt. But some of his books could not be burnt. When the students from Bohemia went back home they took with them some of the writings of John Wycliffe. Soon they were being read by the students in Bohemia. One of them was named John Huss.

John had been born in the year 1369. His home was in the village of Hussinec. That was why he came to be known as John Huss. His parents were peasants and his father died when he was a boy. John's mother took him to the great city of Prague so that he could go to school. When he was old enough he became a student at the famous University of Prague. He was very poor and he lived on porridge. He had to do jobs in his spare time to earn the money for his books and his teaching. He studied hard and he passed all his exams. He became a priest of the Church, and in the year 1402 he was made head of the great University of Prague.

John Huss was now famous. He became even more famous for his preaching at the Bethlehem Chapel in Prague. There he could preach in his own Czech language. For, like John Wycliffe, he wanted the people to understand the Bible and its teachings. There too he could say what he thought was right. He was a fearless preacher. Like John Wycliffe, he said hard things about bishops and monks and about the two Popes both claiming to be the true Bishop of Rome. "How can they be true shepherds of the Church," he cried, "when they care more for riches and power than for their people?" Soon John Huss was very popular with the people. The Queen made him her chaplain and the court ladies came to hear him.

But he made enemies too. The leaders of the Church grew to hate him. They sent a priest to Bethlehem Chapel to write down what he said. The priest hid his face in his hood but John Huss soon found him out. The Pope ordered that the books of John Wycliffe were to be burnt and forbade preaching in private chapels. But John Huss went on preaching what he thought was right. He taught the Gospel of Jesus to the people and attacked those who did not live up to it.

In the year 1412 the Pope sent messengers to the city of Prague to collect money. People could have their sins forgiven if they paid money to the Pope. John Huss spoke out angrily against this for he thought it was wrong. Then the Pope made a law by which John Huss was cast out of the Church. He ordered all the churches in the city of Prague to be closed. There were to be no more services. No one could be baptised or married or buried. The Pope hoped that this would make the people of Prague turn against their popular preacher. But John Huss left the city. He went from place to place speaking to the people in the open air. He was more popular than ever.

The fame of John Wycliffe and of John Huss had spread throughout all the countries of Europe. Everywhere people were hearing how they spoke openly against evils in the Church. Worst of all, there were the two Popes quarrelling with each other. It was decided to call a great meeting or Council of leaders of the Church. The Council was held at the city of Constance in Switzerland. John Huss was ordered to go before the Council to decide whether his teachings were true. The Emperor promised he would be safe. So did his own King of Bohemia. But John Huss said, "I do not put my trust in Kings. I trust in God alone." Bravely he went to the Council. But at once he was seized and thrown into a filthy dungeon. He was kept in prison for nine months. Then he was led before the leaders of the Church. He was accused of false teaching. "I must always follow my own conscience," he cried. "I must obey God, not men." The Council condemned him. His robes were taken off him. Then he was led out into the fields and burned to death. It was July 6th in the year 1415.

The voice of John Huss was dead but his words lived on. Other brave men rose up to follow him and to fight against evils in the Church.

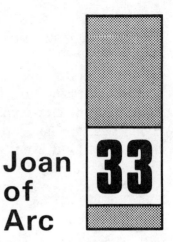

Joan of Arc 33

IN the year 1412 a little girl was born to James of Arc. He lived on a farm in the village of Domrémy in France. He had four children already but he was glad to have another daughter to help on the farm. It lay by the River Meuse in the country of Champagne. There he kept horses and sheep and cattle. He gave his youngest child the name of Joan and she was always a happy child. For she loved her life in the country and she was happiest of all looking after the sheep. There was no school for Joan to go to and she never learned to read or write. She was just a happy peasant girl and, when she was not busy on the farm, she played with her friends in the fields.

Now when Joan was thirteen years old, something strange happened to her. She began to hear voices speaking to her when she was quite alone. Joan was only a simple girl and she was very troubled. She knew nothing except her work on the farm and what she learned at the village church. She began to recognise the voices. They were saints and angels that she had learnt about in church. Sometimes it was St. Michael, the leader of the angels of heaven, who spoke to her. Sometimes it was St. Catherine or St. Margaret. When the voices spoke she seemed to see a great light, too. Their message was always the same. "Joan, you must give yourself to God," they said. "He has chosen you to do a great work for him. One day you must leave your home and go far away. You are to save France."

How strange this message was! How could a simple peasant girl save France? For nearly a hundred years now there had been war between France and England. The Kings of England claimed to be Kings of France too. English soldiers had conquered much of the land. They had taken Paris, the capital city, and now they were laying siege to the great city of Orleans. If they captured Orleans they would hold every great city in France. Charles, the King of France, was a poor leader. Besides, he had not even yet been made King for there was no city where he could be anointed and crowned. Some of the French nobles did not want him to become King so they were friends with the English. It was a terrible time for France with soldiers everywhere and no law in the land.

For three years Joan heard her voices, telling her to save France. She had given up playing games. She spent most of her time out in the fields alone with her sheep. Whenever she could she went into the little church to pray and to be with God. She dared not tell anyone about her voices. No one would believe her. But more and more she knew she must obey them.

When she was sixteen years old Joan went on a journey to the nearest town. Her cousins lived there and they brought her to the Governor of the city. "Will you take me to the King, please?" she asked. "God has sent me to save France." The Governor roared with laughter. "Send her back home," he cried, "and tell her father to whip her!" Joan had to go back home but the next year she tried again. This time another officer of the King was there. He believed her and took her to the town where the King was staying. Joan dressed in the clothes of a page and rode her horse like a boy. Now the King made up his mind to test Joan. He let someone else dress up in his royal robes. He wore the same clothes as the courtiers and stood among them when Joan came to the royal court. But although she had never seen him she knew him at once and went straight up to him. Then he too believed that God had sent her and ordered her to be put in charge of his army.

Joan rode on a fine white horse at the head of six thousand soldiers. She wore glittering white armour and she carried a white banner. On it were just two words—"JESUS. MARY." She led the army

120

to attack the English who were besieging the city of Orleans. They were rough soldiers but they gave up their bad ways when Joan was leading them. When they arrived at Orleans the English soldiers were all round the starving city. Joan tried to make them give up peacefully but they laughed at her. Then, carrying her banner high, she led her army to the attack. The English troops were afraid when they saw her in shining white, like an angel. Nothing could stop the French soldiers for they believed in Joan. That night she led her victorious army through the gates of Orleans.

Now the Maid of Orleans, as she was called, became famous throughout France. God had sent her to save her country and she led her soldiers from victory to victory. Because the English and their French friends were driven back, the King could be crowned at last. The cathedral at Rheims was crowded for the great ceremony. As the Archbishop crowned King Charles VII of France, Joan stood beside him with tears of joy in her eyes.

Now Joan wanted to go back to her home in the country. But she was too popular and the King would not let her go. Her voices no longer spoke to her but she was forced to go on leading the French army. Then came the sad day when she was captured by the French enemies of King Charles. They sold her to the English for money and Joan was thrown into a dungeon in chains. She was tried in the city of Rouen. Her enemies said that she was a witch and that her voices were really evil spirits. She was burnt to death in the market-place at Rouen on May 30th in the year 1431. She was only nineteen years old and she had died for her faith in God. She was made a saint of the Church and May 30th was set aside every year to the memory of Joan of Arc, a faithful soldier of Jesus Christ.

Sir Thomas More

34

Sir John More was very happy when a son was born to him in the year 1478. Thomas soon showed himself to be the brightest child in his family, and Sir John decided that he would be a lawyer like himself. Thomas was sent to St. Anthony's school in Threadneedle Street, near his home in London town. By the time he was thirteen years old he had learnt much from the monks there for he was clever and he worked hard at his books. He left school and went to be a page at Lambeth House. The Archbishop of Canterbury lived there in great splendour. Thomas learnt good manners there. He met all kinds of important people, too. He loved to listen to scholars and wise men. They often talked in the Latin language and in Greek, too, which was becoming popular again. Thomas had learnt both Latin and Greek and already he could understand what they were saying. "Mark my words," the Archbishop said to his friends one day, "Thomas will become one of the greatest men in England when he grows up."

A year later Thomas was sent to Oxford University. He was one of the best students at Christ Church College. He was always reading books by the great Latin and Greek writers of old. But he was very gay, too. He loved music and played on the flute. He was full of fun and he was always jolly and witty. "Thomas is wasting time at Oxford," his father began to think. "It's time he came back to London and studied law instead of all those Greek and Latin books." So when he was sixteen years old Thomas went back home and read his law books. He became a fine lawyer for he was very clever. But he was honest, too, and always just. No one could help liking the wise and witty Thomas More, always so jolly and gay.

But in his heart Thomas was very serious. He loved God dearly and wanted only to serve him. For a long time he thought of being a monk. In the end he decided that he could serve God best as an ordinary man. But he was always very strict with himself, and secretly he lived by stern rules. No one knew that he wore a rough hair shirt under his fine velvet dress. No one knew that often, when they were drinking rich wine, Thomas had only water in his cup. He cared nothing for money and comfort and pomp.

In the year 1504 Thomas became a Member of Parliament. He soon showed what a great man he was. King Henry VII demanded a lot of money. Thomas knew this was wrong and spoke bravely against the King. He was seized and put in a dungeon in the Tower of London, just as he expected. But soon Henry VIII became King and he wanted this wise lawyer to serve him. Thomas was set free and went back home. He had a splendid house in the village of Chelsea and there his four children were born—Margaret, Elizabeth, Cecilia and John. What a happy house it was! Always there was music and dancing and games as Thomas romped with his dear children. They kept many pets in their lovely garden close by the River Thames, birds and dogs as well as a monkey and a fox. Often the house was full of guests, scholars and wise men, and their talk was clever and witty and full of laughter. One of them was a Dutchman named Erasmus. "Thomas is a wonderful friend," he said. "No one could hate him for he loves all living creatures, both men and animals. He is always joking but he is never unkind. Nor is he foolish. He is wise and good and honest." But even his good friend Erasmus did not know that Thomas lived a strict life and that his goodness and joy came from his daily prayers.

But Thomas had less and less time at home. King Henry used him more and more on affairs of state. For over a year he had to live in Holland where he spent his spare time writing books. When he came home he had to help the King more and more in ruling England.

Henry made him Sir Thomas as a reward and in 1529 he made him the Lord Chancellor of England. Now Sir Thomas was the most important man in the land. He was kept busy at the King's court all day long. Henry trusted Sir Thomas for his great wisdom. But he enjoyed having him at court for his wit and gaiety. "Sometimes I pretend to be sad," said Sir Thomas to his dear daughter Margaret. "Then the King doesn't want me around him and I can come back home."

Sir Thomas loved his family much more than power and wealth. He was always very humble for he lived close to God. Every Sunday he sang in the choir in Chelsea church and then went home to a cheerful dinner with his children and friends. But in his heart Sir Thomas was sad and worried. King Henry had no love for his Spanish wife. He wanted to marry Anne Boleyn, one of his wife's maids, who was gay and beautiful. He asked the Pope, the head of the Church, to allow him to divorce his wife and to marry Anne. But the Bishop of Rome refused. The King determined to disobey the Pope. So Sir Thomas gave up his high office and all the money it brought him. He lived quietly at his home in Chelsea. King Henry made himself head of the Church in England and Parliament was forced to agree. Then the King married Anne Boleyn. He made a law ordering everyone to swear that he was head of the Church and that Anne was his true wife.

Sir Thomas had always served his King faithfully but he could not take the oath. At once the King sent him to the Tower of London. For over a year he was a prisoner there, growing thin and ill. But he could still joke when Margaret went to visit him. Then he was tried in Westminster Hall but he still would not take the oath. He was condemned as a traitor and on July 6th he was beheaded on Tower Hill. "I die loyal to God and to my King," he said. "But loyal to God first of all." The Church made him a saint and set aside July 9th in every year to the memory of Sir Thomas More, a faithful servant of God.

35 Erasmus, Scholar of the Bible

ERASMUS was not a very happy child. He had been born in the year 1466 in the city of Rotterdam in Holland. Not long after, both his father and his mother died of the plague. Erasmus had to go and live with a guardian who wanted him to become a monk. He was sent to a good school which he enjoyed best of all. For Erasmus soon realised that he wanted to become a scholar. He worked hard at his studies. In those days books were written in Latin, the ancient language of the Romans. Erasmus became a very good Latin scholar and he wanted to spend his life with books. But he had no money to pay for his food and lodging. His guardian kept on at him, trying to make him become a monk. Erasmus did not want to be shut up in a monastery. He wanted to travel and to see places. He wanted to go to the great universities and to meet scholars. "But at least I could go on with my studies in the monastery," he said to himself. So at last he gave in to his guardian and when he was twenty years old Erasmus became a monk.

For six years Erasmus lived in his monastery. He spent all the time he could with his books. He read the writings of the old Latin scholars. He read books written by the early Christians too. But he was not happy in the monastery. The monks had no love for study and they made fun of him. Erasmus loved God dearly but he thought that many things were wrong with the Church. The monks believed such silly things and he longed to get out into the world and to meet with wise and studious men.

At last his chance came. A bishop wanted Erasmus to be his secretary. He got permission to leave his monastery and at last he was free. He went with the bishop on his journeys and then he settled in Paris, the capital city of France. How he enjoyed life at the great university there! He was very poor but that did not bother him at all. When he had any money he spent it on old books and manuscripts. Erasmus had a new interest now. He had begun to learn the ancient Greek language. For a long time now no one had bothered about the Greek writers of old. Not many scholars even knew Greek. Erasmus studied it hard. It was very exciting to read the books of the wise men of ancient Greece which everyone had forgotten. For a long time there had been none to buy. But now the fierce Turks had captured the great city of Constantinople. The Greek scholars there fled to Europe bringing their precious manuscripts with them. Erasmus read all he could and he was soon becoming famous as a Greek scholar.

It was in the year 1499 that Erasmus first came to England. At the University of Oxford he met Sir Thomas More and his friends. Then he went to stay with Sir Thomas More at his peaceful home in the village of Chelsea. Erasmus had never been so happy. Here he could study as much as he liked and talk with wise and witty men. One of the friends of Sir Thomas was John Colet. He was a Greek scholar too. One day he said to Erasmus, "You are the best Greek scholar in all Europe. Why don't you study the old Greek Bible? Then you can make a new Bible without any mistakes. No one could do it better than you. I am a rich man. I will help you with money so that you can study."

Erasmus went back to Paris with the new plan. What a fine idea it was! The only Bible in all Europe was the old Latin Bible. Erasmus knew there were many mistakes in it. Besides, the four Gospels and all the letters in the New Testament had been written in the Greek language. He could study the old manuscripts and make a fine Greek Bible. Then it could be turned into the language of each country. People in every land would be able to read the exact words of Jesus in their own tongue. It was an exciting task and Erasmus

started at once. He came back to England and went on with his work. Part of the time he stayed with Sir Thomas More at Chelsea. Then he was made a professor at Cambridge University. At last his great work was done. It had taken him sixteen years to finish his New Testament in Greek.

The book was printed in the city of Basle in Switzerland in the year 1516. At the beginning of his book Erasmus wrote: "I should like the people of every country to be able to read the books of the New Testament in their own language. I wish that the farmer should sing verses to himself as he follows the plough; that the weaver should hum them to the tune of his shuttle; that the traveller should brighten his journey with the stories of Jesus." Scholars all over Europe were full of praise for Erasmus. But many leaders of the Church did not like his Greek Testament. They refused to believe that there was anything wrong with the old Latin Bible. Besides, they did not want people to read the Bible at all. They should believe what the Church taught them.

Erasmus went on quietly writing other books. The Pope made a special law setting him free from being a monk. He settled in the city of Basle in Switzerland where his books could be easily printed. He never married. Often he stayed with his friends and wrote many letters to keep in touch with them. But he was a quiet and timid man and he was quite happy living alone with his books. He wrote many other fine works. He made fun of things that were wrong in the Church and made people want to put them right. So he helped to bring about what is called the 'Reformation' of the Church. But Erasmus did not want to put things right himself. He hated arguments and quarrels and he went on living quietly in Switzerland till he died in the year 1536. We can never forget him for our Bible today comes from the work of the scholar Erasmus.

A PRAYER OF ERASMUS

O Lord God,
Whose will it is
That we should hold our parents
In highest honour:
Preserve we pray Thee,
Our parents and homes
In the love of Thy religion
And in health of body and mind;
Grant that
No sorrow may befall them through us:
And as they are kind to us
So be Thou kind to them,
Thou Father of all.

Amen.

Erasmus wrote this prayer for the boys of St. Paul's School which had been founded by his friend John Colet.

36 Tyndale, Father of the English Bible

WILLIAM TYNDALE was born 100 years after the death of John Wycliffe. He lived in a village in Gloucestershire. He went to the University of Oxford and worked hard at his studies. One day he heard that a great scholar had come to Cambridge University, and he went to listen to him. This man's name was Erasmus, and he came from Holland. He was a scholar of the Greek language and he was writing the Bible in Greek. It was far better than the old Latin Bible and soon became very famous. Erasmus wanted everyone to have the Bible in their own language. Then they could read the four Gospels themselves. He said, "I wish that the farmer should sing verses of them to himself as he follows the plough; that the weaver should hum them to the tune of his shuttle; that the traveller should brighten with their stories the boredom of his journey". Tyndale listened eagerly to this great man. If only Englishmen could read this fine new Greek Bible in their own language! Then they would know God for themselves. They would not need the Pope to rule them from far-off Rome. They would not need priests to tell them what to do.

There were many arguments at the University. One day Tyndale was talking with a learned man. The scholar said, "We must always obey the Pope and his laws". Tyndale was angry. He replied, "I defy the Pope and his laws! If God spares my life, before many

130

years I will cause a boy who drives the plough to know the Bible better than you do!" So Tyndale began his great work. He left Cambridge and went to live in a village in the Cotswold hills. He taught the children of the lord of the Manor, and worked on his Bible in the evenings. But soon it became dangerous. The leaders of the Church did not want the people to have a Bible they could read themselves. The priests might betray him. So he went to London to find a quiet home where he could work in secret. A rich cloth-merchant heard him preach and asked him to dinner. His name was Monmouth, an Alderman of the city of London. Tyndale told him his secret. "Come and live with me," Monmouth said, "and be my chaplain. You can work at your Bible here in peace!" Tyndale was very glad to find such a good home. He worked secretly there for many months. Afterwards Monmouth said, "He studied most part of the day and of the night at his book. He lived on simple food and wore plain clothes." Then Tyndale felt it was becoming dangerous in London. Spies were everywhere. He said sadly, "There is no place in all England to translate the New Testament". One night, when it was dark, he crept out of the house. He carried a precious parcel under his cloak. He went down to London docks and found a ship. The next day he sailed away from England never to return. He was an exile because he wanted to give the Bible to English people.

Tyndale had friends at Hamburg in Germany, so he went there. He worked hard for a long time till at last the New Testament was finished. But there were no printers at Hamburg. Printing was a new invention and only a few men could work the strange printing presses. He went to Cologne, where he found a printer who would print his Bible secretly. They worked at night. His friend printed the sheets one by one and Tyndale corrected them. Then one day he found that his secret had been discovered. That night a priest came to the printer's house to arrest Tyndale. But he was already on a boat sailing down the river Rhine. He fled to the city of Worms. Here he was safe, for the people of Worms were followers of Martin Luther, who had taught them not to obey the Pope. At last the printing of the New Testament was finished. 9,000 books were printed in two sizes. They were sent secretly to the coast and smuggled into England in bales of cloth. King Henry the Eighth and his bishops were angry. They ordered that the books should be seized. Many people were tried and punished for having a copy. The books were burnt in public at St. Paul's Cross in London town. Tyndale printed many thousands more. They, too, were smuggled into England and were sold as fast as they came. Priests kept guard at the docks with the customs officer. They burnt all they found. But Tyndale printed his New Testament in a smaller book and it was easier to hide. Soon, all over England men were reading it.

Tyndale was in danger all the time, but he went to Antwerp and started to turn the Old Testament into English. King Henry tried to get him to return to England. Then he was betrayed by a man he had helped. He was put in prison near Brussels, where he was tortured and tried. After some months he was taken out and burnt to death. It was October 6th in the year 1536. His last words were, "O Lord, open the eyes of the King of England". Men could burn his books and his body, but they could not put out the fire Tyndale had lit. In 1539 the King had to give in. A new English Bible was printed, so large that it was called the Great Bible. A copy was to be chained in every church. When King James ordered our Bible to be made in 1611, much of it came from Tyndale's Bible. So when you open your Bible remember how William Tyndale died to give it to you.

Martin Luther, the Reformer of Germany

37

MARTIN LUTHER was born near the town of Wittenburg in Germany in the year 1483. His parents were poor, but they worked hard so that their son could go to the university and become a lawyer. They taught Martin that if he sinned God would punish him. So he grew up to fear God, not to love him. One day when he was a student he went for a walk with his friend. Suddenly a fierce storm broke out. A flash of lightning struck Martin's friend and killed him. Martin fell to the ground sobbing. "God has punished my friend for his sins," he cried. "If he spares me I will give him my life and become a monk!" His parents were sad when he said good-bye to them and went off to a monastery. But the monks were pleased, for he was a clever student and they welcomed him gladly.

No one in the monastery was more serious than Martin. He was always praying, going without food, and punishing himself. He thought he would find forgiveness that way. But his heart was troubled and his mind was anxious. God seemed stern and distant, and he had no peace. One day a kind monk said to him: "Why do you torture yourself? God is merciful and cares for you. Read your Bible. It will show you how Jesus came, not to frighten men, but to comfort them." In those days Bibles were few and written only in Latin. But in any case the Bible was seldom read. Martin himself did not see one till he was twenty years old. The Church told men

133

how to live and worship, the Bible was not necessary. Now Martin began to read it for the first time. He read how Jesus taught men that God is our Father who loves and cares. He read how St. Paul taught that we are forgiven by our faith in Jesus. Then at last Martin Luther knew forgiveness and peace. They did not come to him from the Pope of Rome, nor from bishop or priest as the Church taught. They came from reading the Bible. How joyful he was at his great discovery. Soon after this he was made a professor at the new university of Wittenberg. Now he could teach others how to find the peace of God. People loved to hear him read and teach from his big Latin Bible.

More and more Martin Luther found himself growing angry with the Church. The bishops were rich and powerful. They seemed to care more for their power than for their people. Luther went to Rome and found the Pope just as bad. He hated many things the Church taught, and at last his anger burst out. A monk came to Wittenberg. He was sent to sell pardons by the Pope who wanted money to build a great church in Rome. People could buy a paper document, called an 'Indulgence', which promised them forgiveness of their sins. How wrong this seemed to Martin Luther. He wrote out on a parchment many things against these pardons and against other evils in the Church. He strode into the market-place and nailed his parchment to the church door where notices were posted. People came to read it, and the news spread like fire. Soon everyone in Germany heard how this brave monk had defied the leaders of the Church. Luther wrote books against evils in the Church and they were read all over Europe. Few people bought pardons any more.

The Pope was very angry at being attacked by a common monk and at losing the money that he wanted for his building. He ordered Luther to appear before a Cardinal in the city of Augsburg to be tried. But the stubborn monk refused to be bullied and would not alter one word of what he had said. Then the Pope sent his solemn order casting Luther out of the Church. Martin burnt it on a bonfire outside the walls of Wittenberg before a cheering crowd. Then the Pope ordered him to go to the city of Worms to be tried by a Council of the Church. Luther's friends were anxious for his safety if he went.

"If there were as many devils in Worms as tiles on the house-tops I would still go," he replied. The people welcomed him with their cheers. He spoke boldly in the Council. "Unless you prove from the Bible that I am wrong, I cannot take back a single word," he said. "Councils and Popes have often been wrong. I must obey Scripture, not them. I can do no other. Here I stand. God help me! Amen."

Luther was in terrible danger of being seized and burnt as a heretic. But the ruler of that part of Germany was his friend. His soldiers waylaid Luther and took him to a castle where he would be safe. Here he turned the Bible into German so that everyone could read the precious word of God. Soon many rulers in Germany threw off the rule of the Pope. New churches grew up in Germany, Norway, Sweden, and Denmark, and still today they are called Lutheran churches.

Martin Luther married and had several children whom he loved dearly. He lived the rest of his life quietly in his home, studying and writing. He wrote fine hymns and tunes as well which are still sung today. Through his writings his influence spread. But it was, above all, through his Bible that he made his people free to find the forgiveness and peace which Jesus brought to men.

38 Ignatius Loyola, and the Society of Jesus

In the year 1495 another son was born to the lord of the castle of Loyola. The castle lay in the north of Spain near the mountains called the Pyrenees. The lord was a Spanish nobleman. He loved God and he was a faithful member of the Church. He named his new son Ignatius. Already one of his older sons was studying to become a priest of the Church. But Ignatius would be a soldier. He was sent to the court of King Ferdinand to be a page and to be trained as a Christian knight. Queen Isabella was a good Christian and at the royal court Ignatius learnt to serve God as well as his country. He was such a good soldier that he was made an officer in the Spanish army. He was not a tall man but he was a good fighter and a fine swordsman.

At that time the army of France had attacked Spain. Ignatius was sent with his troops to defend the fortress of Pamplona. Soon it was attacked by the French. Ignatius and his men were outnumbered. They had to surrender but not without a fierce fight. In the battle a cannon ball hit his right leg and broke it. For many months Ignatius had to lie in bed while his leg mended. In those days there were no good doctors or hospitals and he suffered great pain. But Ignatius never grumbled. He wanted to have his leg quite whole again and he had a weight tied to it to make it as long as the other. But it never became right again. He walked with a limp for

136

the rest of his life. This meant that he could not be a soldier any more.

While he lay in bed, with nothing to do, Ignatius asked for some books to read. He wanted exciting books about knights and battles and fighting. But there were not any. Then one day a friend brought him two books. "They were all I could find," he said. "Never mind," said Ignatius. "They'll be better than nothing." Now one of the books was the story of the life of Jesus. The other was full of stories of saints of the Church. Ignatius read these books again and again. For the first time he began to think seriously about God and about what he should do with his life. Then he realised that he wanted to become a soldier of Jesus and to serve him faithfully.

When he was able to walk again Ignatius went to a monastery. There in the chapel he hung up his armour and his sword and made vows to serve God all his life. He stayed there all night praying. Then the next morning he went to the town of Manresa nearby to begin his new life. First he gave away his fine clothes to a beggar and took his rags to wear. Then he limped from door to door, caring for the sick and helping the poor. He had a room in the monastery of Manresa but he did not often sleep in it. Now that he was a soldier of God he must live just as strictly as when he was a soldier of King Ferdinand. He had little food and little sleep. He spent long hours praying and thinking about God. Sometimes he had visions. Gradually he worked out rules for his life of prayer and discipline. He wrote them in a book which he called 'Spiritual Exercises'. For Ignatius was fighting against evil in himself. When he was a soldier he had to exercise his body. Now he had to exercise his spirit. His weapons were the Bible, his conscience and thinking and praying with God. Ignatius wrote his book for those who wanted to fight with him in the battle against evil.

Ignatius stayed for a year at Manresa, writing his book. Then he went as a pilgrim to the Holy Land to see for himself the places where Jesus had lived. Then he came back to study. For as a page he had spent all his time learning to be a soldier. Now he had to learn the Latin language and to read many books. He went to the great University of Paris in France for seven years. There he made friends with six other men who wanted to join him as soldiers of Jesus.

They made vows just as the monks did. They went to Italy where they all became priests of the Church. Then, in the year 1540, the Pope made a law at Rome allowing the seven friends to form a new company. It was to be called 'The Society of Jesus'. Those who joined it were to be soldiers of God. They promised not to own anything and not to marry. They had to obey their leader in everything. He was called the 'General' and of course Ignatius was chosen by the others to be their first General. The rules for their life were those that Ignatius had written in his book. The members of his new Society soon came to be called 'Jesuits', as they still are today.

The Jesuits were organised just like an army. They were to go wherever the Pope sent them. These soldiers of Jesus made wonderful missionaries and soon they were going to heathen lands. They were good teachers too. Wherever they went they taught both children and adults. Soon they set up their own schools and colleges and many of them became great scholars. They wore no special dress but everyone knew they were soldiers of Jesus by their strict life and by their service to others.

Ignatius was never satisfied with his army. He was a fine General and he wanted his soldiers to be ready to fight for God anywhere. First they had to conquer the evil in themselves. Then they were ready to conquer evil in the world around them. Ignatius led his soldiers for the rest of his life. When he died in the year 1556 his army of seven had grown into an army of over a thousand. Jesuit teachers were to be found all over Europe. Jesuit missionaries were in America, India and even in Japan. They were ready to suffer torture and death as loyal soldiers of Jesus. Their founder was made a saint of the Church and July 31st was set aside each year to the memory of Ignatius Loyola, a valiant soldier of Jesus.

A PRAYER OF IGNATIUS LOYOLA

Teach us, good Lord,
To serve Thee as Thou deservest:
To give
And not to count the cost;
To fight
And not to heed the wounds;
To toil
And not to seek for rest;
To labour
And not to ask for any reward
Save that of knowing
That we do Thy will.

Amen.

39 Thomas Cranmer, Father of the English Prayer Book

THOMAS CRANMER was born in the year 1489. His father was a farmer but Thomas was too fond of books to want to work on the land. He would be a scholar and a priest of the Church. So he went to Cambridge University. When he had finished his own studies he stayed there as a teacher. In the evenings he and his friends met at the White Horse Inn to talk together. His best friends were Hugh Latimer and Nicholas Ridley. They all loved God and they were all going to be priests. They often talked about a man called Martin Luther and they read his books together. Luther was a monk in Germany. He had stood up against the Pope, the head of the whole Church. He had spoken out against evils in the Church. Many people had followed his brave lead and they had left the Church of Rome. They were called 'Protestants' because they protested against evils in the Church.

Thomas Cranmer was a very quiet and studious man. But more and more he thought that Martin Luther was right. He became a priest in the year 1523. Some years later he was staying at Waltham Abbey in Essex when King Henry VIII came there on a visit. Now Henry was in great trouble. For many years he had been married to Queen Katherine. She came from Spain and she had been first married to Henry's brother. When he died, the Pope allowed Henry to marry her, though it was really against the law. But their

140

only child was a daughter named Mary and Henry wanted a son to be King after him. He began to think that perhaps his marriage to Katherine had been wrong. He asked the Pope to allow him to divorce her and to marry again. But the Pope refused. Then Henry fell in love with a lady at his court. She was the beautiful Anne Boleyn. King Henry was determined to marry her and have a son. But how could he when the Pope would not let him? "Sire," said Thomas, when they met at Waltham, "Why not ask the wise men at the Universities about your marriage to Katherine? If they all agree that it was wrong then you could marry again."

King Henry at once sent messengers to all the Universities. Most of them said that the Pope should never have allowed his marriage to Katherine. It had been a false marriage and Henry could therefore marry Anne Boleyn. Then King Henry made Thomas Cranmer a chaplain to his royal court. He forced the leaders of the Church to say that he was Head of the Church in England, not the Pope. Then he made Parliament pass laws against the Pope. Now the King could do just what he wanted.

Henry was glad to have Thomas Cranmer to help him. First he sent Thomas to Germany as his messenger. When he came back the King made him Archbishop of Canterbury. Then Thomas ended Henry's marriage to Katherine and married him to Anne Boleyn. Thomas Cranmer did not want to be Archbishop at all. He was a quiet scholar, not a leader. But he served the King faithfully for fourteen years while Henry grew into a terrible tyrant. While he was in Germany Thomas had married a lady called Margaret who was also a follower of Martin Luther. In the new Church of the Protestants the priests were allowed to marry. In the Church of Rome this had long been forbidden. Henry made a new law about this and Thomas Cranmer had to send his wife back to Germany.

When Henry died in the year 1547 his son Edward became King. He was a weak boy, only nine years old, and the great nobles ruled the land. Archbishop Thomas could now reform the Church in England. His old friend Nicholas Ridley was Bishop of London. Hugh Latimer preached to great crowds at Paul's Cross. Thomas Cranmer wanted to change the services in the churches. Already he had helped in seeing that every church had one of the new Bibles

in English. But there were still many things to put right in the worship of God. There were many Service Books. They were all written in the Latin language. There were different books in different parts of the country. Thomas Cranmer decided to make a new Prayer Book that everyone could use. Night after night his candle could be seen burning late in the tower of Lambeth Palace in London. At last his book was finished. It was printed in the year 1549. It cost 3/8d. with a stiff cover and 2/0d. without one. It was the very first Prayer Book in England.

Everyone must have been very excited in church on June 9th that year. It was Whit Sunday and the new Prayer Book was used for the first time. It was written in English and everyone could understand and join in the service. Now there was one book for everybody, not lots of books. All over the country people used the same book, not different ones. It had simple rules and it was easy to follow. In the services the Bible was to be read regularly all through the year. The Psalms were to be sung, too, and Thomas got his friend John Merbecke to write music for the new services. It was so good that it is still used today in some churches. Now people could sing in the services, too.

142

In the year 1553 the young King died and his elder sister Mary became Queen. She still belonged to the Church of Rome and at once she made laws against the new Protestant ways. She hated Thomas Cranmer who had ended the marriage of her mother Katherine to King Henry. He was sent to the Tower of London where the boat landed him at the dreaded Traitors' Gate. Then with his friends he was sent to Oxford to be tried. Hugh Latimer and Nicholas Ridley were burnt to death there and Thomas Cranmer followed them on March 21st in the year 1556. But he could never be forgotten. For Sunday by Sunday his Prayer Book is used in churches in England as well as in many parts of the world.

A PRAYER OF THOMAS CRANMER

O Lord,
Who hast taught us
That all our doings without charity
Are nothing worth:
Send Thy Holy Ghost,
And pour into our hearts
That most excellent gift of charity,
The very bond of peace
And of all virtues,
Without which
Whosoever liveth
Is counted dead before Thee:
Grant this
For Thine only Son
Jesus Christ's sake.

Amen.

Charity—love.

40 John Calvin, the Reformer of Geneva

JOHN CALVIN was born in the year 1509 in the city of Noyon in France. His father was a rich and important man. He decided that young John should be a priest of the Church, for he soon showed that he was a fine scholar and he had a great love of books. When he was fourteen years old John went to the great University of Paris. Many of the students there were lazy and spent all their time enjoying themselves. John Calvin lived a very strict life and worked hard at his books. He was very clever and one of the best students in all the University. He was very serious and would have nothing to do with the others. They made fun of him but John Calvin was far too brave to care about that. He had always loved God dearly and his heart was set on being a priest of the Church of Rome.

But he began to be worried. The books of Martin Luther were very popular at the University for they were full of new ideas. Martin Luther was a monk in Germany who had become a rebel against the Church of Rome. He had spoken out and protested against evils in the Church, so he and his followers were called Protestants. They had broken away from the Church of Rome and they had formed a separate Church. Soon many rulers had joined them. Martin Luther's books were being read everywhere and Protestant Churches were springing up all over Europe. They had nothing to do with the Pope. They believed that the Bible told them how to live, not the Pope.

John Calvin talked about Martin Luther's books with his close friends. Luther had found peace with God in reading the Bible, not in obeying the rulers of the Church. John Calvin began to wonder whether the Bible was the true way to God, not the Church. One day he saw a great crowd in a market-place in Paris. He went to see what was happening. One of the Protestants was being burned to death. John Calvin watched the terrible sight. He walked slowly home, thinking to himself. "That poor wretch had great faith and courage. He was not afraid. He must have felt God to be very close to him. Can Martin Luther be right, I wonder? I must study the Bible as he did and find out for myself." Then John Calvin realised that he could not become a priest in the Church of Rome. He decided to become a lawyer. But he went on studying his Bible. He was already a good scholar of Latin. Now he studied the Greek language too which not many people understood in those days. The New Testament had been written in Greek and before long John Calvin was reading the Gospels just as they had been written. He read many other books, too, written by the first Christians. He decided that Martin Luther was right. Only God could give forgiveness and peace, not the Church of Rome.

So John Calvin became a Protestant and he had to face persecution. One day soldiers were sent to arrest him. His friends found out and warned him just in time. He tied the sheets of his bed together to make a rope and escaped through the window. He went to the city of Orleans to study law for some years. But wherever he went he was persecuted and in the year 1535 he fled to Switzerland where he would be safe. There he wrote a book which became very famous and as popular as the books of Martin Luther. He wanted to remain a scholar and to write books all his life. But a friend asked him to come to the city of Geneva and to build up the Protestant Church there. John Calvin found that Geneva was an evil city. The people had left the Church of Rome and wanted to follow the new religion. But it did not seem to make them better people. There was much drunkenness and gambling and many other evils. John Calvin saw that the people needed to give up their lazy ways. But he was too strict with them and he soon made enemies. One Easter Day many of them came to church wearing their swords. John Calvin was quite unafraid. He refused to give them the sacred bread and wine. "Your lives are too evil," he cried. "You are not worthy to receive it." They rushed at him with their swords as he stood before the holy table. "You must strike down my body if you want to reach the bread and wine," he said quietly. They dared not attack him there but the next day he was sent out of the city.

John Calvin went to stay in the city of Strasbourg. There he built up a fine Protestant church and wrote his books. He married a lady of the city and they had a child. The child died and his wife became an invalid. But John Calvin was happy in his home and went on with his work for God. Then in the year 1541 the leaders of the city of

Geneva asked him to go back there and to lead their Church. He did not want to go back but he felt it was his duty. He lived in Geneva for the rest of his life, leading the Protestant Church there. He was the most important man in the city but he lived simply and strictly. He had never been strong and often he fell ill. He still had many enemies who hated his strictness. But nothing could stop him doing his work for God. Life in Geneva became very stern under his rule. There were strict laws against gambling and drinking, against dancing and games. There were strict rules for going to church and for living pure lives. Soon Geneva became a different city. John Calvin encouraged the people to work hard at their weaving and trading instead of wasting their time and their money. New schools were built and a University was set up. Before long Geneva was famous throughout Europe and Protestants from many lands went there. John Calvin died in 1564, but still today he is remembered in the Protestant Churches which he helped to found.

THE LORD'S PRAYER IN JOHN CALVIN'S BIBLE

Our Father
which art in heaven,
halowed be thy Name:
Thy kingdome come:
Let thy will be done,
euen in earth,
as it is in heauen:
Our dayly bread giue Vs for the day:
And forgiue vs our sinnes:
for euen we forgiue
euery man that is indebted to vs:
And leade vs not into temptation:
but deliuer vs from euill.

Amen.

Geneva Bible 1560

A HYMN OF
JOHN CALVIN'S CHURCH

From Psalm 100

1. *All people that on earth do dwell,*
     Sing to the Lord with cheerful voice;
   Him serve with mirth, His praise forth tell,
     Come ye before Him and rejoice.

2. *Know that the Lord is God indeed;*
     Without our aid He did us make;
   We are His folk, He doth us feed;
     And for His sheep He doth us take.

3. *O enter then His gates with praise,*
     Approach with joy His courts unto;
   Praise, laud, and bless His name always,
     For it is seemly so to do.

4. *For why? The Lord our God is good:*
     His mercy is for ever sure;
   His truth at all times firmly stood,
     And shall from age to age endure.

Words—Scottish Psalter 1564.
Tune—Geneva Psalter 1551 (Old Hundredth).

Michelangelo, the Divine Artist

41

MICHELANGELO was born in the year 1475 in Italy. His home was in the little town of Caprese near the great city of Florence. His father was mayor of Caprese and he wanted his son to become rich and important. "You will become a merchant and make lots of money," he often said to his son. Now Michelangelo was always drawing and painting and making things out of clay and stone. He did not care a bit about trading and making money. "I am going to be an artist," he said, stubbornly. Then his father beat him with a stick. But it made no difference and in the end his father had to give in. When Michelangelo was thirteen years old his father sent him to a famous painter in Florence to be his apprentice for three years and to learn to be an artist. But the painter soon found out how clever Michelangelo was at his art. "This boy knows more than I do!" he exclaimed. Michelangelo was not only good at painting. He made beautiful things out of stone and for the rest of his life he loved sculpture best of all. Ever afterwards he signed his letters 'Michelangelo, sculptor'.

Now at this time a rich man named Lorenzo was ruler of the city of Florence. He loved beautiful things and he saw the very first piece of sculpture that Michelangelo made. "He is a genius!" Lorenzo cried. "Bring him to me." Then Michelangelo went to live in the palace of Lorenzo, who gave him money each month so that he could go on with his art. Lorenzo was called 'The Magnificent', for his house was full of rich and beautiful things. It was a wonderful time for Michelangelo. Famous painters and sculptors, poets and thinkers, met in the lovely gardens of Lorenzo. For many long years the Greek language had been unknown. Now it was becoming popular again. Scholars were reading the books of the wise men of ancient Greece and Rome. Poets were reciting the lovely poems of old. Artists were finding the beautiful sculptures made by the ancient Greeks and some of them were in Lorenzo's garden. Michelangelo gazed at them as he listened to the wise men and poets and artists. He knew that he would spend his life making beautiful things like them.

But there was something else happening in Florence at that time. A monk named Savonarola was Prior of the monastery there. He was a wonderful preacher and the crowds flocked to hear him. He cried out against the evils of the people. "God will punish you for your wicked ways!" he said. "Be sorry and give them up or it will be the worse for you!" Michelangelo was a boy of fifteen when he heard these things and he never forgot them.

When Lorenzo died his foolish son ruled in the palace. He even ordered Michelangelo to make a statue in snow. Michelangelo went away to the city of Bologna where he stayed with wise men and artists, learning more about the beautiful sculptures of Greece. He made one himself, just like them. A cardinal at Rome bought it and sent for Michelangelo. So in the year 1496 he went to Rome where he made more Greek statues. But he spent three years, too, carving a block of marble with his chisel. It was a sculpture of Jesus and Mary. When people first saw it they knew that Michelangelo was the greatest sculptor in the world.

He went back to Florence to make a famous statue of David the shepherd king. But he was not happy there. His family thought he was rich and kept asking him for money. He was glad when the Pope sent for him to come back to Rome. He was ordered to paint the ceiling of the Pope's private chapel. On March 10th in the year 1508 Michelangelo wrote, "Today I, Michelangelo, sculptor, began the painting of the chapel." It was a long and lonely task, especially as he liked sculpture much better than painting. The next year he wrote—"I am wasting my time." For four years Michelangelo lay on his back, high up on the scaffolding, painting the ceiling. Every day

150

he locked himself in, all alone. In the year 1512 he finished and let people in. They saw the most wonderful paintings in the world, telling in 145 pictures the story of the creation of the world, of Adam and Eve, of Noah and the flood. Michelangelo had hurt his neck badly and his eyes too. But still today people go to Rome to see his great great paintings.

Michelangelo returned to Florence to make sculptures for a church there. He spent four years in a quarry cutting the marble. Then he made beautiful monuments for the tombs of Lorenzo the Magnificent and his family. In the year 1534 the new Pope asked him to come and work at Rome. Again he had to paint in the chapel of the Pope. He was sixty years old but again he shut himself up for five years till the work was finished. Once he fell from the scaffolding and injured his leg. "I am so very tired and in great pain," he wrote. "I have no friends here and I don't want any. I hardly find time to eat." On Christmas Day in the year 1541 the chapel was opened at last. The great painting of the "Last Judgement" filled the whole of the end wall. People gaped in wonder at Michelangelo's greatest work. All over Italy his fame spread. One man wrote to praise him. "You are very kind," the great artist said. "You seem to think I am as fine an artist as God meant me to be. But I am not very good. I just plod along, using the gifts God gave me."

Michelangelo was now a very old man. But it was in his last years that he designed the great dome of St. Peter's Cathedral in Rome. A friend visited him when he was eighty years old. "He lives like a poor man," he said. "He eats only a little bread and drinks only sips of wine. He cannot sleep so he works at night with his chisel. He has made a kind of helmet so that he can fix a candle to it and have light to work by." He died in the year 1564. But Michelangelo lives on for ever in his great works of Christian art.

42 Theresa of Avila

THE town of Avila lies in Spain near to the great capital city of Madrid. Long ago Don Alfonso lived there in a magnificent house, for he was a Spanish nobleman. He had a large family of twelve children and they lived happily together. Don Alfonso and his wife were both good Christian people and they brought their children up to love God. The seven boys and five girls went to church together. At home they read stories of the great Saints of the Church. Theresa had been born in the year 1515. Roderigo was her favourite brother and they both decided to give their lives to God. One day when Roderigo was eleven and Theresa was seven years old they went out hand in hand through the city gates. Just as they were crossing the bridge outside the town their uncle met them. "Where are you off to?" he asked. "Oh, we're going to the land of the heathen," Theresa said firmly. "We shall beg for our food on the way. People will give it to us for the love of God. When the heathen Moors see us they will cut off our heads. Then we shall be martyrs. That's what we want more than anything in the world." Their uncle looked serious. "A martyr means a 'witness'," he said, "Some Christians witness to Jesus by dying for him, others by living for him. You must learn to live for Jesus first." Then he took them back home.

Since they could not be martyrs Roderigo and Theresa decided to be hermits. They made little huts of stones in their big garden. They were going to live alone in their huts and pray to God. But the stone houses kept falling down so they had to give that up, too. Theresa could always play at being nuns with her sisters. She was very fond of reading too and she found many exciting books in her father's big library. She loved best reading stories of knights and their ladies. Now she wanted to be beautiful and she grew fond of pretty clothes and jewels.

But when Theresa was twelve years old her mother died. Don Alfonso sent her to a convent school where the nuns looked after her well. But she became very ill and had to go back home. While she lay in bed she read books about the Saints. More and more she felt that she wanted to become a nun and live in a convent herself. Her father hated the idea. But when she was twenty-one years old she left home and went to the convent in Avila. Her father was very sad at first but he knew that Theresa must give her life to God. She was very happy in her new life. She loved best the long hours spent daily in the quiet chapel with God. Once she fell seriously ill and for a long time she could not move at all. But it was then that she felt God very close to her. When she was better she went home to nurse her father and she stayed with him till his death. Then she returned to her life of prayer.

Theresa longed to spend all her time with God but it was not easy in the convent. The rules there were not very strict. The nuns could have visitors and they disturbed the quiet and peace. They could go into the town too and they came back full of chatter and gossip. They did not keep strict rules for eating either. "I was very unhappy in those days," Theresa wrote later. "On one side God was calling me. On the other side the world was calling me." The more she prayed the more she realised her faults. She could not be really happy like that, trying to serve two masters.

When she was about forty-five years old the bishop allowed Theresa to start a new convent of her own. Only four young nuns went with her. But now Theresa could live quite apart from the world and give her life completely to God. She and her nuns lived by strict rules. They wore a simple black veil and dress, and sandals on their feet. They had simple food and ate no meat. They had no possessions. They never married, and they had to obey their Prioress in everything.

They spent most of their time alone with God.

Theresa was never strong and often she was ill. But now she was always close to God. Her convent was full of love and peace and holiness. Soon the bishop asked Theresa to found other convents like her own. She travelled through the land setting up new houses where nuns could live peaceful and holy lives. For fifteen years she made her journeys. In summer the hot sun poured down; in winter she suffered from ice and snow and bitter cold. She went about in a rough cart on the rutted roads. She had to cross rivers which had no bridges and to stay at inns where there was little comfort. Often she was ill and in pain but nothing could stop her in her work for God. She set up 32 new convents all over Spain. Some were in towns like Seville and Toledo, others were in lonely country villages. Monasteries for men, just like her convents, were set up by her great friend John.

When she was back in her quiet convent at Avila Theresa wrote books to teach others how to find God and to live with him. Already she was loved through all Spain for her wisdom and her holiness. Now her fame spread, through her writings, to other lands. Theresa died on one of her journeys in the year 1582. It was not long before the Church made her a Saint and set aside October 15th in every year to her memory. But Theresa lived on in her convents. Still today her nuns follow the life she taught. Some live in their convents at home and others go to foreign lands as missionaries. But wherever they are they teach others both by their example and their words. Still today Theresa's wonderful books teach Christians how to pray and how to live close to God.

THE TEACHING OF THERESA

Christ has
No body now on earth but yours;
No hands but yours;
No feet but yours:
Yours are the eyes
Through which his love
Looks out to the world:
Yours are the feet
With which he goes about
Doing good:
Yours are the hands
With which he blesses men now.

43 The Pilgrim Fathers

IN the year 1493 exciting news spread through all the countries of Europe. Christopher Columbus had sailed to the west the year before and he had discovered a New World. Soon other bold adventurers followed him. One of them was an Italian named Amerigo Vespucci. In the year 1499 he went ashore on the mainland and from him came its name—America. Now from many countries of Europe men went to the New World. Englishmen had always been excellent sailors and from the ports of Bristol and Bideford, Southampton and Plymouth, they sailed away westwards. Sir Walter Raleigh landed in North America in the year 1584 and named the place 'Virginia'. But it was not till the year 1607 that John Smith landed there with a hundred settlers and made it an English colony. They built a settlement which they called 'Jamestown' in honour of the King. Soon Virginia was a growing colony of 5,000 English people.

News spread through England of this rich country where men could make their fortunes. Ships sailed bravely westwards from England carrying traders and adventurers seeking riches and a new life. But in the year 1620 a ship called the Mayflower sailed for Virginia with people who wanted neither riches nor adventure. They wanted to be free to worship God in their own way. They came to be called the 'Pilgrim Fathers' for they were among the first ancestors of the American people.

In England there were bitter quarrels about religion in those days. The Church of England was no longer part of the Church of Rome. Queen Elizabeth I had tried to make it the Church of the whole land. But there were two kinds of people who wanted to change it. Roman Catholics wanted to make it part of the Church of Rome again. Then there were people called Puritans because they wanted to purify the Church, and to make it like John Calvin's Church in Geneva. Each congregation should rule itself, free from bishops. Worship should be simple, without prayer books or set services. Churches should be plain and bare. The Puritans wore dull, dark clothes and they lived simply. They cared nothing about fine homes, beautiful clothes and riches. Their lives were given completely to God.

Laws were made in England against the Puritans and they were fined or put in prison. From Lincolnshire some of them managed to escape across the sea to Holland. There they could worship God freely. But it was hard to earn a living and they were among a strange people. So they decided on a great adventure. They would sail to the New World and make a New England where they could serve God in peace and freedom.

The Pilgrim Fathers agreed with some London merchants to sail in two of their ships. The 'Speedwell' took them from Holland to Southampton and there they were joined by the 'Mayflower'. But the 'Speedwell' soon sprang leaks and they had to put back. They all crowded into the 'Mayflower' and sailed from Plymouth on September 6th in the year 1620. The 'Mayflower' was an old whaling ship with a broad beam, two decks and square rigging. But it was a terrible voyage for the 102 pilgrims. They were shut up below while the fierce Atlantic storms drove the little 'Mayflower' before them. For ten weeks they lived on hard biscuits and salted horse-meat, drenched by leaking water and sick from the rolling vessel. At last on November 9th they sighted land and came into Cape Cod harbour. Pastor John Robinson called the leaders together in the cabin. "We must swear to stand together," he said. "If we separate we shall die." Then they all wrote their names to a solemn agreement—John Robinson, William Brewster, Edward Winslow, William Bradford, John Carver and soldier Miles Standish.

So the Pilgrim Fathers landed in the New World. They knelt down

157

on the beach and gave thanks to God for their safe deliverance. Then they made their settlement and called it 'New Plymouth'. There was no time to lose for already winter was stretching its icy fingers over the land. They built a 'Common House' of planks for meeting together and huts for the nineteen families. Hunters went out every day searching for food. Then in January a terrible sickness attacked the weak and hungry settlers. One after another they fell ill and died. Soon there were only six people strong enough to care for the sick. The dead were buried at night in plain flat graves so that the Red Indians should not know. When spring came only fifty of the settlers were left alive and only four mothers to care for all the children. But now at last they could find plenty of food to eat and sow their own crops.

One day a friendly Red Indian came to the tiny settlement. He had learnt a little English from traders. He showed the Pilgrims how to sow maize, the Indians' corn, how to hunt, and how to catch fish. It was not long before they made a treaty with the Red Indian chief to live as brothers and to help each other. For fifty years there was peace and friendship between the Red Indians and the white settlers, and they lived together side by side.

After the dreadful winter it was a wonderful summer. The storehouse was filled with maize and wheat and there were strong houses ready for the next winter. Then, exactly a year after they had landed, the Pilgrims gathered for a feast with their Red Indian brothers. It was their 'Thanksgiving Day'. Still today in America the last Thursday in November is kept as 'Thanksgiving' in honour of the Pilgrim Fathers.

44 George Herbert, Poet and Hymn-writer

THE Herbert family were rich and important people in England. They had ten children and a very happy home. George was born in the year 1593 and, though he loved his brothers and sisters, he loved his mother best of all. She was wise and witty and full of merriment. Her favourite books were the Bible and the writings of the ancient Greeks and Romans and she taught her sons to read them too. She was fond of music and George learnt to play the lute and the viol. Every night the family made music together. Sometimes they read poetry too. From his mother George learnt to love God. Each morning and evening the whole family met for prayers from the new Prayer Book and the children took it in turn to read lessons from the Bible. On Sunday they went to church together and in the evening they sang psalms.

When George was twelve years old he went to Westminster School in London. There he studied hard. He soon showed how clever he was at writing and speaking in his own language. But he was clever too at Greek and Latin and he went on from school to Cambridge University. He was a fine scholar but he was not a 'book-worm'. He had lots of friends for he was friendly himself. In the evenings they met together for music and poetry. Now George began to write his own poetry and he sent two beautiful poems to his mother. When he had finished his examinations he stayed on at his College as a teacher. He went on reading Greek and Latin books, and books about God too. Then in the year 1620 George was made the 'Orator' or 'Speaker' for the University. This meant that when any important persons came to Cambridge University he had to make the speech to welcome them. But the speeches were in Latin, not in English, so we can see what a good scholar George had become.

Four years later George Herbert became Member of Parliament for his home town of Montgomery in Wales. But it was a very short Parliament for its members quarrelled with King James and it soon ended. George Herbert did not mind much. He was a friend of King James and he hoped to be given an important post in the government. But in 1625 Charles I became King and George Herbert decided to have no more to do with the royal court. He lived quietly in the country with his books. He was never very strong and sometimes he was ill, too. He loved God too much to care for riches and power at court. He went on writing poetry. His first book was made up of poems in Greek and Latin. Then he began his famous book of English poems called 'The Temple'. In the year 1630 he became a clergyman in the Church of England. He went to look after the parish of Bemerton near the town of Salisbury. He lived there with his wife till his death in the year 1633.

How happy those last three years were! He had two churches to look after and they both needed rebuilding. He had a new vicarage built too. But he cared much more about people than buildings. He made sure that all the people in his parish were invited to his house during that year. But most of the time he was visiting them. He went into their homes, bringing a blessing from God. He and his wife looked after the sick. The people grew to love him as their friend. He helped them in their troubles and brought medicines when they were ill. With his Bible and his Prayer Book under his arm he went every day to the homes of his people. If they were too ill to come to church he took the sacred bread and wine to them. Twice every day he said the services, praying to God for his people. When they heard the church bell ring the farm labourers stopped their ploughing and joined in prayer with their beloved minister. He cared for the poor, setting aside part of his own money for them. He was specially fond of children and taught them in church and in their homes.

George Herbert wrote a book about his work. It was called

A POEM OF GEORGE HERBERT

EASTER

I got me flowers to straw Thy way;
I got me boughs off many a tree;
But Thou wast up by break of day,
And brought'st Thy sweets along with Thee.

Yet though my flowers be lost, they say
A heart can never come too late;
Teach it to sing Thy praise this day,
And then this day my life shall date.

'The Country Parson'. "He must lead his people like a shepherd," he wrote. "He must be full of love for them. When he gets up in the morning he plans what good deeds he can do that day and then he does them. He counts a day lost if he has not done a loving act."

He still loved music and played his lute or viol each day. Twice a week he went to the Cathedral in Salisbury. He spent the time there in prayer and in listening to the lovely singing. "It is like heaven to be there," he often said when he returned home. While he was in Salisbury he went to his friends to make music. "One day on his walk to Salisbury he met a man in trouble," his friend wrote. "His horse was weak and it had fallen down. The load in his cart was all over the road. George Herbert took off his coat and helped the man to reload his cart. The poor man was full of gratitude. Mr. Herbert blessed him and he was so like the Good Samaritan that he gave him money to buy refreshment for himself and the horse. He told him to be kind to his beast and went on his way. When he came to his friends' house to make music they were astonished to see him so dirty and untidy. He told them what had happened. 'You shouldn't have done anything so dirty,' one of them said. 'The memory of it makes music in my heart,' he replied. 'If I am to pray for those in trouble I must help them, too. Now, let's tune our viols.'"

At home George Herbert wrote his poetry. He was so full of music that many of his poems could easily be set to music and sung. Some of them make the beautiful hymns that we still sing today. For they were full of praise and joy and love of God.

His life ended in the quiet countryside when he was only forty years old. It seemed to his friends so unimportant compared with life at court. But his work was much greater than theirs, for all over the world Christian people praise God in the lovely hymns of George Herbert.

A HYMN OF GEORGE HERBERT

1. *King of Glory, King of peace,*
       I will love Thee;
   And, that love may never cease,
       I will move Thee.
   Thou hast granted my request,
       Thou hast heard me;
   Thou didst note my working breast,
       Thou hast spared me.

2. *Wherefore with my utmost art*
       I will sing Thee,
   And the cream of all my heart
       I will bring Thee.
   Though my sins against me cried,
       Thou didst clear me,
   And alone, when they replied,
       Thou didst hear me.

3. *Seven whole days, not one in seven,*
       I will praise Thee;
   In my heart, though not in heaven,
       I can raise Thee.
   Small it is, in this poor sort
       To enrol Thee;
   E'en eternity's too short
       To extol Thee.

GEORGE HERBERT'S
HYMN OF PRAISE

1. *Let all the world in every corner sing,*
        My God and King!
    The heavens are not too high,
    His praise may thither fly;
    The earth is not too low,
    His praises there may grow.
    Let all the world in every corner sing,
        My God and King!

2. *Let all the world in every corner sing,*
        My God and King!
    The Church with psalms must shout,
    No door can keep them out;
    But, above all, the heart
    Must bear the longest part.
    Let all the world in every corner sing,
        My God and King!

Vincent de Paul, Friend of the Poor

45

VINCENT was born in the year 1576 in a village near the town of Dax in France. It lay in the south, near the Pyrenees Mountains. The de Paul family were poor and there were six children to feed. But Vincent's father and mother worked hard on their rough land and there was just enough food to go round. All the children helped. Vincent looked after the pigs and took the sheep out to pasture. His father taught him to love God so he was never lonely on the hills with his sheep. He spent his time at an old, hollow oak-tree. He made his own little church inside it and prayed there. He often sang hymns and psalms to himself, too. He was a good boy, kind to everyone he met, and always helpful. Once he was going to the village with his savings. He had sixty little coins called 'sous', worth about half-a-crown. He was going to buy a treasure he had wanted for a long time. But he met a beggar and gave it all away. Already Vincent knew that he wanted to give his life to God and to help the poor. "Then you shall be a priest," his kind father said. Vincent went to be taught by the monks in a monastery nearby. His father gave the monks the little money he could spare in return. Vincent worked hard and became such a good scholar that he taught the children of the village squire. Now he was ready to go to University. His father sold two oxen and gave Vincent the money and he went off to the University in the city of Toulouse. For seven years he worked at his books and then

165

in the year 1600 he was made a priest in the Church of Rome.

Vincent still went on studying for he was very clever. "He will be a bishop one day," everyone said. Then one day he had to go on a journey to the city of Marseilles. He decided to come back by boat along the coast. "We had a good wind and we were sailing well," he wrote later. "Then suddenly three ships swooped down on us. They were pirates from North Africa. In the fight I was hit by an arrow. I still have the scar. The heathen Turks killed the captain and put us all in chains. They took us to the port of Tunis. We were lined up in the market-place to be sold as slaves. The buyers treated us as if we were horses. They opened our mouths to look at our teeth and poked all over us. They made us run up and down to see how strong we were."

Vincent was sold to a kind of chemist who taught him about science and medicine. When he died Vincent was sold to a rich farmer. One day his wife heard Vincent singing to God alone out in the field. She asked him to sing for her. Vincent sang the sad psalm of the Jews in exile, far from their own land, just as he was. The woman told her husband and he came to Vincent and poured out his heart. He was not really a heathen Moslem. He was a Frenchman and he had been brought up in the Christian religion. He made up his mind to turn back to God and to return to his own land. One day Vincent sailed with him across the sea back to France. He went to Paris and cared for the poor. The fame of his goodness and holiness spread far and wide. The Queen wanted him to be her chaplain at the royal court. But instead he went to look after a parish of poor people near the city.

In the year 1613 Vincent was sent to be tutor to the sons of Count de Gondi. He was General of the galleys, a rich and important man. His wife the Countess was a good Christian and she was happy for Vincent to care for all the servants on her lands. France was a troubled country in those days. There was much war, and beggars and cripples roamed the countryside. The peasants were very poor and they had little to do with the Church. Vincent started a new order of priests to minister to the people. It grew quickly. Some of the brothers went round the countryside preaching. Some set up colleges to train priests. Some went as missionaries to other lands. Still today the order carries on this fine work.

But the poor and the sick needed help as well as religion. The few hospitals in France were dreadful places. Vincent gathered together rich ladies who showed their love for God by caring for the poor. They are still called 'Sisters of Charity' and they wear wide, starched white hats. "You must not live shut up in convents," Vincent told them. "The homes of the poor are to be your monasteries, the streets will be your cloisters." The Sisters gave their lives to the care of the poor and the sick. Soon there were homes to train the Sisters for their work. They started hospitals for wounded soldiers, for the sick, and for old people. Above all they cared for children whom Vincent loved dearly. Life was hard for the poor in the city of Paris and almost daily children were left in the streets to beg or die. Now they could go to the 'Hospice des Enfants Trouvés', the 'Home for Foundlings', where they were cared for and brought up by the Sisters of Charity.

One day Vincent went with the Count to visit the galleys. Prisoners were sent to the galleys to pull on the great oars. Each was branded with a 'V' on his shoulder to show he was a 'voleur' or thief. Then he was chained to the seat and lashed by overseers if he did not pull hard. Vincent persuaded the Count to let him care for them. The galley-slaves soon came to love him for his help and kindness and love. One day Vincent saw a young man waiting to be taken on the galley and chained. He was sobbing, for his wife and children had no one to provide for them. Quickly Vincent put his cloak on the poor man and took his place at the oar. Before long he was recognised and at once set free. But by such love he won the hearts of even hardened men to God. He died, worn out, in the year 1660. He was made a saint of the Church and July 19th was set aside to remember him. But Vincent de Paul lives on in the good works of those who follow in his footsteps.

46 John Milton, Poet and Hymn-writer

WHEN Mr. Milton had been a student at Oxford University he had left the Church of Rome and become a Protestant. His father was so angry that he turned him out from home and would have nothing more to do with him. Mr. Milton went to London town and became a lawyer. Soon he had his own home and young John was born in the year 1608. It was a happy home for there were so many things to do. John learnt from his father to love books and art and music. He learnt to love God above all and his favourite book was the new Bible printed in the year 1611. Every morning and evening the whole family gathered to say prayers and psalms together.

John went to the new St. Paul's School in London. It had been started by John Colet, a friend of the fine Greek scholar named Erasmus. The boys studied the books of the Greek and Roman writers. John was always reading, early in the morning and late at night. His father was glad for he hoped that John would become a wise and scholarly man. One day when he was fifteen years old John showed his father a poem he had written. It began,

> 'Let us, with a gladsome mind,
> Praise the Lord for He is kind.'

"Why, this is Psalm 136 turned into a poem!" his father exclaimed. "So you're going to be a poet, too! Well done, John!"

168

Two years later John went to Cambridge University. He never joined in the rough pranks of the students there. From dawn to midnight he was deep in his books. When he was not studying he was writing poetry or arguing with other serious students. There were two important things for them to talk about. One was the new Protestant way of worshipping God. They talked about the books of Martin Luther and John Calvin which had come from abroad. But there was something even more serious going on in England. Charles I had become King and already he was quarrelling with Parliament. Charles believed that the King, being appointed by God, could do whatever he willed. "I have to account to God for my actions, not to Parliament," he said. "The King can do no wrong." But Parliament spoke for the people. They did not like the King's French wife who belonged to the Church of Rome. They did not like the King's favourites who ruled the land. More and more members of Parliament were Puritans and they did not like the Church being ruled by bishops. The King was becoming a tyrant and men wanted to be free. John Milton soon made up his mind which side he was on. He stood for Parliament and for freedom and he did not mind saying so.

When he had finished his studies John went to live at his father's new home near Windsor. There he wrote many fine poems. Then in the year 1638 he travelled through France and Italy. He wanted to go on to Greece. But news from England brought him hurrying home. For the quarrel between King Charles and Parliament was getting worse. John Milton gave up writing poetry. He began to use his pen on the side of freedom. He moved to London town and set up his own home. But he soon quarrelled with his wife for she was on the King's side. He spent all his time writing against the tyranny of the King and against the tyranny of bishops and priests. In the year 1642 war broke out between the King and Parliament. There were no newspapers in those days. But there were the pamphlets or little books of John Milton to read. He wrote twenty-five of these booklets altogether. "Men must be free!" he cried again and again. "Free to worship God in their own way, free to write and say what they believe, free to rule themselves through Parliament."

King Charles was beaten in the war and in the year 1649 he was put to death. Many people eagerly read the diary Charles had written in

prison. John Milton sat up night after night writing a new book saying
that it was right to execute the King. His eyes were already tired and
weak from long years of hard reading and writing. When he finished
the book one of his eyes could see no more. But when he was asked to
be a secretary to the government he at once agreed. He wrote letters
in Latin for the new government of Oliver Cromwell. The doctors
told him to stop. But he went on doing his duty. People in other lands
attacked the English for killing their King. Oliver Cromwell asked
John Milton to write a book to answer them. When it was finished he
was quite blind.

It was a terrible thing for a man who lived by books to be blind.
But John Milton was too brave to give up. His good daughters wrote
down his books and his poems. Sometimes in the night new thoughts
came to him. Then he rang the bell on the table beside him and one
of his daughters hurried out of bed to write them down for him.

When Oliver Cromwell died in the year 1658 many of the people
wanted to have a King again. John Milton wrote against this and
when Charles II became King he was put in prison and his books
were burned in the street. But before long he was set free. In prison
he had started to write the poem he had been dreaming of for years.
Now, with his daughters by his side, he spent seven years writing

'Paradise Lost', the greatest English poem. It told of the battle between good and evil in the world. John Milton wanted to show that God is good and that evil is caused by men's pride. He sold his poem for five pounds. Blind and poor he wrote two more great poems before his death in the year 1674. His body was buried at St. Giles Churchyard in London but his memory lives for ever in his great writings.

A HYMN OF JOHN MILTON
From Psalm 136

1. *Let us with a gladsome mind,*
   Praise the Lord, for He is kind:

   For His mercies aye endure,
   Ever faithful, ever sure.

2. *Let us blaze His name abroad,*
   For of gods He is the God:

3. *He, with all-commanding might,*
   Filled the new-made world with light:

4. *He the golden tressèd sun*
   Caused all day his course to run:

5. *And the hornèd moon by night,*
   'Mid her spangled sisters bright:

6. *All things living He doth feed;*
   His full hand supplies their need:

7. *Let us then with gladsome mind*
   Praise the Lord, for He is kind:

aye—always

47 John Bunyan, and 'The Pilgrim's Progress'

IN England, too, there were men like Martin Luther in Germany who fought bravely for freedom to worship God in their own way. John Bunyan was one of them. He was born in 1628 in a poor cottage near Bedford. His father trained John to be a tinker like himself, going round to farms and rich houses mending tools, kettles, pots, and pans. John seemed a happy lad, joining with the youths in their fun on the village green. He joined in their rounders game called tip-cat, he liked dancing with the girls, and he was fond of ringing the church bells. But he was not really happy. In those days people believed in goblins and demons, and poor John Bunyan was terrified of them. Like Martin Luther he never felt at peace, for he believed the demons were sent to punish him for his sins.

When he was sixteen years old, John joined the army of Oliver Cromwell who was fighting against King Charles I. More than once he was nearly killed. But when Cromwell had won the Civil War and become ruler of England, John returned home to his village near Bedford. He married a village girl and they were so poor that at first they had hardly a plate or a spoon between them, John wrote afterwards in his life-story. But his wife had two precious books and they read them together. They were religious books and John Bunyan was haunted more than ever by dreams and visions. His sins seemed like a great burden on his back. He tried to give things up in case they were

172

sinful. First he gave up his young friends and their games. He even gave up ringing the bells of the village church. But still he was haunted by his sins and could not feel forgiven. One day a neighbour heard him cursing and swearing, and told him how wicked he was and how he was harming the other young men. John was ashamed. He stopped swearing and gave up dancing. Instead, he went to church and read his

Bible. Then at last came peace. He heard some old ladies talking about Jesus and how he brought them forgiveness. Suddenly he knew the answer to all his misery. The burden of his sins fell off his shoulders and he stood up straight, full of joy and peace. How happy he was!

John Bunyan joined the little chapel where these women met together, and he shared in their prayers and praises. He read his Bible with the minister and found comfort in it, just as Luther had done. Now he knew he must tell others the Good News he had found, and soon he was preaching the Gospel of Jesus. It was dangerous to do that. Charles II had become king and the new government persecuted those who would not go to church and who met together to worship God in their own way. John Bunyan and his friends had to hold their services secretly in barns and out in the fields. It was safest in the dark at night. John knew that if he was caught he would be sent to prison, but he went on without fear, travelling round in disguise. Before long he was caught and brought before the magistrates. "If you don't go to church and stop your preaching you must go to prison!" they said. John Bunyan answered them back boldly. "If you let me out today I will preach again tomorrow, by the help of God!" he cried. So he went to prison.

The prison at Bedford was old and dirty and dark. For twelve long years John Bunyan was shut up in his gloomy cell. How he longed to be back at home with his wife and his four dear children. He made things in prison to earn money for them. He worried especially about his poor blind daughter, whom he loved best of all. If he would promise to go to church and stop preaching he could go free any time. But he could not betray God and deny his conscience.

Out of his suffering came something wonderful. John Bunyan spent much of his time in prison writing books. One of them was a parable about Christians seeking the Kingdom of God. It was called *Pilgrim's Progress*. It became one of the most famous books in the world, and it was printed in many languages. Through it John Bunyan still speaks to us today from his prison at Bedford.

At last he was given his freedom and at once began preaching again. For sixteen years he travelled round, spreading the Gospel of Jesus, till his death in 1688. His example had inspired others to fight for freedom to worship God in their own way, and soon new laws were made allowing this. So Christians thank God for this brave tinker and remember him as a valiant Christian who helps them to be better pilgrims.

John Eliot, and the Bible for Red Indians

48

THE Pilgrim Fathers had sailed away westwards to the New World in the year 1620. For the next twenty years thousands of good, sturdy English people followed them. Some of them were farming people, seeking good land to till. Others were traders, seeking to make their fortune in this new land of plenty. But many were Puritans, seeking a land where they could worship God freely in their own way. In the year 1629 a Company was set up in this New England. It governed the land around Massachusetts Bay, near where the first Pilgrim Fathers had landed. The Company had a splendid seal to fix to its documents. It was the image of a Red Indian. Underneath were words from the Bible—"Come over and help us". John Eliot was the first man to answer that call to go to the Red Indians.

John had been born in the year 1604. He went to Cambridge University for he wanted to become a clergyman. But he was a Puritan and he could not be happy in the Church in England. "I will go to the New World," he decided. "There are many Puritans there to care for. There are the Red Indians too. People say they are savages, cruel and treacherous and living only to kill. But they are children of God. How I should love to take them the Good News of Jesus, and to teach them the ways of peace!" So John Eliot left his home in the village of Nazeing in Essex and sailed across the rough Atlantic Ocean. The voyage took three months and at last he landed at the

175

port of Boston, the chief town of Massachusetts. He soon found a church there to look after and people to care for in the name of Jesus. But the very next year something exciting happened. A ship from England was sailing into harbour. John hurried down with the crowd to meet it. How delighted he was to find on board people from his own village of Nazeing! When they had told him all the news from home they discussed where they were going to settle. They decided to live all together in the countryside outside the town of Boston where they could start their own farms. Then one of them said, "John, why don't you come with us? You can be our minister. Why, it would be just like living at home again." John agreed and they settled at a place called Roxbury.

Soon Roxbury was just like the village of Nazeing in Essex. Trees were cut down and the land was tilled and sown. Every family had their own house and garden and the animals grazed in the fields outside. There was a school house for the children and a church on the hill. All the buildings were made of wood by the carpenters and the thatchers made roofs for them. Outside the church were the stocks and the pillory to punish evil-doers. The Puritans lived strict and simple lives and John was happy serving them for they were his own people.

But often John's eyes looked beyond the quiet village to the dark and silent forests. The Red Indians lived there. He must get ready to take the word of God to them. But the first thing to do was to learn their language. He found a Red Indian who had lived for many years with an English settler. John talked with him whenever he had time to spare. The trouble was that no Red Indian words had ever been written down. There were no Red Indian books. There was not even a Red Indian alphabet. Every day John Eliot learnt new words from his friend and compared them with each other to find out exactly what they meant. For three years he went on learning the Red Indian language. Then he took some verses from the Bible and turned them into it.

One day his Red Indian friend took a message into the forest to Waban, the Red Indian chief. The next day John Eliot rode out in great excitement. He came to the clearing where the wigwams were pitched. Waban and his warriors awaited him. They carried toma-

176

hawks in their belts and quivers over their shoulders. They watched silently as John Eliot got off his horse and strode up to them smiling, his arms stretched wide in greeting. How astonished they were when he spoke to them in their own tongue. They gathered round him full of curiosity. Then he spoke to them of Jesus and he read the verses of the Bible which he had turned into their language. When he had ended they cried out together, "We understand!" Then one of them asked him, "How can we come to know your Jesus?" Then John knew that his work was not ended. He must turn the whole Bible into the Red Indian language so that they could come to know Jesus.

Whenever he could, John Eliot rode out to his Red Indian friends. Soon they too had a wooden church and a school house. He taught the men how to till the land and to grow their own crops. He taught the women how to spin and to send the cloth they made to market. Before long there was a Red Indian town near Roxbury. From John Eliot the Red Indians learned the Christian way of peace and of dealing justly with each other.

At home John Eliot went on with his Red Indian Bible. It took him ten years of patient work. At last it was ready and in the year 1663 it was printed. John Eliot rode out to his Red Indian friends in great excitement with a bundle of Red Indian Bibles in his arms. Soon he was reading to them the very words of Jesus in their own language. His work grew quickly and other English missionaries joined him. When he died in the year 1690 there were over 2,000 Red Indian Christians in the land of Massachusetts. His wonderful example inspired other people from England to become missionaries both to the Red Indians and to other peoples of the world.

49 George Fox, and the Society of Friends

MR. FOX, the weaver, of Fenny Drayton in Leicestershire, was a very God-fearing man. Both he and his wife were Puritans. One of her family had been burned to death for being a Protestant. So their son George, born in the year 1624, was brought up in a very Christian home. He became an apprentice to a shoemaker and he was going to be a cobbler. He was a strange lad, tall and strong, with long hair and piercing eyes. He wore sturdy leather breeches for they stood up to hard wear and the wandering life he led. He liked being alone and he seldom played with the other lads.

There were many things for him to think about. There was civil war in England between Parliament and King Charles I. There were quarrels about religion. He went to church but he found no peace there. Other young men in the town were Christians but that seemed to make no difference to the way they lived. He was restless and troubled. We know how he felt for he kept a diary. One day when he was walking in the fields he had some strange thoughts. "The Lord showed me that being educated at Oxford or Cambridge was not enough to fit a man to be a minister of Christ. Yet most people thought it was. Another time, out in the orchard reading my Bible, I realised that God does not dwell in churches built by men. He lives in people's hearts. I had tried everywhere to find someone who could help me. I could find no one. Then one day I heard a voice saying, 'There is only

178

one who can help you. He is Jesus Christ'." So at last George Fox found peace. He knew now that the Church was not enough. The Bible was not enough. A man must have the light of God in his own heart. Then he would live with Jesus and be led by him in everything. Only in that way could a man live the Christian life.

George Fox was now twenty-two years old. He began to preach in the name of Jesus at fairs, in the market places, and even in churches. Sometimes he interrupted the service. Sometimes he stood up and spoke when the service was over. People had to listen to this big man with eyes that seemed to see right through them. "Seek the Inner Light" was his message. "Open your hearts to Jesus. Then you will be his Friends and follow in his footsteps." He told men to do a good day's work and he told masters to pay fair wages. He spoke against evil-doing wherever he found it. He feared no one for it was the Holy Spirit within him that spoke. He spoke against clergymen and ministers who were paid to speak even if they did not have the inner light of God. He spoke against the churches which he called 'steeple-houses'. For a church was not a building but a group of believers, waiting for God to speak to them.

George Fox was very happy for he had the inner light of God within him. "The whole earth had a new smell," he wrote. "I fear no-one for the power of God is a-top all evil." But he had many strange ways. He would not take his hat off and bow and scrape as people did in those days. When he was taken to court he would not swear the oath on the Bible to speak the truth. "How can I swear by the Book that says 'Swear not at all'?" he said. "Then take your hat off!" the magistrate snapped. "The three friends of Daniel went into the fiery furnace with their hats on and their coats as well," he replied calmly.

George Fox began to travel through the land. Other people were beginning to follow him and to seek the inner light of God. He was sure that they must be gathered together in new Societies. Soon there were laws made against these strange people but they made no difference. George Fox was often attacked by a mob or cast into prison. In twenty years he was sent to prison six times. He spent eight years in gaols altogether and they were terrible places in those days. In the year 1666 he was thrown into the Castle at Scarborough. "The wind drove the rain in and the water came over my bed," he wrote. "When my clothes were wet I had no fire to dry them: my body was numb with cold, and my fingers swelled. A threepenny loaf lasted me three weeks and most of my drink was water. I was like a man buried alive. For though many Friends came from afar to see me they were not allowed in. The officers often threatened to hang me over the wall. 'I am ready,' I said. 'I have never feared death or suffering. I am an innocent, peaceful man. I have always sought the good of all men. Bring out your gallows.' "

Nothing could be done with people like that. They would not meet in secret as other Protestants did. George Fox was often imprisoned during his journeys in places as far apart as Scarborough in the north, Nottingham in the Midlands, and Launceston in Cornwall. In the year 1668 he made rules for his new society calling his followers 'Friends of the Truth'. He made his home with his friend Thomas Fell who lived near Ulverstone in the Lake District. When Thomas died George Fox married his widow, Margaret. But he was seldom at home. He travelled all over England and Ireland, Scotland and Wales. He went to Holland, to the West Indies and to North America, setting up new Societies of Friends. Oliver Cromwell was his friend. But George Fox would not swear to be loyal to his government, nor to King Charles II after him. "You should be trying the Bible, not me," he said to the judges. "Put the Bible in prison!"

George Fox died in the year 1691. Harsh laws had been made against his Society of Friends but it went on growing. Richard Chantrey of Shropshire went from meeting to meeting wearing the smock of a farm-labourer with a pitch-fork over his shoulder. Many Friends went to the New World to serve God in freedom. Still today the Society of Friends bears witness throughout the world to the inner light of God that George Fox preached to his followers.

William Penn, and the City of Brotherly Love

50

ADMIRAL PENN had led the British fleet against the Dutch in the time of Oliver Cromwell. His son William, born in 1644, was as brave as his father but in a different way. One night, when he was about twelve years old, he had a wonderful vision of God. From that time onwards he knew that the light of God was within him, and he always obeyed the inner voice of conscience. When he went as a student to Oxford he met others who felt about God as he did. They were nicknamed 'Quakers', but their real name is 'Friends'. He found that they too lived by the inner light of God and soon he joined them. But in those days men were not allowed to worship God in their own way. At first William and his friends had to pay fines for not going to church. Then trouble broke out and William was expelled from the university. His father was very angry and beat him. He sent him to look after some of his land in Ireland, hoping that his son would get over his foolish ideas. But William joined the Society of Friends there and for the rest of his life he was a Quaker. He knew what the cost might be, but he had to obey the inner voice of God.

William was put in prison in Ireland for attending Quaker worship. When he was freed and came back to England, his father would have nothing to do with him. Before long he was a prisoner in the Tower of London. The old Admiral sent a messenger to frighten him. "If you don't give up this nonsense you will be put to death." William

181

sent back his brave answer: "I must obey the voice of God, not men," he said. His father knew now that William was not a lazy, good-for-nothing, nor a coward. He welcomed him back home again and, when the Admiral died, William became a man of wealth and importance in England. As a friend of King Charles II he himself was safe. But he used all his time and money in the service of his fellow Quakers, especially those who suffered for their faith in God.

Many Quakers had left England. They set out on the long and dangerous voyage to America, seeking freedom to worship God in their own way. It seemed to William Penn a fine thing. How good it would be to set up in the rich lands of the 'New World' a kingdom where men could live as Jesus taught us, serving God in freedom. King Charles owed him a debt, so William Penn asked him to pay it, not with money, but with land in the colonies. He told the King he would call it 'Sylvania', from a Latin word meaning forest land. "No," said the King. "You shall call it 'Pennsylvania'." William made laws for his new land. All its people must be free to worship God in their own way. There must be no slavery. There would be no army, for Quakers will never fight. Men would live as brothers in peace and love.

William Penn landed in America in 1682. The settlers welcomed him and soon he was busy planning his new state of Pennsylvania. He found a fine place to build his capital city. He called it 'Philadelphia', a name which comes from Greek words meaning 'brotherly love'.

Now there was something very important to be done. The king had granted the land to William Penn, but the Red Indians lived there. The settlers must live in brotherly love with them as well as with each other. William Penn decided to pay them for the land and to make a treaty with them. One day he arranged to meet them at the place where his new city was to be built. He went there with only a few friends. None of them had any weapons. They carried bales of cloth and goods to pay for the land. All around them were Red Indians in their war-paint, tomahawks in their belts, bows and arrows ready in their hands. William Penn had only a parchment in his hand. The Chief signalled to his braves, and they laid down their weapons. They sat round as William Penn talked with the Chief. "We wish to buy land from you," he said. "We desire to live with you in peace. The Great Spirit sees into my heart. He knows that I want my people to live with your people as brothers." "Let it be so," answered the Chief. "My people will be brothers to your people as long as the sun gives her light." The treaty was made and for many years there was peace between the white settlers and the Redskins. If all the settlers had treated the Red Indians as William Penn had done there would never have been fighting between them.

He died in 1718, but his memory lived on in the state of Pennsylvania. His good laws spread far and wide, and one of the greatest laws of the United States of America gives every man the right to worship God in his own way. In the great city of Philadelphia today the Penn Treaty Park is the memorial of the brotherhood William Penn made with the Red Indians. So his name lives on and the memory of his Christian love can never be forgotten.

51 George Frederick Handel, and 'The Messiah'

MR. HANDEL was one of the proudest men in the little German town of Halle. He had started life as a poor barber. Then he had become a doctor and dentist too. Now the Duke of Saxony had made him his royal doctor. He loved to visit the Court where he came to know Dukes from other parts of Germany. He was an important man and he had great plans for his son, George Frederick, who had been born in the year 1685. "He must have plenty of books and study hard," Mr. Handel said to his wife. "He will go to the University and become a lawyer. How proud I shall be when he is made a Councillor to the Duke!"

One day Mr. Handel went into the nursery to find what all the noise was about. He was horrified. Little George was surrounded by musical toys. There were trumpets and drums and oboes—but not a single book. "So this is what you spend your money on!" he said angrily to his son. "But father, I love music," George cried. "Music is only for wandering singers and vagabonds," his father shouted. "You're going to be a lawyer, not a street beggar. You will start going to school at once. That will end this nonsense!" Then he snatched up the toys and hurled them on the fire.

Little George trudged to school every day with his satchel. He grew pale and miserable for the joy had gone out of his life. Sunday was the only happy day for then he went to church with his kind Aunt

Anna. How he loved to listen to the golden music of the organ. Often he gazed up at the organ loft. "One day I shall sit there," he said to himself. "I shall make music for God." Sometimes, when George was specially good, the schoolmaster let him play on his spinet for a few minutes after school. It was a kind of early piano and George raced over the keys with nimble fingers. Sometimes there was a band or group of wandering minstrels in the town and George followed them through the streets. But he longed to make music himself and he grew paler and sadder. "Why are you so unhappy, George?" his mother asked him one day, taking him on her knee. "It's my music," George wept. "I can't live without it!" Then, on the morning of his birthday, Aunt Anna came into his bedroom with a large bundle. It was an old spinet for George himself. How thrilled he was! They took it up to the attic and wrapped cloth round the strings. Now George could play whenever he liked and his father would never know. He did not notice the dark or the cold as he played there at night in his night-shirt.

When George was seven years old his father had to go on a journey to the court of another duke. There would be wonderful music at the court but his father would not take him. George ran behind the coach until it was a long way from home. Then he showed himself and his father had to take him in. George spent all his time at court with the duke's orchestra. On Sunday after the service he crept into the organ loft and began to play. The duke happened to hear him. "Why, your son's a genius!" he cried to Mr. Handel. "You must see that he gets music lessons." George's father had to give in, and when they returned home George began to study music with an organist. Soon he was composing his own music. Halle had never known such a brilliant musician.

When his father died, George went to Hamburg to play in the Opera House. Soon he was made conductor of the orchestra and in the year 1705 he wrote his first opera, a play set to music. Now he had enough money to go to Italy, the land of music. He wrote operas for Cardinals of the Church, songs for the gondoliers of Venice, and dances for the noblemen. When he went back to Germany he was famous, and the Prince of Hanover set him over the music at his Royal Court.

But Handel loved to travel and in the year 1710 he came to England. His first opera was such a success that he decided to remain in London at his house in Brooke Street, Hanover Square, which is still there today. Queen Anne loved his operas and gave him a pension. He worked very hard but sometimes his operas were failures. When he was 52 years old he had lost all his money and he was very ill from years of hard toil. "Poor Handel," people said, "that's the end of his music." But it was really the beginning. Handel grew well and strong again. He gave up composing operas and made a new kind of music. It is called 'oratorio'. Handel set Bible stories to music. Each oratorio needed solo singers, a chorus of singers and an orchestra. There was no acting or scenery or costume. But the English people loved his sacred oratorios. They were sung especially in the time of Lent.

One day Handel remembered his dream as a boy in the church at Halle. He would set to music the whole Bible story of Jesus—how the prophets had foretold his coming, how he had lived and suffered and died, and how he had risen from the dead. He hurried to his room and closed the door. For 24 days there was no sound day and night but the scratching of his pen. Each morning his faithful servant found trays of food untouched and the candle burnt low. One morning he hurried in at his master's call. The tears rolled down Handel's cheeks. "It is finished," he cried. "I saw the gates of Heaven open and I heard the angel choirs singing the 'Hallelujah Chorus'." So Handel's greatest oratorio was born, and still today 'The Messiah' brings people to the gates of heaven.

Handel died in the year 1759. He was old and blind and paralysed but still full of divine music. His body was buried in Westminster Abbey but he lives on for ever in 'The Messiah', still making music for God.

John Howard, Prison Reformer

52

JOHN HOWARD was born in the year 1726 in London. He was never a strong boy, and instead of going to school he had lessons at home. He grew up to love God and he was kind to everyone. His father made him an apprentice to a grocer so that he could earn an honest living. But when his father died he left John all his money. John Howard could have led the easy life of a gentleman in those days, going to banquets and balls and amusing himself by gambling. But he hated gambling and drinking and his food was always simple. Besides, he wanted to do something useful with his life.

In the year 1756 news came to England of a terrible earthquake at Lisbon in Portugal. John Howard decided to go there to help care for those who had suffered and he set sail from England in the good ship *Hanover*. It was a brave thing to do, for England was at war with France. The *Hanover* was a fast merchant ship and the captain hoped to make a safe voyage. But they were only two days out of port when a French man-of-war came over the horizon and bore down on them. The captain of the *Hanover* strove to out-run the French warship but a cannon-ball brought her main-mast down and she was helpless. French sailors soon boarded the *Hanover* and she was taken into the French port of Brest as a prize. John Howard was thrown with the other prisoners into the town jail. It was a filthy dungeon under the ground, dark and damp and foul. They lived like animals, eating with

187

their hands the dirty food that was thrown to them when the jailer thought of them. The prisoners were moved to other jails but they were just as bad. John Howard never forgot that terrible time. Soon he was allowed to go back home on condition that a French officer imprisoned in England was exchanged for him. At once he wrote to Parliament describing the terrible life of English prisoners in France. He went on writing and speaking until they were all allowed to return home to England in exchange for French prisoners.

John Howard went to live with his wife in a large house at Cardington near the city of Bedford. He was a country squire now but he lived for others, not for himself. He and his good wife built fine cottages for the poor of the city and schools for the children. They learnt to read and to write and to do sums, just as we do. The girls learnt to cook and to sew. John Howard liked to be alone sometimes. He had a summer-house in his garden made with logs, and with a thatched roof. He spent his spare time there, thinking and reading. It had a table and a chair and a bookcase full of books. On the table was a sandglass to tell the time, and a Bible.

In the year 1773 John Howard was made High Sheriff for the County of Bedford, because of his fine character. Now he was an important man. One of his chief tasks was to judge people in the Court and to look after the prisons. First he went to the prisons in Bedford city. They were terrible places, just like his own prison long ago in France. Worst of all he found some of the prisoners had been judged innocent. "Then why haven't they been set free?" he demanded. "Because the jailers are not paid wages," he was told. "They have to get all the money they can from the prisoners. They don't let the prisoners go free till they've paid handsomely for it." "You must pay the jailers regular wages," John Howard said sternly to the magistrates. "But we can't do that," they replied. "Not unless it's done in other counties." Then John Howard set out to find how the prisons were run in the other counties of England. What terrible places they were: damp and dark, dirty and cold! The prisoners were all herded together, men and women, boys and girls, innocent and guilty. They slept on filthy straw, they were dressed in rags, and they bolted greedily whatever was thrown to them as food. They had nothing to do. Many died from the jail-fever which every-

188

one took for granted. No one in England saw them and no one seemed to care.

But there was one man who cared. Wherever he went, John Wesley always visited the prison. "It is a hell on earth," he said after going to the grim Marshalsea Prison in London. One day he preached in Bedford. John Howard never forgot Wesley's sermon that Sunday. The text was "Whatsoever thy hand findeth to do, do it with all thy might." They became great friends and Wesley inspired John Howard to go on with his splendid work for God.

For seventeen years John Howard was a crusader for better prisons. He got up each morning about 3 o'clock and was soon on his horse. Four times he went round Britain visiting all the different kinds of prisons, writing down notes on what he found. Then he went back home and sat in his hut in the garden, writing his book called *The State of Prisons in Britain*. In the year 1777 he sent it to Parliament. The Members sent for him for they could not believe the terrible things he described. When they had heard him they at once made a new law. Innocent prisoners were to be set free at once. Jailers were to be paid wages and not to collect money from prisoners. New prisons were to be built, in place of the old dungeons, where men could work and the sick could be cared for.

John Howard was not content. He went across the seas to France and Holland, Germany and Italy, inspecting prisons and writing another book on what he found. In the year 1790 he died in a prison in Russia from a fever which he caught from the prisoners. Money was given to set up a statue to him in St. Paul's Cathedral in London. But he lives on in the good work of those who follow in his footsteps, bringing hope and care to prisoners.

53 John Wesley, and the Society of Methodists

THE Reverend Samuel Wesley was rector of Epworth in Lincoln-shire. He had a big family of ten children and little money, but his wife was very thrifty and even taught the children herself. John was born in 1703. One night, when he was six years old, the thatch roof of the rectory caught fire and John was the last of the family to be saved, snatched from the burning house. This seemed to his mother to be a sign that God wanted him for some great work and she took special care of him. When he was old enough, John went away to school and then to Oxford University. He became a clergyman and went back to Epworth to help his father. After two years he returned to Oxford to teach students. He found that his brother Charles, who taught at another College, had formed a society of men who loved God and wanted to serve him faithfully. It was called the 'Holy Club', and John soon became its leader. The members had strict rules for reading their Bibles, meeting for prayer, going without food, teaching poor children, and visiting the prisoners in Oxford jail. They were nicknamed 'Methodists' because of their strict life, and the followers of John Wesley are called Methodists to this day.

John Wesley felt he ought to go as a missionary to the settlers in America. He wanted to take the Good News of Jesus to the Red Indians too. He met some fine German Christians on the long voyage and they helped him greatly. But his preaching was a failure.

His heart was not on fire with love. All he had was a hard religion of rules and duties. He was sad when he came back to England. But one night in London he went to a meeting of these German Christians. Suddenly during a reading from the Bible he came alive. "I felt my heart strangely warmed," he wrote in his diary. "I felt I did trust in Christ, Christ alone." It was May 24th, 1738, and Methodists have remembered that great day ever since.

Now John Wesley was on fire and he began his great work for God. For fifty-three years he travelled on his horse throughout the land, preaching the Gospel. They were hard times in England. Machines had been invented and ugly new towns sprang up wherever there was coal and iron. People were herded there like animals with no one to care for them. The churches were far away from the factories and collieries. But the churches themselves were dead and few people cared about true religion. It was John Wesley who changed all that. He went to these poor and rough people—to tin-miners and smugglers in Cornwall, coal-miners in Bristol, weavers in Yorkshire and Lancashire, colliers in Durham and Northumberland. Often he was attacked by mobs, but he showed no fear. Some of the bishops and clergymen were against him and would not allow him and his followers to enter their churches. John began preaching in the open air. At first it seemed very strange to him. But his fine voice and his sincerity won men to him.

Thousands flocked to hear him, and rough working men wept as they heard for the first time the offer of God's love and forgiveness and the promise of a new life. Magistrates and rich squires tried to stop him, and gangs of bullies were sent to attack Wesley when he was preaching. But nothing could frighten him.

Groups of Methodists sprang up all over the land. Men gave up drink and gambling and lived new lives, working hard and caring for their families. They met together for worship and built their own chapels. They had weekly meetings for fellowship and helped each other with prayer and friendship and money. John organised his chapels and trained his preachers carefully. He wrote books for them and edited others, for they had to study regularly. All the money he made was used in his work. There were no schools in those days for the poor. John Wesley started his own and wrote the grammar

books to be used in them. He encouraged others to start schools, too. His brother Charles wrote fine hymns to use in their chapels, and Methodists have always loved singing in their worship.

John Wesley got up every day at four o'clock and, after his prayers, set out on his horse, often reading as he went along. He travelled about 5,000 miles each year, preaching several times each day. He was only a little man, but he was very strong from his open-air life. He lived to be eighty-eight years old, working to the end of his life. When he died in 1791, people all over the country mourned for him.

John himself sent some of his followers to America. "I look upon the world as my parish," he said. Today there are Methodist churches in many parts of the world. England became a different country because of his work. For in his schools and chapels children and adults were brought up in the Christian life and from them came a better England. All this was the work of one man, John Wesley, a great prophet of God.

Robert Raikes, Friend of Children

IN the year 1780 there lived in the city of Gloucester in England a man named Robert Raikes. He was a rich man, for he owned a newspaper called *The Gloucester Journal*. He had a fine house, where his children lived happily and had everything they needed. He loved fine clothes so much that people called him 'Buck Raikes'. But he was not a selfish man. He believed in God and cared about other people. "Jesus went about doing good. I try to follow his example," he said. For some time he had been visiting the poor prisoners in the two dreadful jails at Gloucester. Men and women were kept there like animals. No one else went there for fear of catching fever. Robert Raikes felt so sorry for their children and began to wonder what he could do for them. Gangs of children often rushed past his printing office, fighting and running wild. Jesus loved and cared for children, so he must too.

One night he went to call at a house on the other side of the city where the poor lived. Mobs of children roamed the streets in their filthy rags like wild animals. He asked about them. "They're even worse on Sundays," he was told. "For on Sunday they are let out of the factories." Robert Raikes went home and began to plan what he would do to help the children of Gloucester. There were no schools in those days for the poor. Even little children were sent to work in the coal-mines and the factories. Cruel masters made them work long hours at the machines, beating them when they grew tired. Sunday was the only day on which they were free. No wonder they went wild. Nobody cared for them. They were taught nothing.

Robert Raikes decided to start a school for them. It would have to be on Sunday, so it was called a 'Sunday-school'. He paid people to help him, and soon two schools had been started. He had to be

very strict to begin with, for the children had no idea how to behave. They were made to wash and they were taught their manners. They learnt reading and writing, and then began to read the Bible. Robert Raikes took them to church and taught them how to behave there. It was hard work, but he knew it was God's work and he persevered. People called them 'gutter-snipes' and 'street arabs'. But soon they noticed the difference in the children who went to the new Sunday-schools.

There was something else Robert Raikes could do. He began to write in his newspaper about Sunday-schools. Before long, people all over England were reading about this work begun by Robert Raikes. Many good people copied his example and started schools. His friend John Wesley said that every group of Methodists should have a Sunday-school. So this fine work went on growing.

Robert Raikes found enemies as well as friends. Some people were afraid of losing children from the factories. Others said he was breaking the commandment about the Sabbath day. But he went on with his work all his life. When he died in 1811 there were Sunday-schools all over England. They were different from the Sunday-schools we have today, for children were taught reading and writing and good manners. They were more like our day-schools, and they were the only schools poor children had.

Robert Raikes had shown Christians the great need of schools for children. But one day in the week was not enough. Before long the churches started schools on weekdays as well as Sundays. They collected money to build schools and to train teachers. Now there were day-schools all over the land, built and paid for by Christians. Then the Government realised they must do something for children. Laws were passed by Parliament and money was given from the taxes to build schools. So the education of all children in the land became law, and that is why you have your school today. It all began with Robert Raikes. Think of the dreadful life of children in his days, and compare it with your life today. Then you will realise how much we owe to Robert Raikes, who followed the example of Jesus and 'went about doing good'.

55 Granville Sharp, Friend of Slaves

GRANVILLE SHARP was born in the year 1735 in the city of Durham in England. His father was the Archdeacon of Northumberland. He was a good man who loved his people and did everything he could for them. He brought up his children to love God and to serve him in their daily lives. He had a large family and he was too poor to send all his sons away to school. Granville was sent to London town to be an apprentice to a draper. He made friends with the other apprentices and they used to talk together late at night. Often they talked about the Bible and Granville learnt the Greek language in which the New Testament was first written so that he would understand it better. Then he learnt the Hebrew language too, so as to understand the Old Testament better. He worked hard all day and then he studied his books at night. When he was 23 years old Granville gave up learning to be a draper. He had educated himself by his studies and he was given a post as a clerk under the Government.

Sometimes in the evening Granville went to visit his brother. He lived in Mincing Lane where he was a surgeon. One evening he found a poor negro lying on his brother's doorstep. His thin, starved body was covered with sores and shaking with fever. Granville carried him inside and his kind brother looked after him. When he was better, he told them that his name was Jonathan Strong. "My home was in Africa," he said. "Wicked chiefs among my black

196

people sell us to the white men for guns or drink. The white men live on the coast in settlements. Most of them are British or Dutch. We are chained together and brought to their settlements. Those who fall ill are left to die by the wayside. When we reach the coast we are chained by the white men below deck in their slave-ships. Then we are taken across the Atlantic Ocean to America. Hundreds of us are chained together in the hold. Many fall ill and those who die are thrown overboard. When we reach the West Indies a strong slave is sold for about £60. Men who are weak are sold with the women and children in lots. They are much cheaper!"

Granville Sharp had never heard such a terrible story. He knew he must do something about this dreadful slavery. But first he must find out all he could. "What did you do in the West Indies?" he asked Jonathan. "We had to work on the sugar plantations," the negro replied. "It was hard work all day long. The trouble was that none of us was fit after weeks tied up in the ship. Many others fell ill and died. In the end only about half of those who were taken from their homes in Africa were left!" Granville Sharp clenched his fists. "We must stop this wicked thing!" he cried. "Not all of us suffer so badly, master," said Jonathan Strong. "Some slaves are treated kindly. They are permitted to marry and can even earn their freedom if they work hard and please their masters." "That does not make it any better," Granville Sharp replied. "No man can own another man. We are all children of God. He made us free and we are all precious to him, black or white. To buy or sell a human creature is not only a crime against law. It is a sin against God!"

Jonathan Strong went on to tell Granville Sharp how his master had brought him to England as a servant. His cruel master beat him and starved him. When he was too ill to work, his master had thrown him into the street and that was how Granville Sharp had found him. The two brothers nursed him back to health. Then they found him a good home with a kind Quaker chemist in Fenchurch Street. But one day his old master recognised him in the street. "Why, there's my old slave," he said to himself. "He looks fit and well and able to work. I'll get him back. After all, he is my property." So the negro was seized by his old master and sold to a planter for £30. Granville Sharp was furious when he heard what had happened.

Quickly he brought the matter before the court of the Lord Mayor of London. Both Jonathan's old master and the planter claimed him. "The slave has done nothing wrong that I can see," said the Lord Mayor. "I must set him free." So Jonathan was taken off the slave ship sailing to the West Indies. But he was still in danger. Granville Sharp could not find a lawyer to help him so, once again, he sat up far into the night studying law books. There was no clear law about slavery, he found. So he must go to the courts and argue his own case.

After two years he was ready. He had learned all about the law and all about the slave trade, too. There were 2 million slaves owned by the British planters in America. When the planters had become rich they came back to England, bringing slaves with them. So there were over 15,000 slaves in Britain and newspapers often had advertisements for the sale of slaves. From the ports of London, Liverpool and Bristol sailed 200 slave ships flying the British flag. Everyone took slavery for granted—except Granville Sharp. He wrote a book so that people would know the evils of the slave trade. Sometimes at night he helped to save poor negroes from the slave ships. He began to take cases to court. Each time the judges had to give in to him and say that the slave should go free. But they would not say that slavery was against the law.

Then in the year 1772 the Lord Chief Justice agreed to hear a case himself. Granville Sharp argued in the court for five long months. Then the Judge decided. "No one can be a slave in Britain," he said. "When a slave sets foot on English soil he is a free man." It was a wonderful triumph for Granville Sharp and it was all due to him. But he realised it was only the beginning. He must work to stop the slave trade in British ships and in the British colonies. At his home at Clapham in London he gathered his Christian friends. They bound themselves together to fight against slavery. Their enemies gave them a nickname—'The Clapham Sect'. One of them was William Wilberforce.

William Wilberforce, and Freedom for Slaves

56

In the year 1781 the slave ship *Zong* sailed from Africa to Jamaica in the West Indies with 440 slaves chained in the hold. A disease broke out on the voyage. 60 slaves died and their bodies were thrown into the sea. They were worth over £300. Many others were ill and would soon die, losing much more money. The captain decided to throw them overboard while they were still alive. Then the owners could claim money from the insurance company on the excuse that the water on board had run out. One slave saved himself by holding on to a rope. He hid on board and when the ship reached England the terrible story quickly spread. The insurance company would not pay and the case was brought to court. Granville Sharp accused the captain and the slave owners of murder. The judge decided that the slaves were the property of the owners. "It is only like throwing horses overboard," he said. Many people were shocked by the judge's decision and they helped the 'Clapham Sect' in their fight against slavery.

In his home, at Clapham in London, Granville Sharp's friends met together regularly. One of them was a young man named Thomas Clarkson. He had hoped to be a clergyman like his father. But he gave up his great ambition so that he could give all his time to the fight against slavery. He rode all over Britain, gathering information about the slave trade from sailors and former slaves. He went on the slave ships and measured the holds where they were kept. He collected the chains and fetters, handcuffs and thumbscrews used for slaves and exhibited them in London. His other Clapham friends were busy, too, making people realise the evils of slavery. They had pictures and sayings painted on soup plates. Then, as their guests sipped their soup, they were forced to read—"Do away with slavery". Or there would be a picture of a negro and the words, "A man and a brother". They won thousands of supporters. Many people gave up sugar which came from the slave plantations.

But something more was needed. Laws must be made against slavery. Someone must lead the fight in Parliament. There was no doubt as to who it should be.

William Wilberforce was born in the city of Hull, in Yorkshire, in the year 1759. His father was very rich and, after going to grammar school, William went on to Cambridge University. He was clever and witty and he was very fond of music, having a fine voice. Friends flocked around this gay and charming young man. When he was 21 years old he became a Member of Parliament through his father's money. He was a wonderful speaker and he enjoyed argument and debate in Parliament. But he found plenty of time to be a 'man about town'. He belonged to five clubs and he spent his evenings drinking and gambling, going to balls and parties.

When he was 25 years old a strange change came over William Wilberforce. He began to read serious books and to study his Bible. He became a different person. He gave up his gay life. "I decided to devote the rest of my life to the service of God," he wrote. Soon he had joined the 'Clapham Sect' and it was not long before he knew how he would serve God.

One day in the year 1786 he was staying with his great friend William Pitt at his house near Bromley in Kent. They went for a walk and sat under an old tree at Holwood, looking down into Keston valley. There Wilberforce told Pitt that he had decided to lead the fight against slavery in Parliament. He and his Clapham friends collected all the evidence they could, for he must have facts when he spoke in Parliament. Planters, traders and merchants soon grew to hate him but he never gave up. The last letter John Wesley wrote was to cheer him on—"If God be for you, who can be against you?" Wesley wrote. "He has called you to this great task. Go on, in the name of God!" Some people said he was mad. "My mother and relatives in Yorkshire were very worried," Wilberforce wrote. "I had to go back home and show them how cheerful and happy I was, working for God. One of them said, 'If that's madness I wish other people suffered from it!' "

In the year 1789 Wilberforce stood up in Parliament for the first time to propose a new law to end slavery. He spoke for three hours in his golden voice. He gave terrible facts about the evils of slavery. "I blame no one," he said. "We are all guilty of allowing this dreadful evil to go on!" The Members listened to him quietly, but many of them had grown rich from the plantations and they voted against him. But he went on, both in Parliament and in towns all over Britain, speaking against the slave trade. His new law was thrown out again and again. There was a terrible revolution in France and then followed the war with Napoleon. But Wilberforce went on for nearly twenty years with his crusade against slavery. At last in the year 1807 victory was in sight. Wilberforce spoke for the last time in Parliament. When the votes were counted there were 384 for his new law and only 16 against it. Everyone rose to cheer the great Christian warrior.

The new law ended the slave trade. But the fight had to go on to free slaves in the British colonies. It took another 20 years. Wilberforce lived just long enough to hear that the law of 1833 had been passed. All slaves in British lands were made free. Wilberforce heard the wonderful news three days before he died. With his last breath he praised God that he had lived to see his cause triumphant, and he died peaceful and content.

57 John Williams of the South Sea Islands

JOHN WILLIAMS was born in the year 1796. His home was at Tottenham in London and he played there happily with his sisters. He was very clever with his hands and he was always making things for them. When he was still a boy he read the thrilling *Journals* of Captain Cook, telling of his adventures in the South Seas on his voyage of 1772. John made a ship in his garden and he and his sisters and their friends sailed away on imaginary voyages among the coral islands. But when he was twelve years old he had to leave school and start work. He was made apprentice to an ironmonger so that he could learn to use his clever hands skilfully. He had to serve customers in the shop but, whenever he could, he went into the smithy behind and watched the brawny workmen hammering the red-hot metal on the forge in a shower of sparks. Then, when the day's work was done and the smithy was deserted, John went in to practise by himself. He used old bits of iron to fashion nails and tools and during his seven years' apprenticeship John grew into a fine smith. He grew tall and strong, too, a fine young man.

But all was not well with John. No longer would he go to church on Sunday evenings with his family. Instead, he mixed with a gang of rough young men who wasted their time hanging around the streets and wasted their money on drink. One Sunday evening John was waiting for them in the street when the wife of his master came along, on her way to church. "Come with me, John," she invited. He went with her unwillingly, but he soon felt at home again in church. And it was during that service that John realised he wanted to give his whole life to God. He never missed church again. Once the preacher spoke of the South Sea islands that everyone was talking about through Captain Cook's discoveries. "Some people will tell you how happy these islanders are in their simple ways," he said. "But our missionaries tell a different story. These people live a savage life, worshipping their cruel gods. They kill their little children to please their idols and they sacrifice men on their stone altars to please Oro, their god of war. They live to fight and to kill and they eat their enemies. Is this the good and happy life?" John Williams never forgot those words. He would go where Captain Cook had gone and find adventure in the service of his Master.

John studied hard and offered himself to the London Missionary Society, which had been set up in 1795 to take the Good News of Jesus to the South Seas. In the year 1816 John Williams set sail in a little sailing ship called the *Harriet*. He was twenty years old and his wife, Mary, a year younger. It was a long voyage round to the other side of the world. John loved to be with the sailors, helping them to furl the sails and splice ropes. By the time the year's voyage was over, he knew everything about a sailing ship.

In 1817 John Williams landed on the island of Tahiti where King Pomare and his people had become Christians. Soon he had learnt the language of the people and he was delighted when a message came from King Tamatoa of the island of Raiatea. "Please send teachers to my people," he asked. Before long, John set sail with his wife and another missionary. Raiatea was the biggest of the Society Islands, discovered by Captain Cook. John Williams found the people jolly and friendly. But since they had given up fighting and killing, the men had become lazy. Several families lived together in one long thatched house built on poles. John Williams decided to build his own house. He used coral to make cement and whitewash and distemper. His house had seven rooms and when it was finished he made furniture for it. Soon the men of the island were copying him, while John Williams learnt their language. He translated the Gospel of Luke into their tongue and made copies of it on his small printing press. John and Mary taught 300 children in the new school and the people met together to worship God in the new church they had built. Before long, King Tamatoa and his people were taking the Good News to other islands near by.

John Williams was never content to stay in one place. He studied the charts of Captain Cook, eager to take the Gospel to islands where the Christian message of peace and goodwill had never been heard. He made the long voyage to Sydney in Australia and chartered a sturdy ship for his work. In the *Matamua* he sailed back to Raiatea and then set off to find Rarotonga, one of the Cook Islands mentioned on the charts. The anxious captain wanted to turn back, for food and water were running dangerously low. But John Williams would never give up. At last the island came into view and John Williams went ashore with the people who had come with him from Raiatea to teach the islanders. King Makea seemed to welcome them but that night they were attacked and had to flee back to the ship. Papeiha, one of the native teachers, insisted on going back to the island. John Williams sailed away with a heavy heart but he knew he must not stop Papeiha. He must go on training native teachers so that they could take the Gospel to their own people.

It was not till 1826, four years later, that John Williams returned to Rarotonga. How delighted he was to find that the people had burned their idols and followed Papeiha in the worship of God and in the Christian way of peace. Soon he was busy teaching and preaching, building schools and churches, and translating parts of the Bible into the language of the islanders. After a year he was eager to be off to new islands, but the *Matamua* had not returned. So he built his own ship, *The Messenger of Peace*. In her he sailed to the friendly islands of Samoa and then on to the fierce islanders of the New Hebrides. There in 1839 he was clubbed to death on the island of Erromanga, dying, as he had lived, in the service of his Master. Others carried on the work he had begun, and the foundation stone of the memorial to John Williams was laid by the Christian son of the man who had killed him.

Elizabeth Fry, Friend of Prisoners

BETSY GURNEY lived a gay life in her grand home near the city of Norwich in England. Her father was a rich man and very good to his seven daughters. They had fine clothes and everyone knew them by their scarlet cloaks. Betsy was especially proud of her purple boots with red laces. They all kept diaries and we can read in them of the pranks they got up to and the fun they had together. They loved dances and picnics best of all.

Mr. Gurney was a Quaker. Every Sunday he took his daughters to the Meeting House in Norwich. The service was very quiet and often these lively girls were fidgety. But when Betsy was eighteen years old a Quaker from America spoke at the service and she was very touched by what he said. She knew that God wanted her to give her life to him, and she longed to serve him. She gave up bright clothes, and for the rest of her life wore the plain grey frock, white collar and white cuffs of the strict Quakers. She started a school for the village children at her home, just as Robert Raikes was doing in Gloucester. She too felt it was a special way of serving God.

But her greatest work was still to come. She fell in love with a good Quaker gentleman called Joseph Fry. Soon they were married and they moved to his fine house in London so as to be near his business. There were always visitors and friends at their home, and Elizabeth Fry was kept busy looking after them. Several children were born to her and she was a busy mother as well. But she felt there was more she could do to serve God. She began to visit the sick and poor in London town, bringing them help and comfort and the Good News of Jesus. One day two visitors called on her. They had been visiting the men in the terrible Newgate Prison. It was the worst of the eighteen dreadful prisons in London. The governor would not let them visit the women prisoners. "Will you go?" they asked. The next morning Elizabeth Fry stood outside the grim gates and asked to see the governor. He was amazed at what she asked. "They're like wild beasts!" he cried. "I have soldiers guarding them! I never go there myself if I can help it!" Quietly she insisted, and the governor gave in. The huge bolts were drawn back, the door opened, and the turnkey slammed it shut quickly as soon as she was through.

It was a dreadful sight. Three hundred women lived with their children in the filthy jail, without light or heat, without beds or wash-places, with nothing but their filthy rags. The children were starved and naked. The women fought like cats over any money a kind passer-by threw to them through the bars. As often as they had money they were drunk. The laws in those days were savage. Some were in prison for owing money, others for stealing. A child could be hanged for stealing.

Elizabeth Fry never forgot what she saw and for thirty years never ceased to work for women in prison. The women stared at her that morning. She picked up a filthy baby and nursed him tenderly. Slowly the women came around her and she spoke to them of the love of God. Then she told them that God had sent her to them. "Let us help each other," she said. "Together we can make this prison a better place. God will help us to do it. Let us ask him." Then she prayed to God and many of the women fell down, sobbing and crying.

Elizabeth Fry went to Newgate every day she could. Other Quaker ladies joined her. Soon the women's ward was clean and neat, the terrible smell was gone and fever was much less. The women were busy making clothes for themselves and their children. A girl who was in prison for stealing a watch became teacher to the children, and Elizabeth persuaded the governor to let them have a small cell for their school. She brought food and clothing and medicines. After a time she brought the Lord Mayor of London and other important people to see the women's ward. They were amazed to find the women prisoners so neat and busy and well-behaved. They soon gave Elizabeth what she asked for her women—regular food, clothing, work, more space, and women to look after them.

One of the cruel punishments in those days was to send women to Australia in horrible convict ships. People jeered at them as the open carts took them through London to the docks. Elizabeth did all she could for these poor women. They were taken to the ship in closed carriages. Elizabeth went with them, saw them settled on board, and saw that they had plenty of useful work to do during the long voyage. She arranged for the ships to be met in Australia and for a hostel where the women could stay till they found work and a home in their new land.

She was never content. She used all her influence to improve the prisons. She went to Members of Parliament, judges, and magistrates to seek their help in her work. She visited prisons throughout England and spoke at meetings up and down the country, spreading her new way of treating those who had broken the law. "Prisons are not just places for punishing people," she said. "We must help them to lead better lives. Kindness will do much more than cruelty." Slowly through her tireless work her ideas spread. She went to Europe to visit prisons, bumping in a coach over the dreadful roads of Holland, Belgium, Germany, and Denmark.

Elizabeth Fry died in 1845. She was mourned by her own large family. She was mourned too by a far bigger family of women whose lives she had changed. Her memory lived on in her work. Never again could prisons be as they were when she found them. She showed the love of Jesus to those who had done wrong and by her work changed the prisons of many lands.

59 John Ashley, Apostle of Seafarers

IN the year 1835 the Reverend John Ashley took his small son to Clevedon in Somerset for a summer holiday. He was a clergyman in the Church of England and soon he was going to care for a new parish. One day he took his son for a walk along the Bristol Channel between the coasts of England and Wales. They stopped to look out at the two little islands in the Bristol Channel—Steep Holme and Flat Holme. It was getting dusk and a small light glimmered from a house on one of the lonely islands. "Daddy," said the boy, "how can those people get to Church to worship God?" John Ashley could not answer his son's question and he was troubled. The next day he went out in a boat to the islands and made friends with the fishing folk who lived there. Then he went to the lonely men in the lighthouses, too. How grateful they were to be visited by a friend who brought them comfort and cheer and the Word of God. Just before his holiday ended John Ashley asked one of his new fishermen friends about the ships lying in the Penarth Roads off the coast of Wales. There were 400 sailing vessels there, waiting for a good wind to start their voyages. "No one ever goes to visit them," said the fisherman. The very next day John Ashley hired a boat and went out to the sailing-ships. Many of the seamen gave him a warm welcome and John Ashley now realised what he must do. He resigned at once from his new parish. He was going to give his life to seafarers. If they could not go to Church, then the Church must go to them.

John Ashley gave all he had to the needs of seafarers. With his own money he bought a cutter and named her *Eirene*, a Greek word meaning 'Peace'. He made a chapel below deck and chose his own crew. Then the *Eirene* went wherever there were ships, inviting seamen aboard for friendship and worship. Signals were run up to tell the time for Service. One day in December 1841 John Ashley wrote in the *Eirene's* log book—"Blowing heavy, raining all night, the day continued so tempestuous that we had little expectation of any men coming. But before the time of Service every seat in our chapel was filled. I could scarcely get through to my desk, and when I arrived at it, found two seamen squeezed into my seat."

Soon the 'Bristol Channel Seamen's Mission' was formed and the fine work spread to other nearby ports. It was a hard life for John Ashley, out in all sorts of weathers. Altogether he visited over 14,000 ships, taking Bibles and Prayer Books to the rough seamen. In 1850 he had to give up through ill-health but the work he had inspired went on. In 1855 there were two Chaplains at work, one in the Bristol Channel and the other in the English Channel. Then in 1856 the great Lord Shaftesbury became President of the new MISSIONS TO SEAMEN. A splendid new flag, the 'Flying Angel', was chosen and before long it could be seen flying in ports all over Britain. By 1914, when the First World War broke out, it was flying in ports all over the world.

Life was hard and cruel for seamen in those early days. Men were 'shanghaied' and 'crimped' and dragged off to sea. Food was terrible, discipline was savage, and wages were poor. When lonely sailors went ashore, there was nowhere to go and they were easily made drunk and cheated and robbed. Today there is a Seamen's Institute in many ports where the seamen find comfortable lodging, good food, entertainment and, above all, friendship. Wherever a ship docks, the 'padre' is soon climbing aboard from the Mission launch as a well-known friend. Through him the sailor abroad keeps in touch with home. The Chaplain cares for seamen in hospital far from home and is there to help in any emergency. He is the servant of all seafarers, no matter what their race or religion, because he is a servant of God. He is to be found in 200 ports throughout the world.

In 80 of these ports there is a Seamen's Institute, a 'home from home', and the heart of each one is the Chapel where seafarers of different races kneel side by side in the world-wide family of God. There is the same rule for every Mission Chapel throughout the world— "All may come to Chapel; no one must".

In 1951 the motor fishing-vessel *John Ashley* was dedicated for work in the River Thames. In one year alone she travelled 6,000 miles between London Bridge and Rochester, visiting over 2,000 ships. She carries books and magazines, television and piano, toothpaste and razor blades, shopping, letters, friends, and a tiny Chapel. She is the best known boat on the River Thames.

Some of the loneliest men in the world are the keepers of lighthouses and lightships. The Mission launches visit them regularly. One Easter the *John Ashley* was due to visit the Chapman lighthouse off Canvey Island to take the sacred bread and wine to the two keepers. The Chaplain's telephone rang. "There is a gale blowing and it's getting worse," was the news. "Do you still want to go?" "Of course," replied the Chaplain. "If the boat can make it, I'm going." The *John Ashley* struggled through the crashing, mountainous waves. The Chaplain was soaked as he jumped from the boat to the ladder. Soon he was kneeling in the tiny living-room giving the two men their Easter Communion. It was a grim journey back but the Chaplain had served his people.

During the two World Wars Britain depended on the courage of her sailors for food and life. One of them, H.R.H. the Duke of Edinburgh, became President of the world-wide Missions to Seamen in 1956 when it was one hundred years old. One seaman said, "Wherever I see the 'Flying Angel', I know I am at home." All over the world the Missions to Seamen carries on the work inspired by John Ashley, the Apostle of Seafarers. He first showed that, if seafarers cannot go to Church, then the Church must go to seafarers.

Abraham Lincoln, Fighting Slavery

60

ABRAHAM LINCOLN was born in the year 1809. His home was a rough hut made of logs in the backwoods of Kentucky in the United States. His father was a poor farmer who wandered from place to place. While his sister Sarah helped her mother in the log cabin, Abraham helped his father on the land. He was never much good with a gun because he hated killing. But he became very skilful with the axe and he grew up strong and tall. There was no school or church for many miles. Their mother taught the children to read and to write. When Abraham was nine years old, she died, and it was three months before a minister came that way and gave her proper burial.

Mr. Lincoln married again and from his new stepmother Abraham learnt to love books. The Bible was his favourite book all his life, and *Pilgrim's Progress* was another. Though Abraham had little schooling and no church to go to, he grew up an educated man with a deep love for God. "He read all the books he could lay hands on," his sister said.

When he was 19 years old Abraham left home. His first job was as a boatman on the River Ohio. He had always worked hard, chopping logs and splitting wood. He was very tall and thin, with big hands and long, black hair. He was awkward and gawky and his clothes never seemed to fit him. But he was very strong and hard-working. He was always cheerful and full of fun, although he could be serious

211

too. One day his boat went down the river to the city of New Orleans. It was a fine, rich town, for the wealthy cotton-planters had their great estates all around. They had no wages to pay, for they had slaves to grow their crops, slaves to plant and pick the cotton, slaves to run their homes and to care for their children, and slaves to drive their coaches to town and to wait upon them. Many slaves were happy with good masters and lived with the same family all their lives. But others were treated cruelly. As Abraham Lincoln went round New Orleans, looking at the splendid sights with his friends, he came to the market where slaves were bought and sold like horses. Abraham was horrified at what he saw. The sellers made the slaves run up and down to show their strength and the mean buyers prodded them as if they were animals. "Let's get away from this!" Abraham said in angry disgust. "If ever I get a chance to hit slavery I'll hit it hard!" He never forgot that slave-market.

In the year 1830 Abraham settled in the State of Illinois. For a time he was a labourer and after that a soldier on patrol against the Red Indians. Then he ran a store in a place called New Salem. But he was too busy reading books to care much about trade. He was so honest that he once walked miles to take $\frac{1}{4}$ lb. of butter to a lady who by mistake had not had full weight. The fame of 'Honest Abe' spread far and wide. He moved to the town of Springfield and became a lawyer. Here, too, his honesty and his simple wisdom made him famous. A man who had done wrong once asked Lincoln to defend him. "I can't do it," said Honest Abe. "When I spoke in court I'd be thinking, 'Lincoln, you're a liar.' Then I might say it out loud." When he was 25 years old Lincoln was elected a member of the Parliament of his State of Illinois. Soon he was known throughout the State and in the year 1846 he was elected to the Congress, or Parliament, of the whole United States of America. Now he began his crusade.

The tall, thin, ugly, awkward man was a wonderful speaker and he stirred the crowds when he described the evils of slavery. He made many friends, but he made enemies too. One of them said Lincoln was 'two-faced'. Lincoln laughed it off. "You decide," he said to the crowd. "Do you think I'd wear this face if I had another one?" He was too gentle and kind to hate anyone.

212

In the year 1860 Abraham Lincoln was elected President of the United States of America. He said goodbye to all his friends in Springfield. "I have a great task before me," he said. "Without God's aid I cannot succeed. With his help I cannot fail." From the President's home at the White House in the city of Washington Abraham Lincoln led the fight against slavery. The States of the North followed him. But most slaves were in the Southern States, and they decided to separate. Lincoln would not give way. "Our country cannot go on, half slave and half free," he said. Sadly he saw the quarrel between North and South break out into Civil War in the year 1861. He hated bloodshed but he hated slavery even more, and in the next year he signed a law making all slaves free. When his secretary brought the document to be signed, Lincoln waited a bit. "I've been shaking hands all morning," he said, "and my hand is trembling. If I become famous it will be for this law. I must not sign my name shakily or people will think I was uncertain about it. I have never been more certain about anything. It is the greatest deed I shall ever do." Then he took up his quill and signed the new law.

The four years of war hurt Lincoln terribly. 600,000 men died in battle. "I have to make jokes," he said, "else I'd cry. Every night I kneel by my bed and ask God to make me wise and strong." The Bible was always on his desk. He called it 'The Book of Books'. "It is God's greatest gift to men," he said. He had no hatred for the soldiers of the South and he longed for peace. At last, after four years, the Northern States were victorious. "Now we must bind up the nation's wounds," Lincoln said. But five days later, as he sat in the theatre with his wife, a madman shot him through the back and he died shortly afterwards. All over the United States millions of people mourned his death, but none more than the three million slaves who owed their freedom to him. His body was taken back 1,700 miles to rest at his native Springfield, but his memory could never die. "Now he belongs to all the ages," said one of his countrymen.

John Keble, Poet and Hymn-writer

61

A HAPPY family of five children lived in the vicarage of Coln St. Aldwyn's in the county of Gloucestershire in England. John was born in the year 1792. With his brother Tom he was taught at home by his father, a man who loved learning. John soon showed what a fine scholar he was, and he learnt both Greek and Latin. From his father, too, he learnt to love God and to be a faithful son of the Church. His sisters, Elizabeth, Sarah and Mary were very dear to him and, when he was not at his books, John played happily with them.

When he was only fourteen years old, John won a scholarship to Oxford University. He was a brilliant scholar but he never became proud of his clever mind. He made friends by his gaiety and charm. He lived simply and humbly before God. He was always a bit shy, especially about the poetry he was often writing. He passed his examinations in Greek and Latin and in Mathematics as well. Then he was chosen to stay on at the University as a Fellow or teacher. He made great friends of his pupils. He loved talking and arguing, but he never gave way on what he believed. He was like a saint in his simplicity and his goodness. His fine face showed his character. He could be gay and charming. But he could be very angry, too, when anyone said something he thought was wrong or untrue. In the year 1815 he became a clergyman like his father. "Pray for me," he wrote to a friend, "that God will give me his grace to be worthy of my sacred calling."

The next year John left Oxford University. He went back to his country home to help his father look after his parish. He was happy to be in the English countryside again for he felt the presence of God in the beauty of nature. He was happy, too, because now he was working for God in caring for his people. But he was soon asked to go back to Oxford as a teacher. He agreed to go because he believed that he could serve God by teaching the students and by caring for them. But he always longed for the quiet and simple life of the country and in the year 1823 he gave up his work at Oxford. He wanted to be near his lonely father now that his mother had died. So he went to care for the parish of Southrop, near his father's parish in Gloucestershire. How happy he was there, like a good shepherd to his people! Some of his Oxford students came to stay with him and he taught them gladly. He had time to write poems and in 1827 they were published as a book. It was called *The Christian Year*, for it had poems for every Sunday and holy day of the Christian year. It became very popular and famous, and some of the hymns sung today came from it. John Keble's poems were read in good Christian homes throughout the country and they helped many people to live closer to God.

In 1831 John Keble was chosen to be Professor of Poetry at Oxford University. Now he gathered round him a group of friends. They talked together of the sad state of the Church of England. For a long time now the Church had been ruled by the State and it had no life of its own. The 'parliament' of the Church had not met for over a hundred years, so it had no leaders. Many of the churches were dirty and drab and uncared for. Many of the church services were dull and dreary. The most important service of the Holy Communion was not often held. Now the Government wanted to make changes in the Church. In 1833 a new law was passed ending ten bishoprics. John Keble boldly spoke against this in St. Mary's Church, Oxford. He called all those who loved the Church to stand and fight for its rights. He and his friends became the leaders of a new crusade. It was called the 'Oxford Movement'. They began to publish penny and two-penny pamphlets or 'tracts' to teach people

about the Church. They taught that the Church had been founded by Jesus and could never be ruled by any government. They reminded ministers of the sacredness of their calling. They showed how the early Church had made creeds to teach the true faith. The worship of God must be beautiful, and churches must be fit for him. Services must be held regularly: above all, the service of Holy Communion. Soon churches were being repaired and cleaned and the services were held every day in beauty and holiness.

The Oxford Movement made many enemies, but John Keble and his friends stood firm. They brought back new life to the Church of England and John Keble's hymns were sung throughout the land. His own life, holy and humble, brought many people to love the Church he served so faithfully. In the year 1835 he married an old friend of his childhood. He and his wife went to live in the parish of Hursley, near Winchester in Hampshire. There he lived for the rest of his life. He never wanted to be important and he was happy

217

caring for the people of his village. His church was beautiful and peaceful and the good vicar held services there every day. He loved the children best of all. He taught them in the little village school and he taught them in his church. He was very proud when they had learnt their faith and the bishop came to confirm them. He visited the people in their cottages, going out at night with his lantern if anyone was ill. Half of his money he gave to help those who were needy. His people loved him for he was so simple and he understood them so well. They did not realise that he was a famous author and a Professor of Oxford University as well.

John Keble died in the year 1866 and in 1870 a new college at Oxford was named after him. But his memory lives on, most of all in the hymns he wrote, which help Christians to know God and to serve him faithfully in his Church.

A HYMN OF JOHN KEBLE

1. *Blest are the pure in heart,*
   For they shall see our God,
   The secret of the Lord is theirs,
   Their soul is Christ's abode.

2. *The Lord, who left the heavens,*
   Our life and peace to bring,
   To dwell in lowliness with men,
   Their pattern and their King.

3. *Still to the lowly soul*
   He doth Himself impart,
   And for His dwelling and His throne
   Chooseth the pure in heart.

4. *Lord, we Thy presence seek;*
   May ours this blessing be:
   Give us a pure and lowly heart,
   A temple meet for Thee.

Bishop Patteson of the South Seas

62

JUDGE PATTESON of London Town had great plans for his son John. He gave him a fine education at Eton College and Oxford University, hoping that he would one day enter the law. John had many friends at school, and being captain of cricket made him even more popular. One day when the boys were doing something he thought wrong he walked out of the room and resigned from the team. They came and pleaded with him to come back to the team, promising not to do it again. They respected him for his goodness and his courage.

Some years later, when John was on holiday from Oxford, the Bishop of New Zealand came to stay with his father. He thought what a fine missionary this brave young man would make. The next time the Bishop met him John was a young clergyman in Devon. "I want you, John!" he said. "Come out to the South Seas with me as a missionary! There is plenty of exciting work to do for God there!"

In 1855 John landed at Auckland in New Zealand. He soon made friends with the Maoris, for he had spent the long voyage in learning their language. His first work was to be headmaster of St. John's College, Auckland. Some of the boys were Maoris. The others came from the islands called Melanesia ('The Black Islands'). When they were older they would return to their islands as teachers and preachers. Sometimes John Patteson went with the Bishop of New Zealand on his ship, the *Southern Cross*. They sailed among the islands and John longed to get to know the natives. Soon his chance came. He was made Bishop of Melanesia. Now he could devote all his time to the island people. For ten years he worked among them, seeking by his friendship and his words to teach them the love of God.

It was hard work. Most of the islanders were cannibals. Wherever Bishop Patteson landed, the savages met him on the beach. They carried clubs and spears. They pointed their big wooden bows at him, ready to let fly their arrows. He was quite fearless. He stood and faced them, alone and unafraid, smiling to show he was a friend. He carried no weapons. Once he went to a new island called Santa Cruz ('Holy Cross'). That was the name given to it by a Spanish explorer long before, but the people who lived there were savages. The *Southern Cross* anchored off the island and the Bishop made for the shore in a small boat with two Englishmen and three island boys from the College. He climbed out of the boat, waded through the water and walked ashore. All round him were fierce-looking natives with their weapons ready. The Bishop went bravely into a hut and sat down to talk to them. Then he came out, said good-bye, and made for the boat. No sooner was he in the boat than a swarm of arrows poured into it. The boys rowed hard, chased by the savages in their canoes. Only when they reached the ship did the canoes turn away.

Bishop Patteson went on with his work undaunted. Soon he was able to move the College for training the islanders from Auckland in New Zealand to Norfolk Island. This was much nearer to the other islands, and boys could be trained there to take the Gospel to their island homes. The new school was named St. Barnabas, after the missionary who travelled with St. Paul. For these boys would be missionaries to their own people.

The Bishop never forgot the island of Santa Cruz. One day he determined to go there again. It was in the year 1871. It needed more courage than ever now. For the Bishop knew that evil white men went round the islands, seizing natives and carrying them off as slaves. They sold them to the planters on the Fiji Islands. The natives hated these 'snatch-snatch' boats, as they called them, and they thought all white men must be their enemies. There was something even worse the Bishop knew. The slave-traders sometimes tricked the natives. "Your Bishop is ill," they said, "and wants you to come and visit him." When the natives came on board to go to the good Bishop they were seized and bound. But even this did not make Bishop Patteson afraid.

The *Southern Cross* came to a little island named Nukapu. The boat was lowered and took the Bishop towards the shore. Some canoes lay off the shore, but the natives in them made no move. The Bishop jumped out of the boat and waded ashore. He disappeared among the trees. The boat waited for him. For a time nothing happened. Then suddenly the savages in the canoes leapt up shouting and let fly their arrows. The men in the boat managed to get back to their ship, though all of them were wounded. Later the boat went back towards the shore, everyone anxious for their beloved Bishop. A canoe came towards them, towing another which seemed empty. it went back again and the empty canoe drifted up to the boat. The body of Bishop Patteson lay in it, wrapped in a mat. He had been clubbed to death. There were five other wounds in his body. They stood for the five islanders whom white slave-traders had snatched from the island only a little while before. The savage islanders believed that the white men had killed their five friends. They took their revenge on this white man who loved them.

Today there are very few savages in the South Sea Islands. For the work of Bishop Patteson was carried on by his boys, and by other missionaries who followed him from England. They built schools and churches on the islands, and today the grandchildren of cannibals and savages worship the God of love.

63 David Livingstone, Explorer and Missionary

EARLY one morning in the year 1823 a small boy named David Livingstone started work in the cotton factory at Blantyre, near Glasgow in Scotland. He was ten years old. From six o'clock in the morning till the evening he worked at his loom. But often he had a book propped up in front of him, for he was studying hard to go to college. He wanted to be a doctor when he grew up and go to China as a missionary, spreading the Good News of Jesus and showing his love by caring for the sick. His wages were small and he gave them to his poor mother. But she gave him a little back when she was able so that he could buy his precious books.

At last David was old enough to go to college. He worked hard there and passed his examinations. Then eagerly he went to London to offer himself as a missionary. How sad he was to be told that there was war in China and no missionaries could be sent out. One evening he went to hear Doctor Moffat, a famous missionary in South Africa. "On a clear morning I can see from my mission station the smoke of a thousand villages," the great man said. "No missionary has ever been to them." David's heart leapt. At once he offered to go to Africa, and in the year 1840 set sail on the long voyage.

He landed at Cape Town and travelled in a lumbering ox-wagon the 700 miles north to Kuruman, Doctor Moffat's mission station.

At once he began his work of teaching and healing, but he was eager to cross the Kalahari desert and to take the Gospel into the heart of Africa. No one knew what lay there. The centre of Africa was left blank on the maps of that time. He would have to be an explorer as well as a missionary. He loved adventure and nothing could daunt him.

He pushed on to the north for 300 miles and set up his station at Mabotsa in the country of the Ba-Khatla ('The People of the Monkey'). They were terrified of the lions which haunted their territory. David Livingstone boldly led a party of natives into the jungle to drive them off. He shot and wounded one, and while he was reloading, the lion leapt on him and seized him by the shoulder. "It growled horribly, close to my ear," he wrote, "and shook me like a terrier shakes a rat." The natives came with their spears to help him and at last the lion was dead. But Livingstone's shoulder was badly hurt and his arm never properly healed.

When he went back to Kuruman, Livingstone married Mary, the daughter of Doctor Moffat. When next he set out for the north he took his wife and children with him in the ox-wagon. But they suffered badly from insect bites and fever, from hunger and from thirst. He left them with a friendly chief and went on till he came to the great Zambesi River. It was what he had been seeking—a road into Africa for missionaries, explorers, and traders. He would follow it.

First he made the long journey back to Cape Town with his family and sadly put them on a ship to England. Then he trekked back northwards again to the land of the Makololo people. From their chief village, Linyanti, Livingstone set out by canoe following the Zambesi River to the west. Twenty-seven natives went with him. When the river ended they plunged into thick forest. They struggled on for weeks, often hungry, often in danger, and Livingstone was often ill with fever. At last they reached the west coast of Africa and kindly settlers from Portugal cared for them. An English ship was in harbour there. "Let me take you back to England," the captain said. "No," replied Livingstone. "I promised to take my friends back to their homes in Linyanti." It took a whole year to return. How delighted the Makololo people were to see the White

Doctor again.

Then Livingstone followed the Zambesi River to the east. On his journey he discovered the mighty waterfall which he named Victoria Falls in honour of the Queen of England. At last he came to Quilimane by the Indian Ocean. He had crossed Africa from west to east.

Livingstone wondered why the natives of East Africa were so frightened of him. He soon found why. They thought he must be one of the evil slave-traders who attacked villages, seized the natives and dragged them off in chains, yoked to each other. They took men and women and even little children and sold them as slaves on the coast, where they were shipped to America and the West Indies. Livingstone fought against this wicked trade for the rest of his life.

When Livingstone returned to England he found himself a national hero. The Queen herself sent for him to tell her about his work. He spoke all over the land, calling young men to follow in his footsteps and bring the light of the Gospel to darkest Africa.

Soon he went back again. He discovered Lake Nyasa and Lake Tanganyika. For four years nothing was heard of him. A newspaper reporter led an expedition to search for him. At last he came to the village of Ujiji and found the hut where the great explorer lay ill. He stayed with him, caring for him, and pleaded with Livingstone to come back with him. "No, I must finish my task," he replied.

Once again Livingstone set out. It was the year 1873. One night in April his faithful servants left him kneeling by his bed praying to God. When they came in the morning his body was still there, but his soul had gone home to the Master he had served so faithfully. They embalmed his body and carried it for a thousand miles till at last they reached the coast. It was brought back to England, together with Livingstone's diaries and his possessions. He was buried in Westminster Abbey, where you may see his tomb. But his work went on. Other missionaries, inspired by his example, followed in his footsteps. Today, churches and hospitals and schools in Africa stand as witnesses to the work begun by the brave explorer-missionary, David Livingstone.

64 | Charles Kingsley, Writer for the Poor

CHARLES KINGSLEY was born in the year 1819. His father was the vicar of Holne in Devon and Charles loved his life in the country. When he came home from school there were so many things to see and do. He went walking through the woods or riding over the moor on his pony. He loved all kinds of animals. He knew trees and plants and birds and the tiny creatures in the streams. He loved to go down to the sea, too, and he spent many happy hours with the fishermen. He grew up into a sturdy boy, fond of sports and an open-air life. When he left school he went to college, first to London and then to Cambridge University. He had many friends for he was so manly. He thought he would like to be a soldier. But he had learnt to love God and he wanted to serve him as best he could. At last he knew what he would do with his life. In the year 1842 he left Cambridge University and became a clergyman like his father.

The Reverend Charles Kingsley went to help the Vicar of the parish of Eversley in Hampshire. After two years he became Vicar himself and he stayed at Eversley for most of his life. He was a good parson to his people. When he came, the church was in a dreadful state, falling to ruins. He repaired it himself and led his people carefully in the worship of God. He loved the village children and soon they had a new school. No one could help liking the Vicar for he was full of life and interested in everything. The people found

226

that he knew as much about the countryside as they did. He was very strong, for every day he chopped wood or went for long walks with his dogs at his heels. When the heathland round the village caught fire in the hot summer, he stood side by side with his people fighting the fire. He was a good horseman and a fine fisherman. "A real man's man", people called him.

Charles Kingsley loved the country life for it brought him so close to God. But he loved his people more and he lived for them. His vicarage was open every night to the boys and girls, the men and women of Eversley. There was a club for boys, talks and discussions for the men, needlework classes for the girls and meetings for the women. The Vicar's home was the happiest in the village for he was a gay father to his own children. He joined in their games and took them out into the countryside to teach them all about its beauty, and of course they had many pets in the garden at home. Best of all, he was a wonderful story-teller. The stories he told his eldest children were made into a book called *The Heroes*. Later he wrote other thrilling story-books for his children. There was *Westward Ho!*, the story of brave Amyas Leigh in the adventurous days of good Queen Bess, telling how the Spanish Armada was beaten by the brave seamen of England. *Hereward the Wake* was the story of the gallant fight against the invader, William the Conqueror.

Every day Charles Kingsley spent an hour alone with God. More and more he was troubled at the life of his people. Their wages were very low and many children went hungry. They lived in wretched houses and they were often ill. There was no pure water or good drains in those days and many died from disease. Charles Kingsley taught his own people how to live cleanly. When disease broke out in the village he went round with a bottle of medicine, teaching them to gargle. Once he went to a man ill in bed in a stuffy room. He made holes in the walls to let in the good, fresh air. But all this was not enough. He knew God wanted him to do more. In his daily hour by himself he came to realise that the Church must help people in every part of their life, not only in worship. But what did God want him to do?

In the year 1848 thousands of the poor marched on London. They had made up a 'charter', a list of all the evils they wanted to be put right. The poor people had no votes in those days. They had to try and force Parliament to make things better. But the Government called the troops out and the march of the Chartists was a failure. But Charles Kingsley went to London. He found other Christians who thought, as he did, that social evils must be done away with. They called themselves 'Christian Socialists'. They believed that employers and employees must work together to make a better society. There must be justice for the poor, better wages and good homes. People must learn how to live cleanly and there must be pure water and proper drains in the towns and villages. A 'College for Working Men' was set up in London and even a College for Women, the very first in England. New societies were started for making such things as boots and shoes and even houses. In them, people worked together for the good of all.

Charles Kingsley was busy preaching and giving talks, showing how God has made laws for every part of life. People must live and work together if they wanted his Kingdom to come on earth. But best of all he could use his pen. He wrote poems and songs, pamphlets and books. Soon people all over Britain were learning from his books about the sad life of the poor. One story-book called *Alton Locke* told of the dreadful life of poor needle-women making beautiful clothes for the rich. *The Water Babies* was a story of the sweeps' boys who had to climb hot chimneys in the dark and were cruelly treated. In a song called 'The Three Fishers' he described the dangers and sufferings of the fishermen and their families. Charles Kingsley made Christians realise that they served God best by serving his people.

In the year 1869 Queen Victoria made Charles Kingsley one of her own Chaplains. He became a Canon first at Chester and then at Westminster. When he died in the year 1875, thousands of ordinary folk, as well as important people, mourned the loss of their true friend, Charles Kingsley.

Bishop Selwyn, Apostle of the Maoris

65

GEORGE SELWYN was born in the year 1809. He came from a wealthy home and he went to school at the famous Eton College. He was a very strong boy and he was quite fearless too. At school he played well at all sports and in the holidays he went walking and riding. When he went on to Cambridge University he rowed in the very first Boat Race against Oxford in the year 1829. He could have lived the life of a country gentleman in England. But the call of God had come to him and in 1833 he became a clergyman in the Church of England. He went to work in the parish of Windsor and served his people faithfully. But in 1841 another call came to him. He was asked to become the first Bishop of New Zealand and in the following year his ship sailed into Sydney harbour in Australia. He was too impatient after the long voyage to wait for the ship to be repaired, and he sailed the 1200 miles to New Zealand in the first little boat he could find. Captain Hobson, the very first British Governor of New Zealand, hurried down to the harbour at Auckland when he heard that the new bishop had arrived. He expected him to come in state like the bishops of those days in England. But Bishop Selwyn was standing in the water with the sailors, helping them to drag their boat up on to the beach!

Captain Hobson had not been in New Zealand long himself. It was not easy to be Governor in those days for he had two races to look after. First there were the Maoris, the native people of New Zealand. These 'aborigines' or 'first inhabitants' had come from the South Sea Islands of Polynesia centuries before. They were tall, sturdy people with olive-brown skins and wavy hair. They lived chiefly by hunting and fishing. But they grew crops as well, and had their own native art and crafts. Not many years before, they had been savages and cannibals. But Christianity had come to them through Samuel Marsden, a clergyman of the Church of England who had gone out to Australia to care for the convicts sent there from Britain. He made friends with some Maoris in Australia. He went with them to New Zealand and held the first Christian service there on Christmas Day in the year 1814. Other missionaries followed him and in 1825 the first Maori chief was baptised. When Governor Hobson arrived in New Zealand in 1840, there were 35 white missionaries and over fifty schools in North Island where most of the Maoris lived. They were learning the ways of peace and Christian Maoris gave up their old gods and fierce customs. They could read the Bible and praise God in their own tongue.

But now white people had started coming to New Zealand. Many came not to give but to get, and the missionaries fought hard to protect the Maoris from evil and greedy men. They helped Governor Hobson to make the Treaty of Waitangi with the Maori chiefs in 1840. By the treaty the Maori people became British subjects of Queen Victoria and they were given freedom in their own territory. But some white men cheated them of their lands and fighting broke out between Maoris and white people. There was fighting among the Maori tribes, too, and it was all the worse now that they had fire-arms.

Bishop Selwyn had to be Father-in-God to both Maoris and white people. He went tirelessly through the land, sometimes on horseback, sometimes on foot, hacking his way through the bush when there was no footpath. He swam rivers with his clothes tied in a bundle on his head. Often the Bishop would arrive at a settlement in the bush with his dress in tatters. Wherever he went, he took the Gospel of peace and goodwill to Maoris and white men alike. At Auckland he set up St. John's College to train Maoris and soon the natives had teachers and clergymen of their own race. As Bishop Selwyn

230

went through the land he often risked his life, especially where there was fighting. Sometimes the white people suspected him of being on the side of the Maoris, for when there was fighting he would go out unarmed to carry wounded natives to safety. Sometimes the Maoris suspected him and they would greet him sullenly. At one village he was offered no food and no resting-place except the pig-shed. The Bishop made a bed of ferns and slept happily in the sty. He knew only one side in the wars—God's side, and he treated all men as his children in God.

So the Church of God grew throughout New Zealand. Bishop Selwyn planned it carefully, making new bishoprics of Wellington, Waipu, Nelson and Christchurch. He gathered all his clergy together regularly for a 'synod' or conference. By 1859 the Church of England in New Zealand was properly organized with its bishops, clergy and laity, both white and Maori. By that time, too, almost all the Maori people were Christians.

But Bishop Selwyn's work carried him outside New Zealand. He had been made Bishop of all the islands in the Pacific Ocean called Melanesia as well. In four years he landed on more than 50 islands scattered about the Ocean. His great plan was to take Christian boys from the islands back to New Zealand where they would train at his new College. Then they would return to their own islands as missionaries and teachers. Bishop Selwyn made seven long voyages through the islands, spreading the Gospel, risking his life from savage tribes. From Erromanga Island, where John Williams had been murdered by cannibals only ten years before, he took boys back to train at Auckland. But the islands of Melanesia needed their own leader. Returning from a visit to England in 1855, Bishop Selwyn brought with him John Patteson who spent his life among the savage islanders and became the first Bishop of Melanesia, dying as a martyr.

In 1867 Bishop Selwyn returned to England to attend a conference of bishops of the Church of England. He was made Bishop of Lichfield, where he died ten years later. Selwyn College at Cambridge University was built in his memory and named after this heroic leader of the Church of God in New Zealand.

66 Lord Shaftesbury, Worker for the Poor

LORD SHAFTESBURY was a rich landowner in the county of Dorset. He had a splendid house in London, too, for he had an important post in Parliament. He liked drinking with his friends in the London clubs. His wife was a woman of society, living only for fashion and parties and balls. Neither of them cared about their son, Antony, who had been born in the year 1801. He did not even see them often. But there was someone who loved him. Her name was Maria and she was housekeeper at the house in London. She was little Antony's best friend. At bed-time she tip-toed up to his bedroom and talked to him and taught him to say his prayers. She read storybooks to him, but she loved best of all to tell him stories from the Bible. From her, Antony learnt to know God and to love him. Once she gave him a watch as a present. It was not a valuable one but he treasured it all his life.

When Antony was seven years old, his parents sent him to a London school. "It was a dirty and horrible place," he said later. "I was bullied and beaten and ill-treated. But it taught me to hate cruelty." Antony went on to the famous school at Harrow. One day, on his way home from school, he saw a terrible sight. It was the funeral of a poor man. The men who carried the coffin to the churchyard were drunk. Singing and swearing and staggering about, they dropped the coffin. Antony never forgot that day. He felt as angry as Abraham

232

Lincoln did when he saw the slaves being sold at New Orleans. He, too, vowed to God to end such horrible things.

Antony went to Oxford University and when he was 25 years old he became a Member of Parliament. He came from a great family and of course everyone expected him to become famous and probably even Prime Minister of Britain. He did become very famous but for quite a different reason.

There were terrible evils in Britain in those days. Machines had been invented. They needed coal and iron. The new coal-mines and mills and factories wanted lots of workers, for they were busy night and day making their masters rich. They were used to slavery in the colonies and they wanted cheap labour in their factories. The wages were very small but people lost their old work on the land and they went to live in the ugly factory towns. Women had to work like the men. But boys and girls were the cheapest labour of all. Slaves in the West Indies worked for $11\frac{1}{2}$ hours a day. But in the factories of Britain little children worked for at least 12 hours a day. They started when they were about five years old. Some of them were sent to work by their parents in order to get more money. Other parents had to send them out to get enough money for food. Some of the children came from orphanages. A good Christian, named Michael Sadler, found out these terrible facts. "The children are allowed 15 minutes for each meal," he was told. "They often fall asleep at work. They are paid three shillings a week." Michael Sadler lost his seat in Parliament and he went to Antony. "Will you fight for new laws to protect the poor?" he asked. "It would be a work for God," Antony said to his wife. "Then it is your duty to do it," she replied.

Lord Cooper, as Antony had now become, spent the remaining fifty years of his life in the service of the poor. He had no pay and he had to live on his small family income. Sometimes he had to borrow money to feed his ten children and send them to school. Though he was his heir, his father would not help him. Lord Cooper refused high posts in the Government so that he could carry on his crusade. He went round the factories and told Parliament what he had found. New laws, called 'Factory Acts', were passed, ending these dreadful evils.

But Lord Cooper found even worse evils in the coal mines. Children

234

of six and seven worked 12 hours a day in the dark mines, opening the doors to let in air and to let the coal trucks pass. "I haven't a light and I'm frightened," said one little girl. "I work from four o'clock in the morning till five o'clock at night." Bigger children pulled the coal trucks with chains. Some had to crawl along; others stood working in water. There were girls and women as well as boys crawling in the dark, narrow passages under the ground. "Some children are carried to the mines in their nightclothes," Lord Cooper told Parliament. His new law was passed ordering that no women or girls were to work in the mines, and no boys under ten. That Sunday Lord Cooper wrote in his diary—"I went to church and received the holy bread and wine. My heart was full of thankfulness to God for my success in helping his children."

But there were many others to help, especially the chimney-boys. Small boys were apprenticed to chimney-sweeps. Their masters made them climb the hot, narrow chimneys to sweep away the soot. Their bodies became crooked and covered with sores. Sometimes they died. "I know of a boy aged $4\frac{1}{2}$ years who is forced to climb chimneys," Lord Cooper told Parliament. He had a law made against this evil but it still went on. Thirty years later his new law ordered the police to see that it was stopped, once and for all.

When his father died he became Lord Shaftesbury. He was famous all over the country as the friend of the poor. The costermongers in London gave him a donkey to show their love for him, and made him a member of their Union. The shoeblacks were his friends, for they were often poor orphans. "I knew one boy who slept in the big iron roller in Regent's Park," he said. Lord Shaftesbury started his 'Ragged Schools' for boys like him. When he died in the year 1885, he was mourned throughout the land. For Lord Shaftesbury had won love as well as fame by his life of service.

67 General Gordon, a Christian Soldier

CHARLES GORDON was born in the year 1833 at Woolwich in London town. All his family had been soldiers and his father was an officer in charge of the guns at the great Woolwich Arsenal. There were eleven children, all full of mischief, and Charles was as wild as any of them. One of his tricks was to push his little brother Freddy through the front door of a stranger's house, then ring the bell and hold the door so that Freddy could not escape. The workers at the Arsenal made little guns for the boys and one Sunday afternoon they broke 27 panes of glass with them. "I feel like a man sitting on a barrel of powder," said their harassed father.

Charles loved his mother and his eldest sister, Augusta, best of all. From them he learnt to love God and to believe in the Bible as His word. Charles went to boarding-school at Taunton in Somerset and then, when he was sixteen years old, he joined the army. He was a wild cadet, often in trouble. But when he became an officer, he was happy with his work and he settled down. Soon after, when England was at war with Russia, Charles Gordon got himself sent out to the Crimea where the fighting was going on. It was a dreadful winter that year and the British soldiers suffered terribly. Miss Florence Nightingale had set up her famous hospital and she was doing all she could for them. Charles Gordon did not bother much about the terrible cold and lack of food. He thought only about getting

236

on with the fighting. He soon showed himself a born soldier and a fine leader of his men. He had no fear and he was soon famous for his courage. He stood calmly among a hail of bullets to encourage his men. God was so close to him that he believed he was perfectly safe. He thought of nothing but his duty and he never wanted to marry. His life was given to God and to the service of his country.

When the war was ended, Gordon came back to England. But he was too full of energy to live a quiet life. There was a war in China and he quickly volunteered for it. During his four years in China he won great fame. He led the soldiers of the Chinese Government and they were called 'The Ever Victorious Army'. In two years he led his men into action over thirty times. He never carried any weapon when he led them against the enemy. He had only his short officer's cane under his arm. The Chinese thought it was a magic wand, but it was Gordon's courage and faith that won his battles. He soon ended the rebellion but he would not take any of the presents which the Emperor offered him.

When Gordon returned to England in the year 1865 he found he was a hero. The newspapers had been full of stories of the brave General Gordon. They told how he won his battles by his courage, how he never took his clothes off for months, and how he slept only in two blankets sewn together like a sack. The thin, wiry General with the bright, piercing eyes was the pride of England. But he hated being famous and would not accept any of the invitations which showered upon him. For six years he was in charge of the forts being built at Gravesend. He was soon forgotten, and though there were several wars in Africa he was not asked to lead the army. But he found a wonderful work for God among the street urchins of Gravesend. His house was open to them every evening and some of them lived with him. He taught them to read and to write. He told them stories of heroes and adventures. Above all, he taught them the Bible and to love God as he did himself. When they were old enough, he found work for them. Most of them went to sea and Gordon kept a big map on his wall with flags stuck on it to show where his boys were. Out of his own money he bought clothes and boots for hundreds of his poor boys and sat up at night mending their clothes himself. He was a teacher in the Ragged School set up by the great Lord Shaftesbury.

He called his boys 'Kings' for he believed that every one was as precious to God as a King is to his people. But in spite of his busy days and nights, he spent long hours alone with God.

Gordon cared little for money and he was always poor. He was a very humble man and he never pushed himself forward. The Government forgot him and he did not seek new posts. In the year 1873 he was asked by the Turkish Governor of Egypt to bring law and order to the southern part of the land. It was called the Sudan and the chief town there was Khartoum. Gordon had to travel among the fierce tribes who had never known proper government. "Like King Solomon, I ask God to give me wisdom to rule over this great people," Gordon wrote. He was horrified to find slavery going on and he fought against the slave-traders. "I will stop them even if it costs me my life," he vowed. Often he was ill but he never gave in and for seven years he brought law and order to the land.

Gordon came home to England worn out and ill. For some years the Government could find no use for this strange General. But in 1884 he was sent for urgently. The desert tribes of the Sudan had found a new leader. He claimed to be a Prophet and the fierce tribesmen flocked to him. General Gordon was asked to go out and lead the thousands of British troops back. He went at once and reached Khartoum safely. But soon the town was surrounded by the savage warriors of the Prophet. For ten months Khartoum was besieged. An expedition was sent to relieve the town but it arrived two days late. A deserter had shown the Prophet how to get into Khartoum and the tribesmen burst through the defences. General Gordon met his death, through a hail of spears, with the courage that his faith in God had always given him.

Father Damien, Friend of Lepers

68

IN the year 1840 a second son was born to a poor peasant family who lived near the city of Louvain in Belgium. His mother and father called him Joseph. They brought their children up to love God. Joseph grew into a strong and fearless boy, fond of adventure. Like Jesus, when he was a boy, Joseph loved to go out with the shepherds when they took their flocks to pasture. Like Jesus, too, he loved to be in his Father's house. When he was eighteen years old he knew he wanted to give his life to serve God in a special way. Already his elder brother had gone away to the city of Rome, studying to be a priest. When Joseph visited him there he knew that he must do the same. When he was made a priest in 1863 he had a new name—Father Damien. Not long afterwards his brother decided to go as a missionary to the islands of Hawaii in the South Seas, far west of America. Father Damien went to the harbour to say good-bye to his brother. But when the time came to sail his brother was too ill to go. At once Father Damien offered to go in his place. So in 1864, after the long voyage, he landed at Hawaii to begin his great work.

Father Damien loved the islanders and they soon grew to love him. He shared their troubles and was always ready to help them. He showed them the love of God in his life as well as in his words. But there was one thing he could not share, and it made him sad. Some of the islanders caught the dreadful disease of leprosy. When this

239

happened they had to leave home. They were sent to the island of Molokai where all the lepers were forced to live, far from their homes and friends and with no one to care for them. The bishop who looked after the islands said one day to the missionaries, "I am very worried about Molokai. The lepers there badly need a priest to care for them. Whoever went to the island could never come back. He might become a leper himself. But what a wonderful work he could do for God!" At once Father Damien cried out, "I will go!"

So in 1873 Father Damien landed on the island of Molokai where no one else ever dared to go. What a dreadful state the lepers were in. There were six hundred altogether. Most of them lived in a valley, but those who were full of disease were made to live apart in a corner of the island. Father Damien went to them first. They made a strong drink from roots and were often drunk. They quarrelled and fought with each other. They lived in huts made of branches. They had no proper food or water and they lived like wild animals. Father Damien slept at night under a tree and all day long laboured among them. He seemed like an angel as he went among them, bringing them comfort and cheer. His friends sent him the things he asked for, and it was not long before the island began to be a different place. The lepers lived now in proper houses, water was brought in pipes from the spring, and they ate good food. The strong drink was done away with. Their wounds were cared for by a doctor and nurses who had come to join Father Damien. He himself lived among them, teaching them how to live the good life with God.

Then, after twelve years of loving service, Father Damien found that he was a leper himself. "People feel sorry for me," he wrote to his friend. "But I am glad. Now I am one of them. I would rather be a leper than give up my work for God here. It is his will. I am very happy."

After three years of suffering, Father Damien died in 1888 and was buried under his tree. His loving example inspired others to follow him, and today Christians care for lepers in fine hospitals and with wonderful drugs. But they need above everything else the love which Father Damien showed in his life and in his death.

Thomas Freeman, Apostle of the Ashanti

THOMAS FREEMAN was born in the year 1809, just two years after William Wilberforce had won his great battle for the slaves. Already Granville Sharp had won a verdict that any slave setting foot on English soil was free. The law of 1807 ended the slave trade and by that law Thomas Freeman's negro father became a free man. His mother was an English lady so that young Thomas was a 'mulatto', part white and part negro. He grew up in an English village, full of mischief and fun. Once he climbed the roof of the cobbler's cottage where he knew the Methodists of the village were holding a prayer meeting. While the boys watched him admiringly, he let a brick down the chimney tied to a string. As he jerked the string it would scrape soot off the chimney into the fire, causing sparks to disturb the worshippers. It seemed great fun at the time to play jokes on the 'Methodies'. But later Thomas listened quietly to the simple prayers of the villagers and he felt ashamed. The next day he went to apologise and it was not long before Thomas Freeman was taking part in the weekly prayer meeting at the cobbler's cottage.

Thomas grew up into a fine, upright young man. He was a gardener by trade and he educated himself in his spare time. He was always courteous and friendly and gentlemanly in manner. He worked in the lovely park of a country mansion and there he fell in love with the young housekeeper. She shared his love for God and his secret

241

longing to serve God in spreading the Gospel. Every month Thomas read eagerly the magazine of the Methodist Missionary Society, especially news of his own negro people in Africa. The law of 1833 had freed all slaves in the British Colonies. The dreaded Gold Coast in West Africa was no longer to be the haunt of slave-traders. Now white missionaries were going there to take the Good News of Jesus to the freed slaves, seeking to make up for the evils done to negroes. But already the Gold Coast had earned another grim name—'The White Man's Grave'. For Europeans could not endure the climate and the mosquito bites that brought the weakening fevers of malaria. Thomas read a letter in his magazine from Mr. Wrigley, a white missionary on the Gold Coast. In two years five out of six missionaries had died and he alone was left, pleading for help from Britain. Thomas Freeman knew that this was the call of God. He was part negro, and he might stand up to the climate when white men died. With his wife at his side he sailed for Africa and in 1838 he landed at Cape Castle on the Gold Coast. As he came ashore in the canoe he was met with sad tidings. Mr. Wrigley, too, was dead.

Thomas Freeman set to work at once, building the little church that Mr. Wrigley had started. Within six weeks his wife had died from fever. "I stand alone," he wrote sadly, "but with quiet confidence in God." He threw himself into his work among the Fanti tribe who lived along the coast, making many friends. As soon as the church was finished he began taking regular services and training Christian natives so that they in turn could teach their own people.

Already Thomas Freeman was restless. 200 miles inland, beyond the dense forests, lay the kingdom of the mighty Ashanti people and their capital, Kumasi—'The City of Blood'. For many days he travelled through the thick jungle till at last he came to Kumasi. His Fanti friends had thought 'Kwaku Anan' must be mad to risk his life among the warlike and pagan Ashanti. For they believed in spirits who must be worshipped with human sacrifice. The very day Thomas Freeman reached the city, two men had been beheaded under the fetish tree to ward off any evil that he might bring upon the people. King Kwaku Dua was suspicious of the stranger. First he made a great display of his power to impress Thomas Freeman. 70 chiefs and 40,000 warriors passed before him in a procession that took 1½ hours. Then for days the King refused to see him while he made up his mind.

But Thomas Freeman was not alone. There were some Fanti traders in Kumasi who were Christians and one day they brought the first Ashanti Christian to him for baptism. At last King Kwaku Dua sent for him. "You may come again to my city," he said. "Then I will decide whether you may teach your religion to my people."

Thomas Freeman went back to the coast, happy at least to have won the King's favour. In 1840 he had to visit England through illness, taking with him a young African Christian. People in England had not forgotten how the Ashanti had broken their treaty of 1817 with the British traders on the coast and how in 1824 they had wiped out the white forces sent against them. But Thomas Freeman spoke movingly of the great opportunities for taking the Gospel to the Ashanti. He took back another English missionary with him and a present for King Kwaku Dua from the Methodist Missionary Society. He took also two young Ashanti princes who had been taken as hostages and educated in England. Now the King knew that the white man sought only the good of his people and he gave permission for a missionary to be stationed at Kumasi.

Thomas Freeman was never content to stay in one place. In 1843 he was asked to go to Abeokuta, a settlement of Yoruba people who had escaped from the Spanish and Portuguese slave-traders. Chief Shodeka sent horses and guides to lead him to their township in the rocks, and there Thomas Freeman established a Christian mission. He visited the terrible King Gezo of Dahomey and opened his country to the Gospel of peace and goodwill. For 52 years Thomas Freeman taught and lived the Christian life among the tribes of the Gold Coast. As the Gospel spread, the evils of slavery, idol-worship and human sacrifice to the spirits slowly died. Missions, schools and hospitals grew up and men who had lived for war tilled the ground in peace. Thomas Freeman died in 1890, mourned by the many tribes of West Africa who knew him as the friend and teacher. Today the many churches of Ghana, as the Gold Coast is now called, are the finest memorial to Thomas Freeman, Apostle of the Ashanti.

70 Alexander Mackay of Uganda

In the year 1849 a son was born to the minister of the village of Rhynie in Aberdeenshire, Scotland. He was named Alexander and he grew into a fine, sturdy lad. His mother hoped that he would become a minister of the Free Kirk like his father. But Alexander found too many interesting things around him to stay indoors with his books. It was exciting to visit the forge, where his friend George the blacksmith hammered the glowing metal. Alexander loved machines of any kind. If he was not at the smithy he was at the gasworks or with the carpenter or saddler. He would walk eight miles just to see the railway engine on the railway. If he was at home he would be experimenting with his hand printing-press.

Sometimes Alexander went walking with his father. Mr. Mackay told him of the famous Scotsman, David Livingstone, the missionary and explorer. The middle of Africa was quite empty in Alexander's atlas at school. Livingstone was going where no white man had ever been before, opening up the heart of darkest Africa and taking the Good News of Jesus to savage peoples. What adventures he had! But he only came from a poor cottage home near Glasgow. "I wish I could be like him," Alexander said to himself. But soon he was off to grammar school in the city of Aberdeen. Then he went to study engineering in the great city of Edinburgh and to work in noisy shipyards at Leith. Alexander loved his work and he became a skilled engineer. In 1873 he was offered an excellent post in Berlin, the capital city of Germany, designing new engines.

While he was in Germany Alexander Mackay read a book written by Stanley, the African missionary. It was called *How I found Livingstone,* and it brought back to him his boyish ambitions. Then one day he read a letter from Stanley in the Scottish newspaper sent out to him. "There is a great work to do in Uganda," it said. "King M'tesa is sympathetic to the white man's God. What we need is a practical Christian, a missionary who would teach these people farming and building and hygiene. Such a man would become the saviour of Africa." Alexander Mackay's heart leapt. This was the call of God. Again and again, whenever he thought of his hero David Livingstone, some words of Jesus kept coming into his mind—"Go, and do thou likewise." At once he wrote to the Church Missionary Society in London and in 1876 he set sail for East Africa.

Mackay and his missionary companions landed at Zanzibar. They set off on the long march into the interior through swamps and jungles, along rough tracks, for there were no roads. Everything had to be carried, including all the pieces of a boat for their use on Lake Victoria. Mackay was stricken with fever and had to be carried back to the coast by African bearers. When he was better again, he decided to make a road from the coast to the mission headquarters at Mpwapwa, 230 miles away. "Our work is to spread the Gospel to the ends of the earth," he wrote. "Where we do not find a way we must make one." The work took over four months of toil with shovels and picks and axes. At last it was completed. "This will be a highway for the King himself," wrote Alexander Mackay. When he reached the shore of Lake Victoria he found that his companions had sailed north to Uganda in an Arab ship. The *Daisy,* the boat on which they had pinned their hopes, lay blistering in the sun, broken and twisted and warped. Mackay at once set to and repaired it. But no sooner had they sailed than a storm drove it ashore. For another two months Mackay worked on the shore re-making the *Daisy,* and then sailed north. So at last he reached Uganda in the year 1878.

King M'tesa received Mackay in state, sitting on his royal stool in his white robe, surrounded by his chiefs. Soon Mackay had set up his workshop and forge to build his own house. The natives gathered round, amazed to see the sparks and steam and red-hot metal. "He is a great wizard," they cried. They gave him a new name—"Mzungu-wa Kazi"—"White Man of Work". The men of Uganda were lazy. "Work is for women," they said. "Men talk with their chiefs and fight." So the first lesson Mackay taught them was the dignity of hard work. And when he had turned the Gospel into their Swahili language he read to them about Jesus who had worked with his hands as a carpenter before he began the Father's work. Soon Mackay was teaching boys to read their language which he printed on sheets with the printing press he had brought from his home in Scotland. The first three to be baptised as Christians were given new names—Samweli (Samuel), Yusufu (Joseph) and Lugalama. So the church in Uganda began.

One day an Arab slave-trader came to the royal court. He brought bales of cloth, muskets and ammunition to exchange for slaves. King M'tesa looked at them greedily. He could easily send his men to raid the hill-tribes of the north, as he had often done before, to get slaves to sell. How useful those guns would be in conquering the tribes around him! Then Mzungu-wa Kazi stood up and spoke. "King M'tesa, you are the father of your people. Will you sell them as if they were animals? They are made by the one great Father-God. Will you exchange his handiwork for bits of cloth and metal?" Then M'tesa went into palaver with his chiefs. "My people shall never become slaves again," he decided.

M'tesa never became a Christian but Alexander Mackay was free to go on with his work. But in 1884 the king died, and his young son M'wanga succeeded him. He was ruled by the chief of the court and the captain of his army. The Moslem Arab traders were jealous of Mackay too and they turned the king against him and his God. Christian natives were tortured and brutally put to death. Alexander Mackay was cast out after three years and he went to live at Usambiro on the south of Lake Victoria. There he translated the whole Bible into the language of Uganda. He died there through malaria in 1890, but his memory lives on still today in the thriving churches of Uganda.

Samuel Crowther, the First Negro Bishop

71

IN the year 1808 a boy was born to a negro family in West Africa. They belonged to the Yoruba tribe and their home was in a native town called Oshogun. The boy was named 'Adjai', which means 'Lucky', and he seemed very fortunate to his friends. His father was a well-to-do weaver and he had bought a small farm. Adjai grew yams there and sold them in the market for cowrie shells which were used for money by his people. He was a good leader, too, and before long he was leader of all the boys of Oshogun. Adjai was clever and brave, and when his father's house caught fire he ran in through the flames to rescue the idols which his family worshipped.

But his happy boyhood came to a sudden and dreadful end. All his people feared the fierce Fulah tribesmen who had come from North Africa and who lived by selling slaves. One morning when all the families were sitting round the cooking-pots outside their huts, eating breakfast, a man rushed out of the forest. "The Fulahs are coming!" he shrieked. The men rushed to defend the fence round their town and the women snatched up their children. But the fight was soon over and the slave-traders came pouring into the town. Everyone ran for the bush but few escaped. Men, women and children were roped together and dragged off to be sold. Poor Adjai was only a boy of thirteen and he was separated from his family. He was sold for a horse and then sold several times more. Finally he was taken to the city of

247

Lagos on the coast and sold to the heartless Portuguese slave-traders. He was fastened to the other slaves with iron chains. Then they were rowed out to the slave ship which would take them to America where slaves fetched a good price. Adjai had never even seen the sea before. He lay chained in the dark hold, sick and miserable.

Adjai could not know that across the seas in England William Wilberforce and his Christian friends had been fighting for years against slavery and all its evils. At last in 1807 a law had been passed by the British Parliament forbidding the slave trade. British men-of-war patrolled the coast of West Africa, hunting down slave ships and setting free the captives they found. That was why Adjai suddenly heard the sound of cannon firing and, before long, shouting and scuffling on the deck above. Then the hatches were thrown open and the slaves were brought up on deck. When their chains were struck off, many of the slaves fell on their knees before Captain Leeke who had saved them from so terrible a fate.

Adjai was put ashore with the others at Freetown in Sierra Leone. It was a colony where former slaves could settle in freedom. He was taken into the home of the schoolmaster in the village of Bathurst, who had been sent from England by the Church Missionary Society. There he learnt his alphabet, side by side with Asano, a former slave-girl. Adjai was an eager student and skilful with his hands, too. Before long he and Asano were reading the New Testament together and in December of the year 1825 they were baptised together into the Christian Church. Adjai was named Samuel Crowther and Asano was christened Susanna Lawrence.

The following year Susanna went to train as a teacher. Samuel was taken by the schoolmaster on an exciting visit to England. When he came back he went to the new Fourah Bay College to train as a Christian teacher. In 1828 he became a village schoolmaster and the next year he and Susanna were married. Samuel was a good teacher, always kind and patient with his mischievous piccaninny scholars. His pay of one pound each month came in fruit and vegetables, corn and palm oil.

In 1841 came a new adventure for Samuel Crowther. A law had been passed in England, eight years before, ending all slavery. But

248

the evil trade still went on. A British expedition was being sent up the River Niger to open up unexplored territory so that trade could take the place of slavery. Samuel Crowther was chosen to go with it. The hot, steamy swamps on either side of the great river brought fever and death to the white people on board the three steamships and they had to turn back. Samuel Crowther realised that the Good News of Jesus could only be taken by black people like himself to the jungle villages. Soon he was on his way to England to become a minister of the Gospel.

In 1845 the Reverend Samuel Crowther came back to Sierra Leone to begin his missionary work. It was hard to win people from their pagan ways. Even Christian negroes sometimes kept their magic fetishes and still believed in the juju of evil spirits. But Samuel Crowther was one of them and he spoke in their own dialects, and many turned from heathenism to worship the Christian God. Yet he was not satisfied, and the next year he set off for Yoruba territory to go to his own people. It was a long, hard journey through the jungle with his wife and his four children. Once they crossed a swollen stream in the wooden bath-tub that Susanna had refused to leave behind. At last they came to Abeokuta, 'Under the Stone', a settlement built among the rocks by those who had escaped from the slave-traders. They were people of the Egba tribe and they listened eagerly to one of their own race. Soon a church was built and pagans were turning to the Christian faith. One day an old woman was led into Abeokuta by her daughters. It was Samuel Crowther's mother, from whom he had been dragged away by the slave-traders forty-five years before.

Samuel Crowther was asked to go on another expedition up the River Niger and, as a result, the Niger Mission was set up in 1859. Everywhere churches sprang up and soon a bishop was needed there, for Sierra Leone was 2,000 miles distant. On June 29th, 1864, Samuel Crowther was made the first African bishop, in Canterbury Cathedral. Among the congregation was Admiral Leeke who had rescued him from the slave ship forty-two years before. Bishop Crowther ministered to his people for 27 years, till his death in the year 1891. The many Christian churches of Nigeria today stand as memorials to the slave-boy who became a Christian bishop.

72 Louis Pasteur, Fighting Germs

LOUIS PASTEUR was born at a little village in France in the year 1822. His father was a poor tanner, but Louis soon showed himself to be a clever boy. His father taught him to love God, and Louis always wanted to serve other people. One day his teacher let him look through his microscope which makes things look much bigger. How excited Louis was to see every detail of tiny insects and plants through the microscope. He knew then that he wanted to spend his life finding out about the world of nature. He worked very hard at his science and by the time he was a man he had become a professor at a college in Paris. He was never content. All through his life he studied hard, making new discoveries.

In those days men knew very little about science. Using his microscope, Louis soon discovered the tiny creatures we call germs or microbes. He believed that they caused things like food and drink to go bad, and brought sickness to animals and men. They might be small but they were very dangerous. When he spoke about this discovery, doctors and scientists laughed at him. They believed that decay and disease came from inside the food or the animal. Louis knew he was right and went on with his studies. One day a way would come of proving it to them. He had been studying wine, which many people in France made from their fine vineyards. Much wine went bad, no one knew why. Louis believed it was through germs. He soon found that the wine remained good if the air, full of germs, was kept away from it. He found too that heat killed the germs. Milk is heated today to destroy germs. We call it 'pasteurised milk', and we owe this discovery to Pasteur.

Soon his great chance came. Silk fibre was made in France from silkworms. One year thousands of them died, and many people were faced with ruin and poverty. They pleaded with Louis Pasteur to help them. He went gladly to the little town where the silk was made and found an old shed to work in. For five years he worked till he found the tiny germs that were killing the silkworms and discovered a way to kill them. The silk industry of France was saved.

In 1873 something very sad happened. One of Louis Pasteur's little daughters died from a disease called typhoid. He did not just mourn her death. He decided to study the diseases like typhoid which attack animals and men. He would find cures for them and save people from suffering. He began to work in a hospital. The doctors mocked him for the nonsense he talked about germs, but he went on undaunted. In those days hospitals were dreadful places. Out of every hundred people who had operations, sixty died. Pasteur knew it was because of germs. He used disinfectants to kill them and kept everything clean. After that, very few people died in hospital. He had shown he was right, and doctors began to copy him. A surgeon named Lister brought his ideas to Britain. That is why our hospitals today are so clean and safe.

Soon Louis Pasteur was able to show that germs caused disease in sheep. While he was trying to find how to prevent it he noticed a strange thing. When animals had once had a disease they never caught it again. He thought he knew the answer. It must be because the dead germs in the blood saved the animals from new, living germs. So if he put some harmless germs into the animal's blood it would never be attacked by live germs. We call this vaccination. He gathered doctors and scientists to watch his experiments on some sheep. They laughed when they came, but they went away astonished. Louis Pasteur had made a wonderful discovery which would save animals from suffering and disease.

But he knew his discovery must be used to save people from suffering, too. No one would believe him unless he could prove it,

but he dared not risk killing a human being. He had to wait for an opportunity. He began to study dogs. In those days anyone bitten by a mad dog died from the poison. He must get some of the poison and see if he could find and kill the germs in it. A mad dog was brought to him one day. He sucked the poison out of its mouth through a tube, risking his own life. Then he made harmless germs ready to use. At last his chance came. A mother brought to him her little boy of nine years old, named Joseph. He had been bitten twelve times by a mad dog, and everyone knew he would die. "It was two days ago," she wept. "Is it too late?" "Only God knows that," replied the great man. "I will do all I can." Day after day he put harmless germs into the boy. Then he injected the living germs. Now he had to wait seven days. They seemed awfully long days, for he was very anxious. On the seventh day the boy jumped out of bed full of life. He had been quite cured. By his hard work and his faith Louis Pasteur had given a great blessing to mankind.

Soon he was famous and the Pasteur Institute was built in Paris to honour him. He worked there till his death in 1895, always humble because of his Christian faith. He had spent his life in the service of God and man.

James Chalmers of New Guinea

JAMES CHALMERS was born in the year 1841 in Scotland. His home was in the village of Ardrishaig near the town of Inverary. He grew up sturdy and fearless, a born leader of the children of the glen. He had many adventures sailing his own little boat on Loch Fyne and twice he saved a child from drowning. Every Sunday he went to kirk where the minister, Mr. Meikle, sometimes told the children stories of the adventures of missionaries in far-off lands. After one story, from the island of Fiji in the South Seas, the minister said, "Perhaps one of you boys will become an adventurer of Jesus when you grow up." James never forgot that story. When he was eighteen years old he knew he must give his life to God. He went to work in the slums of Glasgow before training to become a minister of the kirk. But deep inside him was the call of the South Seas and, instead of becoming a minister, he offered himself to the London Missionary Society. He was sent to train at Cheshunt College in Hertfordshire and in 1866 he set sail for the far-off Pacific Ocean.

James Chalmers was a big, strong, brawny man. His wife Jane was thin and delicate but she was determined to share all his adventures. Their boat was the *John William II,* a new ship named after the first great missionary of the South Seas who had been clubbed to death by savages in 1839. James Chalmers was very useful on board for he knew so much about sailing. At last they put into

253

Sydney Harbour in Australia, but that was not the end of the voyage. Each of the missionaries had to be landed at mission stations on islands scattered throughout the South Seas. When they reached the island of Niue, 2,500 miles from Sydney, tragedy struck. The fine new ship was sucked by the current towards the island and, despite all the efforts of the crew, it was wrecked on the rocky shore. James Chalmers was going to Rarotonga Island, 600 miles further on. He and his wife found a ship which took them to the island of Samoa, where they hoped to find another boat going on to Rarotonga. There was only one, the *Rona*. It belonged to Billy Hayes, a famous pirate of the South Seas! James Chalmers soon made friends with the buccaneer and sailed with him. Billy Hayes liked the big, strong missionary who could sail his ship as well as any of his crew. He went to the services James Chalmers held every day, and he made his men join in the prayers too. When they said goodbye at Rarotonga Island they were firm friends.

Rarotonga was one of the islands discovered by Captain Cook and named after him. When John Williams first went there in 1822, the islanders had been cannibals, sacrificing human beings to their wooden idols, fighting and killing. But one of his brave native teachers had won them to the Christian faith and they had put away their idols and their savage ways. Soon they had schools and churches and they could read the Gospel turned into their own language by John Williams. Now it was the year 1868 and canoes full of happy, laughing islanders shot out from the beach to welcome their new teacher and his wife and to carry them ashore through the surf.

James Chalmers spent ten years on Rarotonga Island. He went round the villages teaching and setting up churches. Much of his time he spent teaching children in his schools so that they would grow up in the Christian faith. He trained native pastors to care for the churches and to take the Good News of Jesus to neighbouring islands while his quiet, gentle wife made friends with the womenfolk. So the church grew strong on Rarotonga, for it was the church of the natives and it did not rely on white missionaries.

But James Chalmers soon longed to take the Gospel where it had never been heard before. He had set his eyes on New Guinea which, next to Greenland, is the biggest island in the world, and in 1877 he sailed for Australia with his wife. From Sydney they sailed north and landed at Suau on the south coast of the huge island. There was only one white man there, Mr. Lawes, who had set up his mission station at Port Moresby. Nothing was known about the many tribes who lived inland, save that they were cannibals and head-hunters who spent their time fighting and killing. James Chalmers was met by natives who painted themselves hideously and wore strings of human bones. In their huts were piles of human skulls. It was dangerous to go among them, but James Chalmers had no fear and never carried any weapon. The fame of the huge white man spread along the coast. 'Tamate' the natives called him. He went from bay to bay, taking presents for the chiefs and slowly winning their friendship. Then he travelled to the inland villages along jungle tracks. His wife Jane grew ill and had to sail back to Sydney, where she died in 1879. While Mr. Lawes studied the languages of the tribes, so as to translate the Bible for them, James Chalmers travelled around the island, risking his life among these warlike people.

He was usually met by fierce-looking natives armed with spears and clubs. If there were children in the crowd he knew they were not going to attack him. He would open his shirt to show his white skin or roll up his sleeves to show his huge white muscles. The natives were amazed for they had never seen a white man before. "Never send little men out here," James Chalmers wrote home. "The natives like, big, strong men." In such simple ways he made friends with the tribes of Papua, as that part of New Guinea is called. Then he could tell them the Good News of Jesus. Soon there were little churches springing up in the villages.

But other white men had their eyes on Papua where they could buy land cheaply, cheating the natives. James Chalmers sought the help of the British Government and in 1888 Papua was made a Crown Colony. He made two trips home to England but soon came back to Papua to explore new territory along the Fly River. There in the year 1901 he met his death at the hands of savages, giving his life for the sake of the Gospel.

74 Dr. Barnardo, Friend of Homeless Children

THOMAS BARNARDO was born in the year 1845 in the city of Dublin, the capital of Ireland. When he left school, he went to work in an office. He was rather a prig and he did not care about God. But when he was seventeen years old, his heart was changed and he became a Christian. He soon found work to do for God. Every night he went into the slums of the city to help to care for the poor and needy. When he was twenty years old, a famous missionary came to speak in Dublin. His name was Hudson Taylor and he had spent years away in the East, taking the Good News of Jesus to the people of China. That very day Thomas Barnardo offered himself as a missionary. But before he could go to China he must study medicine. For a missionary showed the love of God best by caring for his people. So he gave up his work in Dublin and sailed to England. Soon he was settled in London town, studying to be a doctor.

Thomas Barnardo worked hard all day but at night he loved to go out to help others, just as he had done in Ireland. He soon found that the slums of East London needed him just as much as the slums of Dublin. The great Lord Shaftesbury had started the 'Ragged Schools' for poor boys. Thomas Barnardo started one of his own. It was called 'The Donkey Shed Ragged School', for that was where it was held. One cold winter's night in the year 1866 a new boy came. His name was Jim Jarvis. When the evening was ended and the boys had drunk their cocoa, they said "Good night" and rushed out. Thomas Barnardo went to turn out the lamp. Then he saw Jim Jarvis, hidden behind a box, curled up beside the embers of the fire. "Please let me sleep 'ere," he pleaded. "Why, you must go home," said Thomas Barnardo. "I ain't got no 'ome," the boy replied. Barnardo took him back to his lodgings and saw that Jim had a good supper. He bolted down the good food like a wolf. Thomas Barnardo felt sorry for Jim as he watched him. He said he was ten years old, but he was so small and thin that he looked much younger. He had no shoes or socks, no underclothes and no cap. He had only a ragged coat and torn trousers. He had no home or friends. "There's lots of boys like me," he said. "We eats anything and sleeps anywhere." "Come and show me," said Barnardo.

They went out together into the night. Jim hunted round for an hour but he found no one. "I'm beginning to think this is just a story," said Barnardo. "No, Gov'nor," said Jim earnestly. "We'll find 'em." Then they went down an alley and climbed a high wall. "Look, Gov'nor!" Jim whispered. In the pale moonlight Barnardo saw eleven ragged boys, huddled together to keep warm, fast asleep on the flat roof of a shed.

Every night after that, Thomas Barnardo went out searching for street urchins. He found many like Jim. He made friends with them and found out all about them. He knew he must do something for them. Some weeks later he went to a missionary meeting. The hall was crowded when a message arrived that the speaker was ill and could not come. The Chairman knew Barnardo and he had already heard about his work in the slums. He hurried over to him. "Tell them about your orphan boys," he said. For an hour Barnardo told the great crowd about the terrible lives of orphan boys in the East End of London. The people listened in silence, horrified at this story. The next day the papers were full of it. But some people wrote to the papers in anger. "It isn't true," they said. "Barnardo's just making it up." The great Lord Shaftesbury read Barnardo's story. He invited him to eat with him one evening. He invited the people who disbelieved him, too. There was a long argument between them. Then Lord Shaftesbury said, "We can soon settle this. It's nearly midnight. Let's go and see for ourselves." Cabs were called for and

the whole party set off to the slums. They found 73 boys altogether, huddled asleep wherever they could lie out of sight of the police. As they went back home Lord Shaftesbury turned to Thomas Barnardo. "I think you have found your 'China'," he said. "You can be a missionary in London. God bless you in your work. You can rely on me to help you all I can."

Doctor Barnardo set up a home for orphan boys in the year 1866. He had to rely on his Christian friends for money to buy food and clothes and beds for his 'family'. At first he could only take a few boys. One day a boy named Ginger came and pleaded to be taken in. He was thin and ragged and hungry and looked so ill. But Doctor Barnardo had to turn him away, for there was just no room. A few days later came terrible news. Ginger had died. Doctor Barnardo was heart-broken. He made a solemn vow. "We will never again turn any child away," he said. "Ours will be an ever-open door." More and more children came to him. He had no money of his own. He trusted in God to provide their needs. People heard about his fine work and their gifts enabled the Home in Stepney Causeway to go on. Even babies were brought there or left on the doorstep, and they were all taken in. One day came a wonderful gift. A large house at Hawkhurst in Kent was given to Doctor Barnardo. He called it "Babies' Castle" and from that day his orphan babies have found a good and happy home there.

As Doctor Barnardo's children grew up, he had to think of their future. His boys and girls were trained to earn their living. A kind merchant gave him a house to start a school for boys who wanted to enter the British Navy. Many went out to the British Colonies, especially Canada, to become farmers. Doctor Barnardo died in the year 1905. By that time 60,000 children had been brought up in his Homes. But his work still goes on today in the many fine "Doctor Barnardo's Homes" in our land. He never went to China. He found his work for God at home. He showed his love for God by caring for his children. His name lives on still as the founder of 'the largest family in the world'.

75 Bishop Bompas, Apostle of the Red Indians

WILLIAM BOMPAS was born in London in the year 1834. His father was a lawyer and a member of the Baptist Church. He taught his eight children to know God and to love the Bible. William was educated by a tutor at home and so he did not have many friends. He was shy and often went for walks by himself, sketching churches. For William loved God and already he wanted to spend his life in his service. He had a clever mind, but his father had died when William was ten years old and there was no money to send him to University. William went to work for a solicitor. When he was ill and had to stay at home, he went on studying by himself and he learnt three languages— Latin, Greek and Hebrew. Now he could read the Bible as it had been first written.

In the year 1859 he was ordained a clergyman in the Church of England. For six years he worked as a curate among rough smugglers in Lincolnshire and lace-workers in Nottingham. But he had a growing desire to spread the Gospel abroad and one day in 1865 he went to London to a missionary meeting. A bishop from Canada spoke of the savage life of Red Indians and Eskimos in the frozen north, and of the lonely mission by the great Yukon River where one aged clergyman worked alone. "Will no one come forward to take up the banner of the Lord from his hands?" the bishop cried. At once William Bompas offered himself and eight weeks later he sailed for

New York. He gave away all his possessions so that nothing would remind him of home. He was determined to give himself completely to his new work for God.

On Christmas Day in the year 1865 William Bompas reached Fort Simpson on the Mackenzie River. It had been a long journey by train, steamer, canoe and sledge. Three years before, the Sioux tribe had massacred over a thousand white people and there was great fear in the land. But William Bompas was eager to take the Gospel to the wild North-West. No white man had ever been there except for a few adventurous fur-traders of the Hudson Bay Company, who had set up lonely trading posts where the Red Indians traded their furs. William Bompas began at once to learn the language of the Indians. Soon he went northwards to Fort Norman near Great Bear Lake, teaching the Indians. "I visited their wigwams, telling them the Good News of Jesus," he wrote. "Living in Indian tents is not hard for me. The Indians have regular hours for eating and sleeping and they spend their time in useful occupations— fishing, snaring rabbits, making nets and snow-shoes and sledges, while the women work on deer-skins." With his sledge he travelled to Great Slave Lake, visiting the 'Forts', as the trading-stations were called, and meeting new Indian tribes. He followed the sledge in his light snow-shoes or 'northern slippers', wearing mittens for his hands and moccasins for his feet in the bitter cold. He lived mostly on moose during his journeys between Fort Simpson and Fort Vermilion.

In 1870 he set off to Fort Yukon in the far north, crossing the Rocky Mountains. On his journey he met Eskimos for the first time, and he stayed with them at Atlavik, in the Arctic Circle. He admired their cleverness in making tools out of old iron and their skill in building snow-houses. But they believed in charms and magic, some were thieves and liars, and sometimes treacherous killers. Now William Bompas had another language to learn as he went with the Eskimos on their hunting and fishing expeditions and slept with them in their crowded summer tents and winter snow-houses. The old Eskimo chief, Shipataitook, became the great friend of William Bompas, the 'Child of the Sun', as the Eskimos called him. When the young men of the tribe plotted to kill him, it was Shipataitook who

261

saved his life. Soon William Bompas had to say goodbye to his Eskimo friends along the Mackenzie River. But he left behind him some hymns and prayers and parts of the Bible in their language.

On one journey alone in the year 1870 William Bompas travelled 4,700 miles by canoe. He had grown lean and bronzed after years of hard life in the frozen north, always pioneering and facing death daily. Many Red Indian tribes knew him as their friend and brother, sharing their life and ministering to their needs. In summer he travelled by canoe along the Mackenzie, Slave, Peace, Red and Hay Rivers. In winter he used snow-shoes and sledge. "I must have walked more than 1,000 miles among the Indians this winter," he wrote in 1873. More and more Indians were turning from their medicine-men to worship the Christian God.

In 1873 William Bompas was called back to England. The huge diocese of Rupert's Land, more than half the area of Canada, was to be split up into separate dioceses. William Bompas was to be made Bishop of the new diocese of Athabasca. He hated the idea of becoming a Bishop and determined to protest against it. He took home with him the Gospel of Mark and other parts of the Bible, as well as prayers and hymns, which he had turned into seven different Indian tongues. They were printed while he was in England. Reluctantly he was made a Bishop and within a week he sailed back to Canada with his newly-wed wife, Charlotte. Mrs. Bompas was soon 'Yalti Betzani', 'Bishop's wife', to the Indians. She gladly shared the hard life of her husband. When they arrived at Fort Simpson, the new Bishop's headquarters, they found everyone starving from food shortage, and it was often like that. When they did have food, it was only frozen fish, or moose-meat as hard as leather.

The Bishop's new diocese of Athabasca stretched for one million square miles. "Both the length and breadth of 3,000 miles equal the distance from London to Constantinople," he wrote. While he was away during the long winter, living with the Indian tribes, Mrs. Bompas taught the girls in school. Their house was always full of orphan babies and needy children. The Bishop set up mission-farms to teach Indians to grow food instead of just hunting. He persuaded the Hudson Bay Company to provide a steamer for the huge Mackenzie River.

262

In 1884 William Bompas became Bishop of Mackenzie River diocese and in 1891 Bishop of Selkirk along the Yukon River, over the Rocky Mountains. He died at Carcross in 1906 after forty years of selfless service as the Apostle of the Red Indians.

A RED INDIAN VERSION OF PSALM 23

1. *The Great Father above the Shepherd Chief is. I am His, and with Him I want not.*

2. *He throws out to me a rope, and the name of the rope is love. With it He draws me to where the grass is green and the water is not dangerous, and I eat and lie down and I am satisfied.*

3. *Some time—it may be soon, it may be a long time—He will draw me into a valley. It is dark there, but I will be afraid not, for it is between those mountains that the Shepherd Chief will meet me, and the hunger I have had in my heart all through this life will be satisfied. Sometimes my heart is very weak and falls down, but He lifts me into a good road.*

4. *His name is Wonderful. Sometimes He makes the love rope a whip but afterwards He gives me a staff to lean upon.*

5. *He spreads a table before me with all kinds of foods. He puts His hand upon my head, and all the tired is gone. My cup He fills till it runs over.*

6. *What I tell is true. I lie not. These roads that are away ahead.will stay with me through this life, and afterwards I will go to live in the Big Tepee, and sit down there with the Shepherd Chief for ever.*

Psalm 23 as known to the Pointe Red
Indians of Canada

76 Florence Nightingale, Friend of the Sick

MR. AND MRS. NIGHTINGALE were rich English people with two fine country houses and many servants. Often they travelled abroad, especially in Italy. When a daughter was born to them in Florence in the year 1820 they named her after the city. She and her sister were brought up as gentlewomen. They would never need to work. Instead, they would live a busy life in the high society of London. In rich, fashionable clothes they would go to balls and theatres and parties, marry rich men, and then run their own fine houses. As soon as they were old enough, the sisters were presented at Court to Queen Victoria. Their gay life had begun.

Soon Mrs. Nightingale was worried. Florence was a clever girl and she did not enjoy the life of a fashionable young lady. She would have been more worried if she had gone into Florence's bedroom. Late at night and early in the morning Florence sat with her shawl wrapped around her reading by the flickering candlelight. She studied books and papers about hospitals and the care of the sick. Mrs. Nightingale was horrified when one day Florence told her that she wanted to be a nurse, for in those days nurses were despised. They had no training and very little pay. They were dirty and ignorant and rude and often drunk. "Mama was terrified," Florence said. "It was as if I had wanted to be a kitchen-maid!"

The family fought against Florence. They travelled abroad hoping

264

that she would forget her crazy idea. But wherever they went, in France and Germany and Egypt, Florence managed to creep out and visit hospitals. She learnt all she could from the nuns who were trained to care for the sick. How angry the family were when they found out! But nothing could stop Florence with her strong will. When they got back to England they had to give way and let Florence look after a Hospital 'for Gentlewomen during Illness' in Harley Street, London. "We are ducks who have hatched a wild swan," Mrs. Nightingale wept.

Soon after, a war broke out between England and Russia. It was the year 1854 and Florence was thirty-four years old. The armies of Britain and France sailed to the Crimea in the south of Russia. They tried to capture the port of Sebastopol, but after three fierce battles it was still unconquered. Then came the dreadful Russian winter. A newspaper reporter wrote home of the terrible plight of the wounded, with no one to care for them. A letter went from the War Office to Miss Nightingale. But the very same day she had written to the War Office herself. She was going to the Crimea. Within two days she set off with thirty-eight carefully chosen nurses.

She reached the hospital at Scutari in November. The wounded were taken there from the Crimea in ships, many dying on the way. Florence found that the hospital was an old barracks, with four miles of corridors. It could hold 1,000 wounded. But there were 4,000 there already and more arriving every day. The building was damp and rotting, filled with the awful smell of the sewers and foul air. The wounded were jammed together, dirty and uncared for. Out of every hundred men in the hospital forty died from fever. There were only a few army doctors and even they had to do without bandages and medicines, for the army was in a dreadful muddle. There were no blankets, and very little food.

Florence had brought money collected in England, and soon she and her nurses were hard at work, cleaning and scrubbing, nursing the wounded, and providing good food and clean clothes and blankets. Some of the army officers and doctors disliked these nurses, but nothing could daunt the 'Lady-in-Chief'. She was everywhere, looking after her huge family. At night she went through the long wards, carrying her lamp, seeing that everyone was comfortable.

The soldiers loved her and kissed her shadow as she passed. When at last she reached her room she spent the cold, night hours writing her letters. Some were to ask for more help from England, others were to send news to the mothers and wives of her men. For two years she laboured on. What a different place the hospital was because of her work. Soon all England rang with the fame of the 'Lady with the Lamp'. When the war ended she stayed till her hospital was empty. Then she came home. A wonderful welcome was prepared for her, and a warship was sent to bring her from France. But she took a small boat and came home without anyone knowing.

Queen Victoria sent for Florence and gave her a lovely brooch. On it were the words, 'Blessed are the merciful'. Parliament gave her £50,000. Florence used it to build a School for Nurses at St. Thomas's Hospital, London. She settled in a quiet house in London, where she lived for fifty years. The fever she had caught in the Crimea made her an invalid and she had to lie on her sofa, seldom going out. But nothing could stop her going on with her work. She had many important visitors and wrote endless letters. Her influence was very great. Through her work nursing became a fine and honourable profession, and hospitals became the clean and comfortable places we know today. When she died in 1910 all England mourned for her.

Once Florence Nightingale was asked how she could go on with her work when she was tired and ill and people criticised her. "I do my Master's work," she said. Few people knew to which church she belonged. But someone said, "She belongs to the sect of the Good Samaritan."

77 General Booth, and the Salvation Army

ONE day in the year 1842 a boy of thirteen years started work in the city of Nottingham in England. His name was William Booth and he worked for a pawnbroker. He soon got used to the long hours and the little money he was paid as an apprentice. But he felt sorry for the poor people who came to pawn anything which they possessed. They went straight off and got drunk with the money the pawnbroker lent them on their goods. Times were hard, they were paid poor wages, and their lives were wretched. William Booth soon came to hate strong drink, for it ruined people's lives and broke up their homes.

When he was fifteen years old William Booth decided to give his life to God. At once he gathered friends and they went into the streets of the slums, singing hymns to gather a crowd. Then William stood on a chair and spoke of Jesus. He knew the poor people and the way they lived. He had a wonderful gift for speaking and they listened to him. When he had finished his time as an apprentice he went to London. There he spent more and more time in the slums, preaching the Good News of Jesus to the poor. In 1855 he married, and his wife Catherine always shared his love for God and his work. He became the minister of a Methodist church, but he was not happy in it. He longed to be out in the streets of the slums instead of in a respectable church. The church-people looked down on the slum-dwellers for their drunken lives. They were shocked at a minister spending his time with these evil people, taking services in the streets instead of in church. William Booth gave up his church in 1861 and began to preach on his own.

For four years he went from place to place preaching. He had four little children now and they were very poor, but William Booth trusted in God. In 1865 he was invited to preach in a tent in Whitechapel, London. When the mission was over he knew he must stay there, ministering to his beloved slum-dwellers, his wife beside him. When a storm destroyed the tent he preached wherever he could, in the street, in a dance hall, in an old hut. For six years he went on with his 'Christian Mission'. Then at last he got an old hall for his headquarters. He gave his Mission a new name—the Salvation Army. The men wore red and blue uniform, the women wore blue costumes and poke bonnets. Bands led them as they marched through the slum streets, the army of God.

For a long time William Booth had been laughed at. Sometimes his meetings were broken up by noisy hooligans and he himself was attacked. Now it became worse. The men who made strong drink and the inn-keepers who sold it knew that William Booth would do all he could to destroy their trade. Then these brewers and publicans and the slum-landlords would lose the money they got out of the poor. They paid men to attack William Booth, to stop his services, and to destroy his 'Army'. But nothing could daunt the brave warrior of God. Some of his followers were put in prison on the excuse that they were causing trouble. Many church-people were disgusted with the Salvation Army and thought it was blasphemy to sing and shout about God in the streets. But the Army went on growing and spreading throughout the land. Men who had led wicked, drunken lives became followers of Jesus, and every one became an active soldier in the war against evil. Thieves and drunkards led new lives, and slum hovels became Christian homes.

In 1890 Catherine Booth died. During her illness General Booth sat by the bed of his beloved wife writing a book. It was called *Darkest England and the Way Out*. Many people were shocked when they read of the dreadful lives of the poor. They gladly gave the money William Booth asked for to spread his work. He received £100,000. At last he could do what he wanted for the poor. Homes were built for homeless and needy people in England so that no one need go without food and shelter. People who had been saved from evil ways went to the colonies to begin new lives. The Salvation Army began to spread throughout the whole world.

In 1904 King Edward VII sent for General Booth. He should have gone in ordinary clothes, but the King received him in his 'Army' uniform to honour him. Other honours were given to him, but he remained to the end a humble soldier of Jesus Christ. When he died in 1912 the famous warrior was mourned throughout all the world.

General Booth's work goes on spreading through the world. In towns and cities the Salvation Army marches through the streets, bands playing and banners flying, proclaiming the Gospel of Jesus Christ.

Captain Scott of the Antarctic  78

ROBERT FALCON SCOTT was born in the year 1868 in the County of Devon in England. His family were seafarers but it did not seem that Robert would be strong enough for the sea. Besides, he was a day-dreamer. But his secret dreams were of life in the Royal Navy and of great adventures. He grew up into a fine boy. He had a pony named Beppo that he rode to school. Sunday by Sunday he sang in the choir of St. Mark's Church at Ford, near Plymouth. When he was thirteen years old he joined the training-ship *Britannia* as a cadet for the Royal Navy. He worked hard at his profession and passed his examinations with honours. He was a good officer and a born leader and he was promoted to be a Commander by the time he was thirty-two years old.

Soon afterwards, Scott heard that an expedition was being arranged to go to the Antarctic, the vast unknown continent of ice around the South Pole. He had never thought of becoming an explorer but this was just the kind of exciting adventure he had dreamed about. It wasn't long before he was chosen to lead the expedition. No man had ever set foot at the South Pole. In the year 1773 the brave explorer, Captain Cook, had discovered the frozen continent and sailed across the icy sea surrounding it. In the year 1841 another Englishman named Ross had driven his ships even farther south. He named the land he found after Queen Victoria, and the two moun-

271

tains he saw he named after his two ships—'Erebus' and 'Terror'. Now Norwegian adventurers were becoming interested in exploring the unknown continent. In their own country they spent the long snowy winter on their skis so that they were used to a frozen land.

Scott sailed from London in the year 1901. After a voyage of six months his good ship, the *Discovery,* reached the Ross Sea. Scott found that the two mountains were on an island. Behind it was the Great Ice Barrier, a solid rampart of ice rising out of the sea. Scott went up in a balloon and he could see the land of glaciers and mountains that stretched for miles to the distant South Pole. He and his companions spent the bitter winter in a hut on the shore of McMurdo Sound. Then, when winter broke, Scott chose two companions to set off over the land. One was Ernest Shackleton who was to lead his own expeditions later. The other was Doctor Wilson, a fine Christian and a scientist, who found God in the wonder of nature. They travelled by sledge for nearly a thousand miles. But their dogs grew weak and died, and they had to drag the four sledges themselves. Shackleton fell ill and the others were frost-bitten. They had to turn back and pull Shackleton on a sledge. They only just got back to the *Discovery* alive. But they had been nearer to the Pole than any man before.

The ship was ice-bound all winter and it was not till 1904 that Scott reached England again. He returned to his work in the Navy but his one ambition was to go back to the South and to reach the Pole. At last in the year 1909 his new expedition was ready. He chose his men carefully. Scott had been experimenting with the new motor-sledges. He took three of them with him, as well as 34 dogs and some hardy, Siberian ponies. His ship was the *Terra Nova*, a tough old whaling boat with a total company of 59 men. They sailed first to Australia. There Scott received a telegram from the Norwegian explorer, Amundsen. "Beg leave to inform you proceeding Antarctic", it read. So it was going to be a race to the South Pole! A terrible storm struck the *Terra Nova* on the way south but she battled through it. On Sundays Captain Scott led divine service on deck, the men's strong voices breaking the white stillness. Early in the year 1911 they reached McMurdo Sound and began to prepare for their adventure. The motor sledges soon broke down. They would have to rely on the dogs and ponies. They heard that Amundsen and his party were going by skis on a shorter route, taking dogs with them.

When the Antarctic winter ended, all was ready for the 700 mile journey over the frozen land. Depots of food and oil had been laid along the route. On November 1st Scott set out with his men. The weather was against them and before long the ponies could struggle no more and they had to be shot. When they reached the grim Beardmore Glacier, the dog teams had to return. Now the remaining twelve men pulled the loaded sledges themselves. They struggled up the Glacier and made a depot at the top just before Christmas Day. There four others turned back, as had been arranged. On New Year's Day in the year 1912 there were eight hardy adventurers left. They were 170 miles from their goal. Two days later Scott chose the men to go on with him. They were his old companion, Doctor Wilson; Petty Officer Evans from the Navy; Lieutenant Bowers and Captain Oates from the Army. The others watched the five men disappear into the white distance. They had a month's supply of food.

Captain Scott's Diary tells us what happened. His companions were fine men—Wilson "tough as steel", Evans "a giant worker", Bowers "a marvel", and Oates "goes hard the whole time". They made a mile an hour as they plodded on. By January 16th they were nearing the Pole when Bowers thought he saw something ahead. Soon they came up to the remains of a camp. "The Norwegians are first at the Pole!" They were bitterly disappointed but they had no ill-feelings. They planted the Union Jack at the Pole and turned back. They had 950 miles to travel.

The weather was terrible as they trudged on. First Evans fell ill and died. Then Oates suffered from frost-bitten feet. He drove himself on. One morning he struggled to his feet. "I am just going outside and may be some time," he said. He staggered out into the blizzard to die so that his friends might go on quicker. The remaining three plodded on. By March 21st they were only eleven miles from their big depot of food and oil. But the blizzard raged, and one by one they passed away in their little tent. Eight months later their comrades found them and buried them. They set up a cross in memory and wrote on it— 'To Strive: To Seek: To Find: And Not To Yield'.

THE BARRIER SILENCE

by

Dr. Wilson
(who died with Captain Scott)

The Silence was deep with a breath like sleep
  As our sledge runners slid on the snow,
And the fateful fall of our fur-clad feet
  Struck mute like a silent blow.
On a questioning 'hush', as the settling crust
  Shrank shivering over the floe;
And the sledge in its track sent a whisper back
  Which was lost in a white fog-bow.
And this was the thought that the Silence wrought
  As it scorched and froze us through,
Though secrets hidden are all forbidden
  Till God means man to know:
We might be the men God meant should know
  The heart of the Barrier snow,
In the heat of the sun, and the glow
  And the glare from the glistening floe,
As it scorched and froze us through and through
  With the bite of the drifting snow.

South Polar Times

Lord Lister, and War on Germs

79

JOSEPH LISTER was born in the year 1827. His home was at Plaistow, in the East of London town. His father was a scientist and young Joseph soon showed that he loved finding out about things, too. But his interest was in living creatures, animals as well as people. While he was still a schoolboy he used to collect animals. He cut them open—'dissected' them—to find out all about their bodies. His most precious possession was the skeleton of a cat! He was always reading books about the human body and the art of healing. His father soon realised that Joseph was going to be a doctor. He must go to a university to study.

Joseph's father belonged to the religious Society of Friends. These 'Quakers', as they were nicknamed, were good people who loved God and served him in their daily lives. But in those days they were not allowed to go to Oxford or Cambridge Universities. So Joseph went to the new University of London to study medicine. By studying hard he became a doctor when he was 24 years old. Two years later he went to work in Scotland where he stayed for 25 years.

Doctor Lister was a surgeon at the Royal Infirmary in the city of Glasgow. We just cannot imagine what hospitals were like in those days. In Doctor Lister's hospital nearly as many people died as those who were healed. Operations caused many deaths. Lister hated all this. He was a disciple of Jesus and he wanted to be like his Master,

275

healing sickness and disease. He hated suffering. What could cause all these deaths in hospitals? They were mostly due to cuts and wounds becoming poisoned. Already he thought he had found a clue. People who had broken a bone never suffered from poisoning. This must be because they had no open wounds; their skin was not often cut. Then the poisoning must be caused by something entering wounds from outside.

At once Doctor Lister began to attack dirt in his ward. In those days hospitals were dirty, and smelly, too. Surgeons used to operate in their long black 'frock-coats', and often their clothes were dirty as well as their instruments and their hands. Doctor Lister had his ward scrubbed every day. He made his doctors and nurses scrub their hands too. He soon made lots of enemies but he took no notice. Other doctors thought he was crazy. But they had to admit that fewer people died in his ward than in any other.

Doctor Lister was not content with this. He went on searching to find the cause of wounds turning poisonous or 'septic'. Then one day he read of the great work of Louis Pasteur. This great French scientist had discovered that disease is caused by tiny germs or 'microbes'. "That's it!" cried Lister. "The germs get into the open wounds from the air, from dirty clothes and instruments." Now, more than ever, he made certain that everything was clean in the hospital. He used so much more soap, towels and bed-clothes than any other doctor that he was accused of wasting money. But he had something much more important to think about. How could he kill the germs to prevent them getting into wounds? He found that carbolic acid killed germs. But it was too strong to put on the human body. So next he invented a spray. He used it everywhere to spray carbolic acid on his clothes and his instruments and on the walls of the room where he operated. Even fewer patients suffered from septic wounds in his ward.

His next task was to find some kind of 'anti-septic' that he could put on the wounds themselves to kill germs. Carbolic acid was much too painful. Besides, it could cause poisoning itself. After many experiments Doctor Lister found how to mix it with other things. Now he could safely put this on the wounds themselves. He had found how to keep germs away from the sick. No more would

276

people in hospital die from poisoned wounds.

In the year 1860 Doctor Lister had been made a Professor at Glasgow University where his work was known. But as his fame spread, many doctors opposed him. They laughed at his ideas about germs and cleanliness. He took no notice of them. He spent his time teaching his students and writing about his new methods of 'anti-septic' surgery. In the year 1869 he moved to Edinburgh University where he went on with his teaching. He was never content. He studied germs to find out more about them. He invented new dressings to put on wounds. They had been 'sterilized' or made free from germs. There was so much to do. He had invented 'anti-septic' surgery—that is, destroying germs already there. What he aimed at was 'aseptic surgery'—operating, that is, without any germs being present at all. Louis Pasteur was already doing this at his hospital in France. Lister would never be content till it was done in Britain too.

In the year 1878 Doctor Lister moved to London to teach his new anti-septic surgery. He had few enemies now for his teaching was spreading both in Britain and abroad. His fame spread, too, and he was honoured everywhere. But he was a very humble man. When people said how grateful they were to him he would say—"Don't thank me. Thank Louis Pasteur. I only put his discovery into practice." In 1897 Queen Victoria honoured him on behalf of his country. Lord Lister retired from his post as Professor in London, but he could never give up working. A new kind of hospital was built in London to carry on his work. It is called the 'Lister Institute of Preventive Medicine'.

Lord Lister died in the year 1912. He needed no statue in his memory. Every hospital in the world is his memorial. He had saved millions of people from suffering and pain and death. He had spent his life in the service of mankind, following in the steps of Jesus, who went about doing good and healing the sick.

80 Mary Bird of Persia

MARY BIRD was born in the year 1859 in the county of Durham in England. Her father was a clergyman who cared for the parish of Castle Eden. Mary lived happily in the rectory with her four brothers and sisters. Sometimes visitors came to speak at her father's church. Mary never forgot how, when she was five years old, a missionary from Africa came to her home. She sat on his knee while he told stories of the black children of Africa. From that very day she knew that, when she grew up, she would be a missionary and carry the Good News of Jesus to other lands. But it was a long time before that happened.

Mary's mother was not very strong and she had to help look after the home. As she grew older she helped her father, too, in his parish. She was quite a small person but she was full of energy and always worked very hard. She was full of joy, too, for she had a good sense of humour. She was very determined and always finished what she set out to do. At last, when she was thirty-two years old, she was able to leave home and to train at a college for missionaries. In the year 1891 she set off on the long journey to Persia.

Mary Bird had always hoped to go to Africa, but the Church Missionary Society asked her to go to Persia where a woman missionary was badly needed. For hundreds of years the people of Persia had been followers of Mohammed. Then, in 1815, the New Testament had

278

been turned into the Persian language by a fine Indian missionary named Henry Martyn. Copies of it had been welcomed by many people in Persia, including the Shah himself. So, in 1875, the first missionary was sent out. It was not easy for Mr. Bruce to win Persian men to Christianity for if a Moslem changed his religion he should be put to death. He could never speak to Persian women for they were jealously guarded by their menfolk. At home they lived in a separate part of the house called the 'harem'. When they were allowed out of doors they had to be completely covered in long cloaks with veils over their faces, so that they should not be seen by any other men. Mr. Bruce believed as a Christian that women are just as precious to God as men but he could do nothing for them. So, when his mission was well established, he asked for a lady missionary to join him and to be the first to bring Christianity to the women of Persia.

Mary Bird made the long journey over the mountains to the village of Julfa where Mr. and Mrs. Bruce had their mission. Mr. Bruce told her all about the religion of Mohammed but he could tell her nothing about the women or how to get to know them. First Mary had to learn their language. One teacher taught her Persian but she had to have another teacher to help her to learn Arabic. For the Koran, the sacred book of the Mohammedans, is written in the Arabic language. Mary made friends with the children when she went out. One day she met the mother of some of her child friends. She was crying, for her son was ill with fever. Mary Bird took him some quinine and soon he was better. Her fame spread as a wonderful 'hakim' or doctor, and other women brought their children for healing. So at last Mary Bird had found a way of making friends with the women. But it was not an easy way for she knew little about medicine. She could teach the women how to keep their homes clean and how to care for simple cuts and sores. But she had to send home to England for medical books and to study them far into the night.

Mary set up a dispensary in Isfahan, the old capital of Persia, two miles from Julfa. Every day it was crowded with women and children who had come to seek healing from 'Khanum Maryam'—'Lady Mary', as they called her. Every day she began her work with prayer and read to them the words of Jesus in their own language. Now she could go into the homes of both rich and poor and she soon found how very sad was the lot of women and children. There was much poverty in the land and even little children were forced to work at making the famous Persian rugs. Mary Bird made many friends and they listened eagerly to the message of God's love for them.

But the mullahs, the Moslem Teachers, soon came to hate Mary Bird and her Christian teaching. They spoke against her in their mosques and tried to stop her. As she rode on her donkey every morning from Julfa to Isfahan, angry Moslems were stirred up by the mullahs to attack her. "Christian dog! Infidel!" they shouted. But Mary Bird showed no fear. Nor was she ever angry. "God watch over you," she said, using the polite Persian greeting, and went on her way. Then her enemies decided to try to silence her in another way. One of them sent her an invitation to go to his house where his wife would welcome her. Mary went there and the lady of the house greeted her courteously as the custom was. "Welcome in the name of God," she said. They sat on cushions on the floor. In front of the mullah's wife was the 'samovar' or tea-urn and cakes and sweetmeats. She poured a glass of tea and the servant took it to Mary Bird. Now Mary knew that the mullah hated her and she wondered why she was being given such warm hospitality. Then she noticed that the mullah's wife did not have a glass of tea. Quickly she remembered the Persian custom of asking a superior person to honour the drink by sipping it first. "Will you bless my glass, my lady?" she asked, holding it out. The mullah's wife had to take it. She held it without drinking while Mary looked silently away from her. Then she handed it to a servant. "Take it away, it's too cold," she said. "Bring us fresh tea." As Mary went out of the house later the servant whispered, "How did you know that it was poisoned?"

Mary Bird went on to work at two other towns, Yezd and Kerman, where carpets were woven. When she died in Persia in 1914 there were hospitals and dispensaries where Christian love was shown in word and in deed. They stood as memorials to the faith and courage of Mary Bird who gave her life to the women and children of Persia.

Mary Slessor of Calabar

MARY SLESSOR was born in Scotland in the year 1848. With her five brothers and sisters she lived in an ugly and dismal house in Dundee. Like William Booth she soon learnt to hate strong drink, for her father was a drunkard and her home was poor and unhappy. Like David Livingstone she went to work in the mill when she was only eleven years old, and like him she had a Bible propped up on her loom. She worked from 6 o'clock in the morning till 6 o'clock at night, and soon became a fine weaver. Her wages kept the family and she helped in the house too. She had a good mother who taught her children to love God. When Mary was old enough she led a Bible class at her church for the rough children from the slums of Dundee. Gangs of wild boys tried to frighten her when she took services in the open air, but she never gave way to them. She was fearless and always stood firm for her faith in God.

Mary had often heard about missionary work in Africa. Two of her brothers wanted to serve God in this way but they died from ill-health. No one had thought of lady missionaries. But Mary had never forgotten the stories she had heard of West Africa, and secretly she longed to go there. In 1874 the news of the death of David Livingstone swept through Britain. Who would follow him? Mary decided to offer herself as a missionary. Her mother gladly agreed. Her sisters' wages would keep the home and Mary would send home all

281

she could from her small pay. In 1876 Mary Slessor sailed from Liverpool to West Africa. She was twenty-six years old.

Mary went to Calabar, a part of Nigeria. In those days West Africa was called 'the white man's grave', for so many died there. She knew what dangers faced her. There were swamps full of poisonous insects, and dark jungles where wild beasts lurked. The natives were fierce and cruel, believing in evil spirits and ruled by their witch-doctors. For years white slave-traders had snatched their people and carried them off in their foul boats. They had no love for white people. This was no place for a white woman.

Mary began her work at Duke Town on the coast, which was already a missionary centre. Here she learnt the language of the people and soon made friends with them. She told them of Jesus, led them in worship, and showed the love of God by living with them and caring for them. She was the first white woman they had ever seen. Soon they were calling her 'the great white Ma' and her fame spread. She loved children best and before long she had a family of her own. One day a native rushed up to her mud hut shouting, "Run, Ma, run!" She hurried after him and he led her to a hut where a woman had just given birth to twin children. Mary knew what would happen. The black people believed that twins brought an evil curse upon the home. They were put into a round pot called a calabash and left in the jungle to die. Mary took the children to bring them up herself. The natives were scared of the evil this would bring upon them. When Mary was out one day they took one of the twins and killed him. But the little girl was safe. Mary called her Janie, and she became the first member of her family.

In 1883 Mary Slessor was very ill and had to go back to England to get better. She took Janie with her and told many people of her work for God in Africa. Two years later she saw her mother settled in the country and sailed back to Calabar. For a time she worked in another settlement called Creek Town. But Mary longed to go to the tribes inland who had never seen a missionary. She wrote home, "I am going to a new tribe up-country, a fierce, cruel people, and everyone tells me that they will kill me. But I don't fear." She set off by canoe to the wild Okoyong tribe and plunged through the forest to their village. Their chief had long been an enemy to the Christian king of

283

Creek Town whose name was Eyo. But Mary got Eyo to invite all the chiefs to a palaver. When they were getting into the royal canoe Mary said, "You must leave your swords and guns behind!" The chiefs would not go without them. "Ma, you make women of us!" they cried. But Mary stood firm and at last they got in. Then she noticed some swords hidden under the cargo. Angrily she threw them out. The chiefs dare not say anything. They went to Creek Town and king Eyo spoke to them of peace, and they all became friends.

Mary fought against the savage customs of the Okoyong tribe. She hated the strong drink which made them quarrel and fight and kill. Soon she was ill again and must return home to get well. She was all ready to leave when news reached her of a quarrel between two tribes. A man had been murdered and the other tribe wanted revenge. At once Mary hurried to the chief. He hid from her and sent this reply to her message: "I have heard of no war. In any case a woman couldn't help." She hurried to the village, where the soldiers were shouting their war-cries. She went fearlessly among them. "Don't behave like fools!" she cried. When they were quiet she went to the other side. An old chief knew her, for she had once looked after him when he was ill. "Speak for us that there may be peace," he said. Mary Slessor arranged a palaver and stayed there till the quarrel was ended. She had stopped a war by her courage.

Mary's fame spread far and wide. The Government honoured her. She was made a magistrate and judged cases in the native courts. Once she boxed the ears of a chief who kept interrupting when she told him to be quiet! The black people respected and feared the 'great white Ma'. But they loved her too because she loved them. When she died in 1914 many of them had come to worship her God. For forty years she had served them and they could never forget her. But her memory lives on best of all in the lives of the Christian people of Calabar.

Pandita Ramabai of India

82

RAMABAI was born in the year 1858 in Western India. Her parents, like most of the people of India, belonged to the Hindu religion. Her father was a 'pundit', a religious teacher. He was a kindly man and he named his daughter 'Ramabai' or 'Giver of Delight'. He was generous, too, especially to the pilgrims who came to his house. Before long all his money was gone. He had to sell his home and become a wanderer himself. Little Ramabai was carried about in a cane basket and she grew up without a home.

But her father was an honoured man. In the Hindu religion there are hundreds of different 'castes' or classes into which people are born. The castes could not mix with each other. The lowest were the 'outcasts' or 'untouchables'. The highest were the 'Brahmans' or 'Priests'. So Ramabai's father was one of the highest caste and he was welcomed wherever he went. People gladly listened to him reading the holy writings in the old, sacred language called 'Sanskrit'. He travelled round India to the temples of the gods and his family lived on the gifts of the people. But the people of India live from hand to mouth and if the crops fail there is dreadful famine. While Ramabai was still young, both her parents died of starvation. She and her brother were left homeless wanderers.

Ramabai was a clever girl. In those days women were less important than men, but her father had even taught her the sacred Sanskrit language. As she travelled through India she had learnt other languages too. She longed to use her life in the service of others. As a good Hindu she read the scriptures, she prayed to the idols in the temples, and she bathed in the sacred rivers. But slowly Ramabai grew discontented with her religion. The gods never seemed to answer her prayers, and the idle priests at the temples would not help her. But she felt something even worse about her Hindu religion. Everywhere she went she saw the dreadful unhappiness of Indian girls. By Hindu custom marriages were arranged by parents and girls were married by the time they were twelve years old. Then, if the boy 'husband' died, the girl was left a widow and she could never marry again. In old times a Hindu widow had died with her husband on his funeral pyre. This grim custom had been forbidden by the British rulers of India in 1829, but widows were still despised. For Hindus believe that we live over and over again. To be a child widow must be a punishment for evil-doing in a former life. Throughout India Ramabai saw these poor girl-widows harshly treated when they had done nothing wrong. She determined to give her life to helping them.

When she was 20 years old Ramabai, now a fine woman, went to Calcutta, the largest city of India. No one could sneer when she spoke about the sad lot of Hindu women. Scholars were astonished that she was as clever as they were in the sacred language and in the Hindu scriptures and teachings. For women were not allowed to learn the holy Sanskrit language. Besides, Ramabai was not even married. But they recognised her learning and wisdom and called her 'Pandita' or 'Lady Teacher'. Soon afterwards Ramabai married the man she loved and a little girl was born to her whom she named 'Manorama-bai'—'The Joy of my Heart'. Ramabai had broken the custom by marrying a man from the lowest caste of all. When her husband died she was left a widow. But she refused to live in misery or to give up her great ambition.

Ramabai went to the city of Poona. There for the first time she met Christian missionaries and read the Gospel of Jesus in her own language. The Sisters of St. Mary the Virgin showed her Christian love and encouraged her in her work. Ramabai wrote books about it and, when she had saved enough money, she went to England to study and stayed at the Convent of the Sisters at Wantage in Berkshire.

286

Ramabai went on to America, too. When she returned to India to take up her life's work, she went as a Christian. For she had found in the Good News of Jesus the answer to all her prayers.

In 1889 Ramabai set up her first Widows' Home in Bombay. She was helped by gifts from friends she had made in England and America. Her Home grew so quickly that she needed a bigger house. She found one in Poona and there unhappy girl-widows found happiness. Ramabai never tried to change their religion but it was not long before the girls wanted to share the joy that Ramabai found in the worship of Jesus. The fame of her Home spread and more girls came to it. Ramabai herself travelled round the cities, disguised as a beggar, rescuing girl-widows from cruelty and starvation.

When plague broke out in Poona, Ramabai moved her Home out into the countryside. She had bought a piece of land there with money from her friends abroad. It made an excellent settlement for her girls and before long it became famous as 'Mukti Sadan'—'The Home of Salvation'. Ramabai had three women to help her teach and train her 300 girl-widows. One of the three was her own daughter, Manoramabai. She could refuse no one in need and by 1900 Ramabai had 700 girls in her country Home. It was a Christian village with its own church and houses, fine wells, and its own orchards and vegetable gardens. There Ramabai's girls grew into fine young women. There was much to be done in the houses and out on the land, in the laundry and in the bake-house. On the looms the girls learnt to weave their own clothes. They helped to print the Bible which Ramabai had turned into their own language. They joined in the worship of the village church and many of them were baptised into the Christian Church.

The fame of Ramabai and her work spread far and wide. In the year 1919 King George V honoured her with a gold medal for her devoted service to the women of India. From 'The Home of Salvation' her girls went out to marry and to set up their own Christian homes. Ramabai died in 1922 but her influence lives on still today in the new India. For Pandita Ramabai brought new hope and respect for the women of her country.

83 Chief Khama of Bechuanaland

CHIEF SEKHOME was very proud when Khama was born in the year 1828. For he ruled over the Bamangwato tribe and now he had a son who would become Chief after him. There were five tribes who lived in that part of Africa. They were called the Bechuana tribes and the Bamangwato were the most powerful of them all. Sekhome ruled over his people through his soldiers and his witch-doctors. His word was law and he was fierce and cruel. He owned many cattle for he was rich. He had many wives, too, and they lived with him in the royal 'kraal' or village. The kraal was made up of many native huts in a circle. In the open space in the middle the cattle were kept at night so that no enemy could steal them. Around the kraal was a high fence. The Bamangwato people feared their Chief for he had power over their lives. He was a witch-doctor himself so that he had power over the evil spirits too.

Africa was a wild country in those days. The tribes often fought against each other and bloodshed was common. There were wild animals lurking in the forests and roaming the plains. People lived in fear of animals, fear of men and fear of evil spirits. One day in the year 1842 Chief Sekhome heard something very strange that made even him afraid. A white man was coming through the forests. Sekhome went to meet him, taking young Khama with him and his warriors. The white man's name was David Livingstone. He

288

had no fear of the black warriors and Sekhome could not frighten him away. Livingstone was a great explorer as well as a Christian missionary. He travelled through the land of the Bechuanas on his journeys and wherever he went he took the Good News of Jesus.

Khama grew up tall and strong. Among all the Bamangwato people there was no better runner or hunter or rider than he. He was called 'Khama the Antelope' by his people. He had great courage too. Once he killed a lion by himself, and no one was braver when the Bamangwato warriors went out to battle against the fierce and warlike Matabele tribe. Sekhome was very proud. "He will be a great Chief like me," he thought. But Khama had never forgotten the white man and his strange new teaching. When he was a young man he went to stay with another Chief who had become a Christian through David Livingstone. He taught Khama to read and to write and told him what it meant to be a Christian. When Khama came back to the royal kraal he asked his father to let a white teacher come to his people. Sekhome agreed, for he wanted to know what this strange medicine was that the white men had. A missionary came to the Bamangwato people and in 1860 Khama and his brother were both baptised and became Christians.

The old chief Sekhome soon changed his mind. He grew very angry when he found Khama going against him and his ways. Khama refused to have many wives, as his father did. He married a good woman of his own tribe and he loved her dearly. Her name was very long so she was called 'Ma-Bessie' by her friends. Khama and Ma-Bessie needed only one hut in their kraal.

Sekhome grew even more angry when Khama would not join in the ancient customs of his tribe. Savage and evil things were done at their feasts and the witch-doctors danced around in power and glory. Only Khama had no fear of them for he believed in the one God of both heaven and earth. "He is no son of mine!" Sekhome thought angrily. He hated Khama now and decided to kill him. He ordered his chief witch-doctors to cast a spell over Khama so that he would die. One night Khama awoke suddenly, hearing voices and the crackle of flames outside his hut. He crept outside. There were the wizards, crouching over the flames, muttering horrible magic spells against him. Khama leapt out of the darkness and they fled in terror.

289

Khama and his brother had to hide in the hills to escape from their father. But in the year 1872 the savage old Chief died and the Bamangwato people chose Khama to wear the leopard's skin and to rule over them. Now he could teach his people to live good lives. But he always taught them best by his own example. He led his people away from witchcraft and their evil customs. But there were other enemies to fight.

Khama knew how, when he was a boy, the white people had made laws against slavery. But his people had fallen into another kind of slavery. There were other white people in his country now and they sold strong drink to the Bamangwato tribe. When they were drunk with the 'fire-water' the people did dreadful things. Khama told the white traders that they must sell no more of it to his people. They went on doing it secretly and they were often drunk themselves. Khama sent for them and told them to leave the land of the Bechuanas. "To you I am only a black man," he said sternly. "But I am Chief and my laws must be kept. I try to lead my people to God. You try to lead them to evil. Pack your waggons and go!"

When the white traders were gone there was still drunkenness among the Bamangwato. The people made their own drink from corn. Khama called them together. "We pray to God for corn," he cried. "God answers our prayer and sends us the good grain that we may live. You use it to bring evil and death. You will do it no more!" Many people were angry but Chief Khama stood firm. Slowly he led his people into the ways of peace.

Other white men came up from the south, searching for gold and diamonds. Khama soon saw that his people would lose their land if they took the rich bribes offered to them. So in the year 1885 he sent a message to Queen Victoria asking her to protect his people. Bechuanaland became a British Protectorate and ten years later Chief Khama travelled to England and knelt before the great Queen, offering her his loyalty. When he died in the year 1923, the Bamangwato people wept for their great Chief who had led them to goodness and to God.

Aggrey
of the
Gold Coast

PRINCE KODWO AGGREY was the most important man at the court of the King of the Gold Coast. He was wise and good and was the King's chief minister. When his tribe was at war he was the only man who could pass to their enemies, for everyone trusted him. Always he tried to bring peace. One day in the year 1875 the drums sounded the news from afar. Their dread enemies the Ashanti tribe were coming to attack them. Now a little son had just been born to Prince Kodwo. He must be named before the warriors marched out. At sunset everyone gathered for the ceremony. He was sprinkled with water from the sacred spring to protect him from the evil spirits and he was named Kwegyir. All night there was feasting and dancing. Then in the morning came good news—the Ashanti were going back to their own country.

The little boy grew up to be very clever and always happy. He loved to listen to his father's stories of their people. Some of them were sad. They told how greedy white men came to their land for gold and for slaves. But his father had no hatred. What a fine man he was, and how the little boy longed to be like him, always seeking peace. One day his father filled his own special jug with water and bade him drink from it. "As thou drinkest, thy father's wisdom and powers of speech will pass into thee. When thou becomest a man thou shalt do in a great way what I have done in a small way." Kwegyir never

291

forgot his father's solemn words.

His father sent him to a Christian school at Cape Coast. He loved the Bible best of all and even slept with it under his pillow. Soon he was baptised as a Christian and all his family too. When he was thirteen years old he went to a Christian boarding-school. He was quick to learn with his books, but he learnt to use his hands as well, especially at the printing-press. It was there that he decided to give his life to God. He would be a peace-maker like his father, not just between black men but especially between black and white people. He was so clever that he became a teacher at his old school and, by the time he was twenty-one years old, he was made Headmaster.

But Aggrey wanted to learn more so that he could serve his people better. For that he had to go to America. He studied at Livingstone College in North Carolina. It was named after the great David Livingstone and negroes could get a good education there. He worked at printing to earn money for College. "I made myself blacker than ever with printer's ink!" he laughed. He passed many examinations and went on to the great Columbia University. But he never grew proud. Wherever he went he taught his fellow-negroes to live at peace with white people. "Keep your temper and always smile," he said. "That's what Jesus meant when he told us to turn the other cheek." When he spoke to white people he told them that black and white people needed each other. He told them the parable of the piano keys. "You can play a simple tune on the white keys. You can play a simple tune on the black keys. But if you want a really fine harmony you must use both the white and the black keys. God has made white keys and black keys. He wants us to make fine harmony together."

Aggrey was always proud of being a black man. Once he said, "If I went to heaven and God asked me if I would like to return to earth as a white man, I would answer, 'I have work to do as a black man that no white man can do. Please send me back to earth as black as You can make me'." He was never bitter when he was ill-treated as a black man. He always laughed about it. He loved to tell the story of what happened when he was once on a crowded ship. In the dining-room he had to sit at a table by himself. "It was very funny," he said. "There were the white people packed at their tables with only one

292

steward to serve seven. I had a whole table and a steward all to myself!"

Aggrey became very famous. He was chosen by the Government to join a group of white people from England and America. They were to go through Africa making plans for the education of the African people. He did wonderful work, for like his father he was wise and just and everyone trusted him. A fine College was built at Achimota on the Gold Coast for African children, and Aggrey agreed to be Vice-Principal of it. There he could help educate his countrymen to work side by side with white people in building a fine, Christian Africa. Its badge shows the black and white keys of the piano.

Aggrey died suddenly in 1928, but his wonderful example could never be forgotten. Achimota has become a University and carries on the work he began. In 1957 the Gold Coast became a new and independent state called Ghana. Its first Prime Minister, Dr. Nkrumah, was educated at Achimota College. Ghana is one of the family of countries which we call the British Commonwealth. In that family the black people of Ghana are equal with white people and live side by side with them. That is what Aggrey longed for and worked for. He believed that all men are brothers in the great family of God.

85 Dr. Nansen, Citizen of the World

FRIDTJOF NANSEN was born in the year 1861 in Oslo, the capital city of Norway. The men of Norway have always been hardy and adventurous, for Norway is a hard country. In the long dark winter it is very cold, especially in the frozen North of the land. In summer the days are long and the nights are never really dark but only twilight. The coast of Norway is cut by many creeks called 'fiords'. From these fiords the fierce Vikings of old sailed in their long-boats to plunder England and the other countries of Europe. From them still today the hardy Norwegian fishermen sail far out into the stormy North Sea. The land of Norway is covered with high mountains, deep lakes and thick forests. In winter the whole country lies under a blanket of snow and the men of Norway travel everywhere on their skis. They love games and their winter sports, such as hunting, shooting, fishing and, of course, ski-ing.

No wonder Nansen grew up to be a hardy sportsman. He was soon talked about for he was the champion skater of Norway. But he could do many things besides sports. He worked in a museum to earn his living. He could write and draw, and during the holidays he spent ski-ing in the mountains there were many things to sketch. But soon he wanted more exciting adventures. In 1882 he sailed across the icy sea to Greenland to collect plants and living creatures for his museum. This gave him a new idea. Greenland is a huge

294

island, nearly fifteen times bigger than England. But it lies in the Arctic Circle and it is covered with ice and snow. No one knew what the country was like inland, for only a few Eskimos lived there in their settlements on the coast. Nansen decided to cross Greenland on skis. It was a dangerous adventure, but that was just what Nansen wanted. In the year 1888 he set off with five friends. They landed on the east coast of Greenland and then set off on their skis into land where no man had ever been. After four months of hard, lonely travelling through snow-storms and blizzards they reached the west coast. Even the Eskimos were astonished to see them. The travellers spent the winter with them in their snow-houses, called 'igloos'. Nansen and his friends had to live with them for six months till winter was over. There were no openings in the igloos. The smell was horrible inside, but he gladly shared the bitter winter with his Eskimo friends.

When Nansen returned to Norway he wrote a book about his adventures called *The First Crossing of Greenland*. But now he had an even greater ambition. He decided to go to the North Pole. While he was in Greenland he had seen the wreck of a ship, held fast in the ice. But it had been lost in the northern part of Russia, called Siberia. "However did it get here?" he wondered. He found branches from Siberian trees, too. Then he had a wonderful idea. First he had a good, strong ship made, named *Fram*. Her sides were two feet thick for she was going to live in ice for a long time. In 1893 his expedition was ready. He sailed with his twelve hardy companions to northern Russia. There he deliberately set his ship in the ice floes. If his idea was right, the current would carry his ice-bound ship right through the Arctic Ocean and so they would be carried over the North Pole. For nearly three years the *Fram* drifted slowly but surely, about two miles a day. When they were nearest to the Pole, Nansen set off across the ice with only one companion. Their dog-sledge did not reach the Pole but Nansen came nearer to it than any man had ever been. The *Fram* came out of the icy sea near the Spitzbergen Islands north of Norway. Nansen's great courage had made a wonderful discovery.

When he came back to Norway, Nansen was a greater hero than ever. He was made a Professor at Oslo University where he studied the oceans of the world. Then in 1905 Norway separated from Sweden and had a King of her own. This was decided in a friendly way. Doctor Nansen was sent to London for two years to represent his country there. But his greatest work was yet to come. From 1914–1918 the great nations fought against each other in the First World War. Norway did not have to fight. But when the war ended, there was terrible suffering in many other lands. Good people in many countries wanted to make sure that such a war would never happen again. They decided to join together in a family of nations in which they would all be friends and settle their quarrels peacefully. It was called 'The League of Nations' and it was set up at Geneva in Switzerland. One of its biggest tasks was to help people who had suffered from the war and had no homes. Who could lead this great work for the refugees? The hero of Norway was asked to do it and he gladly undertook this new adventure.

Nansen went at once to Moscow, the capital city of Russia. There were thousands of prisoners there to be brought back to their homes. He made a treaty with the leaders of Russia. They agreed that prisoners should be exchanged between countries that had fought against each other in the war. Then Nansen had to get ships and food and clothing for all these men. Within a year, half a million prisoners had been safely returned to their homes.

Hardly had Doctor Nansen completed that great task when a new one arose. The Turks were fighting against the Greeks. Over a million Greek families in Asia Minor were homeless. At once Doctor Nansen went to their aid. He collected money and food, and soon ships were bringing the necessities of life to the homeless Greeks and taking them back to safety in their homeland. Then Nansen went to Greece and planned new settlements for them where they could live in peace and happiness.

Doctor Nansen died in the year 1930. Not only in Norway but in every land people mourned his loss. For he was not only a hero of his own country. He was a 'Citizen of the World'.

Ronald Ross, Conqueror of Malaria

86

R ONALD R OSS was born in the year 1857. Because his mother and father lived in India he was sent to boarding-school in England. His father wanted him to be a doctor, so when he left school he went to St. Bartholomew's Hospital in London to study. But Ronald Ross was interested in other things. He was very fond of music and he loved writing poetry. "I'll do what my father wants and learn to be a doctor," he thought. "But one day I'll be able to give up medicine and be a poet and a musician." He thought of being an artist, too, for he was good at drawing and painting.

When he had finished his studies, Doctor Ross went out to India, as his father wanted him to do. His work was to look after the British soldiers who were stationed in India in those days. He took his piano to India and lots of books as well. He had plenty of spare time. He played music and wrote poetry. Sometimes he went out shooting with his friends or fishing by himself. But he was not happy. He felt sorry for the people of India who suffered from so many things. One of the worst was an illness called 'malaria'. Thousands of people suffered from it and many people died from it. Ronald Ross felt more and more that he must try to find the cause of it. For, once he knew the cause, it would be easy to find a cure. He had been brought up a Christian. He had learnt how Jesus went about healing the sick. He decided he must serve his fellow-men. As a doctor he could follow closely in the steps of Jesus.

The word 'malaria' means 'bad air'. It was an illness that had been known for thousands of years. People knew that it came from the hot mists that were found around swamps, so they thought it was caused by this 'bad air'. Even 500 years before Jesus was born, a Greek who lived in Sicily tried to stop malaria. His name was Empedocles. He had the swamps drained and there was no more malaria in his town. But he had not found the real cause of it.

Doctor Ross was very troubled by mosquitoes in India. They are only tiny insects but they are a big nuisance for they bite human beings. Doctor Ross was often bitten in his bungalow and he tried to find where they came from. He found lots of them and their eggs in a garden tub outside his window. He emptied out the tub and then told the officer what he had done. "They are even breeding in the flower vases," Ross told him. "Let me get rid of them all." The officer was scornful. "Certainly not," he said. "They are part of nature. They must be here for some purpose. We must just put up with them." But Doctor Ross secretly decided not to put up with them.

When he had his leave in England he studied more about insects instead of enjoying himself at parties and dances. He had a wonderful idea and he wanted to see if it could be right. People now thought that malaria came from drinking impure water—especially water with dead mosquitoes in it. "I know they're wrong," Doctor Ross said to himself. "I'm sure it is the bite of the live mosquito that causes malaria." He spent all his spare time studying these insects. His friends soon gave him a nickname—"Mosquito Ross'. But he never gave up. More and more he felt that this was a work he was doing for God. If only he were successful he could save millions of people all over the world from their sufferings.

Doctor Ross collected mosquitoes and learnt all he could about them. He studied them under his microscope. It was lonely work, and unpleasant, too, in the hot climate of India. His microscope grew rusty from his perspiration. He could not have the cooling-fan turned on, for the breeze it made would blow the insects about. He got drops of blood from people who had malaria and found in it the malaria germs. Now he had to find them in the mosquito, too, and then he would have the answer. His patient work went on for years. It

298

was not easy because he was moved from one place to another in India. He did not bother about getting better jobs. All he wanted was to go on with his work.

Doctor Ross found there were different kinds of mosquitoes. But he had to find the one that caused malaria. Late one night he was examining a new kind under his microscope. He found inside it malaria germs, exactly the same as the ones he had found in the blood of people with malaria. At last he knew the answer. Malaria is caused by the bite of a certain kind of mosquito. The insect sucked blood from a man who had malaria. Then it bit a healthy man and gave him the germ. That was how malaria spread.

Doctor Ross was very happy. He wrote a splendid poem in which he thanked God for his wonderful discovery. Now he had to make his discovery known and to get doctors to act upon it. He gave up his

work in India, even though it meant losing a lot of money. But when he arrived in England he found that doctors would not believe him and the Government would not do anything about ending malaria. He tried hard to persuade them but it was no good. "Then I will fight malaria myself," he said. He went out to West Africa and put his discovery into practice. Wherever he destroyed mosquitoes, the dreaded malaria disappeared.

It was in the year 1897 that Doctor Ross made his discovery. It was not till twenty years later that it was believed. When the first world war broke out, he was asked by the Government to care for the British armies abroad. After the war, money was given to set up a new hospital in London. It was called 'The Ross Institute and Hospital for Tropical Diseases'. Doctor Ross went on studying there till his death in the year 1932, always searching for new cures to end suffering. Still today the Ross Insitute carries on its wonderful work. It honours the memory of Ronald Ross who followed in the steps of Jesus, healing the sick and caring for those who suffered.

A POEM WRITTEN BY RONALD ROSS

ON DISCOVERING THE CAUSE OF MALARIA

This day relenting God
Hath placed within my hand
A wondrous thing; and God
Be praised. At His command,

Seeking His secret deeds,
With tears and toiling breath,
I find thy cunning seeds,
O million-murdering Death.

I know this little thing
A myriad men will save.
O Death, where is thy sting?
Thy victory, O Grave?

Apolo, Apostle of the Pygmies

87

ONE day in the year 1864 twins were born in a village of the Baganda people in East Africa. The witch-doctor was sent for at once, for they believed that twins brought a curse upon the village and the evil spirits must be driven away. Often twins were killed. But the witch-doctor said that the boy twin would grow into a great man, so even the girl twin was allowed to live. Apolo grew into a fine boy in his poor village home. He loved to go exploring and to find new adventures. How excited he was when he heard that white men had come to his country of Uganda.

In the year 1874 the first missionary had appeared at the court of M'tesa, King of the Baganda tribe. He was an explorer named Stanley who had followed in the steps of the great David Livingstone. King M'tesa worshipped idols and believed in evil spirits. He had heard about the Moslem religion from the Arab slave-traders. Stanley told him about the God of the Christians and he read some of the Bible in the language of the King. M'tesa wanted to know more about the powerful white men and their God. Stanley wrote to England about the King's desire and in 1876 a party of missionaries set sail for Africa. Two years later the most famous of them, Alexander Mackay, came to live in Uganda. Apolo was now twelve years old and he heard exciting stories of the white wizard who made sparks and steam with red-hot metal, and who taught boys to read in their own language from his sacred book. How powerful the great God of the white men must be! Besides, he was a God of goodness, not of evil. He wanted men to love him, not to fear him.

Apolo longed to visit the white man but it was not easy. In 1884 King M'tesa died and his young son M'wanga became King. He was turned against the Christians by his pagan chiefs and by the jealous Moslem Arabs. They told him the white men would seize his land, and M'wanga persecuted the followers of the white men's God. Three of Alexander Mackay's boys were burnt to death, and the first Bishop of East Africa, James Hannington, was murdered before he reached Uganda. Alexander Mackay was allowed to remain because of his cleverness at making things with metal. One day Apolo set off alone through the forest and secretly visited the white man. Apolo never forgot those precious days with the missionary, Alexander Mackay, who told him the Good News of Jesus who had come to save men of all races. He read to Apolo the Gospel of St. Matthew which he had turned into Luganda, the language of the Baganda people, and Apolo's heart was full of joy.

When he got back home, Apolo found there was war in Uganda. The Moslems were trying to win the country and Apolo's father made him join their army. But Apolo escaped and went into hiding. He found a Christian friend who had a copy of the Gospel in their own Luganda language and they studied it together. In 1894 Uganda was brought under the rule of Britain and peace came back to the land. In the following year Apolo was baptised into the Christian Church.

At once Apolo began to preach the Good News of Jesus, going from village to village among his own people. But he longed to go among tribes who had never heard the Gospel. When he heard that the King of Toro wanted Christian teachers he offered to go at once. It was a long journey of 200 miles through lonely country. Apolo risked his life from dangerous swamps and wild animals. After ten days he reached Toro safely and at once he began his work. He soon won people by his love for them and by the joy which shone in his face. For nine months he stayed among the people of Toro, telling them of the Christian God of goodness and love. The King and Queen of Toro were baptised and many of the people too. Churches sprang up through their land and soon there were others to teach the Gospel.

Again Apolo grew restless. Toro lay at the foot of the great Ruwenzori, the 'Mountains of the Moon'. He longed to take the Gospel to the tribes beyond the mountains. "You would die of cold on the mountains," said the King. "Besides, there are demons in the mountains. Beyond them, in the dark forests, live savage cannibals, dwarfs with poisoned arrows and evil spirits." Nothing could frighten Apolo. He climbed the mountains and saw stretched out before him the hill country of Mboga. He hastened on his way to take the Gospel to its heathen people. Apolo set up a little church

at Mboga and there, early in 1898, baptised a woman named Debola, the first Christian in Mboga. The witch-doctors ruled the land and they soon grew jealous of Apolo. They easily persuaded the evil chief, Tabalo, to side with them against Apolo. One night they set fire to his hut and spearmen waited for him to be driven out. But they thought they heard the voice of his God and they were too afraid to kill him. The angry chief told Apolo to leave the land. "God sent me to Mboga," Apolo replied. "I cannot go unless He sends me." Then the chief's bodyguard were ordered to flog Apolo to death with a rawhide whip. He was beaten unconscious and thrown out into the jungle for the beasts of prey. Debola found him there and nursed him for six weeks in a lonely hut. Then one Sunday the church drum sounded again. Chief Tabalo trembled when he heard that it was Apolo, alive from the dead. He hurried to the little church and knelt before Apolo, asking forgiveness. "I too will be a man of Jesus," he said. At his baptism chief Tabalo was named Paul, and from that time he led his people in the Christian way.

Once more Apolo set out into the unknown. He went ever deeper into the forests seeking out the shy little pygmy people. Apolo showed the love of God to the pygmies in both word and deed. They are only four feet high, with dark skins and crinkled hair, and they live a simple life. Apolo made them his friends and soon there was a little Christian church in the depths of the forest. So Apolo laboured on for thirty years till his death in 1933. The thriving Church in Uganda today is the finest memorial to Apolo, the first Apostle of the Pygmies.

Madame Curie, Discoverer of Radium   88

MARIE SKLODOWSKA was born in the year 1867. Her home was in Warsaw, the capital city of Poland. Her father was a teacher and, though he was not rich, he had a happy home for he loved his children dearly. In a cupboard he kept the tubes and weights and measures with which he did experiments. Marie often wanted to play with his 'apparatus', as these things are called, but of course they were too precious. But when she was older and went to school, her father taught her many things. Marie soon knew that she wanted to be a scientist and she worked hard at her studies. She was a very clever girl, too. She worked as a governess in Warsaw, teaching children, in order to earn money. But she went on studying in all the spare time she had.

In 1891 Marie left her own country and went to Paris, the capital city of France. During the long train journey on a hard wooden seat she had plenty to think about. She loved her native land dearly. Poland was a sad country for it had been divided up by other countries. The Polish people longed to be free and Marie wanted to help all she could. But first she had to go to the University of Paris to study science. Then one day perhaps she would be able to help her beloved Poland.

Marie went to stay at first with her sister who was married to a doctor. Then she found a room of her own. It was an attic room and

305

all the furniture she had was a bed, a table and chair, her trunk and her precious books. She lived for her science. Often she was cold and hungry for she never bothered to look after herself. She never went out to enjoy herself. She was happiest when she was studying. She grew very thin and sometimes she fainted for she was too poor to buy good food. The other students were astonished by her. She was a pretty girl, with long fair hair. But they could never get to know her for she was always working. They were not surprised when she passed all her examinations with high honours.

But one scientist did get to know Marie. His name was Pierre Curie. He too lived only for his science. He was 35 years old and, like Marie, he had never thought about marriage. How surprised he was when he found he could talk about his experiments with this charming young lady. He went to her bare attic and soon realised how devoted she was to science. He wanted to have Marie as his life-long companion so that they could share their work together. But when he asked her to marry him, Marie was horrified. She had decided never to marry for it would interfere with her work. Besides, Pierre was a Frenchman and she lived for the day when she could return to her dear Poland. For nearly a year she refused to marry Pierre. But by then she knew that gentle Pierre loved science as much as she did. They were married and lived in a little flat in Paris. They had a shed in the garden for their experiments.

The flat was very bare but neither of them bothered about that. Marie made meals that could be left on the stove cooking by themselves. She spent every minute she could with Pierre in the shed. It was their 'laboratory' or work-room. Soon Marie had a baby, named Irene, but still she went on with her work. Now Pierre and Marie could no longer cycle round the countryside together. But they had something much more exciting to do. They knew that a mineral called uranium gave off rays—that it was 'radio-active'. Marie wanted to find out why this was. First she examined every known substance. Only one other, called thorium, gave off these strange rays. But Marie found that the rays in minerals were too strong to come from the uranium and thorium alone. There must be another substance or 'element' that no one knew about. She decided to find out what it was and Pierre gave up his own work to help her. They were given an old

307

hut to work in. It was cold and damp and it had no floor, but they worked there for four years. From Austria they got altogether eight tons of earth full of minerals called 'pitch-blende'. They boiled it in a big pot. "Sometimes I spent all day stirring it with an iron bar," Marie said later. "The bar was as big as me. But working there with Pierre was the happiest time in my life." The shed was full of jars containing the products from the pitch-blende. Pierre wanted to give up sometimes but Marie would never stop. Slowly she was getting purer minerals. At last, in the year 1902, her work was finished. From the eight tons of pitch-blende she had got a teaspoonful of a new element. It was a white powder that looked like salt, but it glowed in the darkness, for it gave off rays. Marie called it 'radium' because it was radioactive.

Life was still very hard for the Curies. Marie had to teach at a girls' school to get money for their work. But the news of the great discovery spread. Scientists in other lands wrote to ask them the secret of getting radium. If Marie and Pierre had kept the secret they would have become very rich. But they never thought of that. "We are scientists," said Marie. "We must tell the world."

Soon the Curies were famous. They were honoured in England. Then in 1903 the famous Nobel-Peace Prize was awarded to them in Sweden. With the money they received they bought presents for all their relatives, and for themselves just a new bathroom. Marie hated all the publicity. "It spoils our home-life," she said. "It gets in the way of our work, too." In the year 1904 Marie had another child named Eve but she went on with her work just the same. Next year Pierre was made a Professor. At last they could have a fine laboratory. But not long afterwards Pierre was run over in the street and killed. Marie was made Professor in his place. Madame Curie was famous throughout the world. After the war she travelled in America. But she was glad to return to her laboratory at the new 'Institute of Radium' in Paris. She died in the year 1934 from an illness caused by working for years with radium. Madame Curie had given her life in the service of mankind.

Sir
Wilfred Grenfell
of Labrador

89

WILFRED GRENFELL was born in England in the year 1865. His home was near Chester, by the River Dee, and often he went exploring with his brother. They made their own canoe and often camped out for the night. Wilfred loved the water and the fishermen, and was always ready for adventure. He never tired of hearing the story of Sir Richard Grenville, his ancestor. In 1591 the brave Sir Richard had been surrounded in his little ship by fifty-three great Spanish galleons. He fought them for fifteen hours till he was killed. Wilfred, like the heroic admiral, was strong and hardy and loved the sea.

When he was fourteen years old, Wilfred went to boarding-school. He was a fine sportsman and game for any adventure. Four years later his family moved to London, and Wilfred studied at the London Hospital to be a doctor. One night on his way home he saw people going into a big tent for a meeting, and out of curiosity he followed them. The speaker was C. T. Studd, a famous cricketer who had become a missionary. That night Wilfred Grenfell decided to give his life to God. He began to work among the boys of the East End of London, teaching them in Sunday-school and running a club for them. He spent his holidays in an old fishing-boat with his brother, sailing around the Irish Sea.

In 1886 Wilfred passed his exams and became a doctor. He asked a famous surgeon at the hospital where he should work. "You get on very well with the North Sea fishermen who come here as patients. Why not work with them?" the great man said. "There's a little ship goes out to the fishing-fleet to look after the men. It is their shop, their church, and their hospital all in one. They want a young doctor on board. Why not try it?" Wilfred Grenfell jumped at this exciting work. Soon he was at Yarmouth and on board the little fishing-smack. It belonged to the Mission to Deep Sea Fishermen, and painted on its sides were the words, 'Heal the sick' and 'Preach the Word'. He did both those things and many more, always ready to help the 20,000 men and boys who lived the hard life of the North Sea fishermen. Before long he was working with the fishermen off the coast of Ireland, too.

For six years he stayed with them. Then came a new adventure. The Mission wanted to help the fishermen on the other side of the Atlantic Ocean, on the dread coast of Labrador. Dr. Grenfell was the man to see what could be done for them. In 1892 he sailed across the Atlantic in a little ship called the *Albert*, and came into the harbour of St. John's, Newfoundland. He soon found how terrible the coast of Labrador is with its thick fogs, fierce storms, huge, dangerous icebergs, and bitter cold during the long winter. But at once he sailed north after the fishing-fleet, coming up with it at a tiny harbour called Domino Run. How excited the fishermen were! A real live doctor had come to them in his floating hospital! Before long Dr. Grenfell was hard at work, caring for the injured and the sick, and leading the fisherfolk in the worship of God. When he came back to St. John's the chief men of Newfoundland promised to help build at once the hospitals he so badly needed. One would be at Battle Harbour, and the other further north at Indian Harbour.

Dr. Grenfell sailed back to England to tell of the exciting work waiting to be done for the fishermen of Labrador. He had shown what could be done. Next year two doctors and two nurses sailed back with him and the first hospital was soon crowded with patients. Grenfell went north in a little steam launch, the *Princess Mary*, puffing into the bays where the settlers lived their lonely lives. How glad they were to see the hardy doctor with his twinkling eyes, bringing comfort and cheer and the word of God. He went to Okkak in the far north before turning back. He met the Eskimos for the first time, and it was not long before his fame spread among them, too.

Gradually the work grew. More doctors and nurses came out to help the famous doctor, and money was raised to buy more ships. When hospital stations had been set up, Dr. Grenfell went on to explore new territory. He reached Cape Chidley in the farthest north of Labrador, and went out with the seal-hunters on their dangerous work. Winter was a terrible time in Labrador. Fierce blizzards cut off the tiny settlements and there was no help for the sick. Dr. Grenfell travelled hundreds of miles across the ice and snow during the winter. His sledge, made of black spruce wood, was long and swift. His fine team of Labrador dogs ran swiftly along in the bitter cold, taking their master on his errands of mercy. One day as they sped across the ice to a sick man it began to break up beneath them and the sledge was sinking, taking the dogs with it. Grenfell slashed the reins to save the dogs, and after a long struggle reached a sheet of solid ice. But he had lost everything and faced death in the bitter night. He had to kill three dogs for their skins to keep warm and he huddled close to the others during the long hours of darkness. When light came he made a flag, but there was little hope of being rescued five miles out at sea. After some hours he thought he saw a boat, but he was snowblind and dared not believe it. But it was his brave friends, and soon they had snatched him and the dogs to safety. When he got back a bronze tablet was put up in the hospital at St. Anthony. It read: "To the Memory of Three Noble Dogs, Moody, Watch, Spy, whose lives were given for mine on the ice, April 21st, 1908."

There was a Children's Home at St. Anthony as well as a hospital. "I used to collect stamps and butterflies and birds' eggs," said the Doctor. "Now I collect babies!" Poor orphan children found a good home there. Schools were needed next, and today there are three schools as well as five hospitals and the Children's Home. In 1927 the world-famous doctor was made Sir Wilfred Grenfell by King George V. He went on with his great work till his death in 1940. The Grenfell Association carries on his work today from its headquarters at St. Anthony. So his memory lives on, as he would wish, in the service of the fishermen of Labrador.

90 Prebendary Carlile and the Church Army

WILSON CARLILE was born in the year 1847 in the country near London. He had eleven brothers and sisters altogether, and they had plenty of fun in their big garden with each other. Though Wilson was the eldest of the children, he was not the strongest and he often missed school through being ill. His father was an important business man in London. He carried Wilson on his shoulder to see Queen Victoria in Hyde Park. Once David Livingstone, the famous missionary, came to his house with a little black boy. The children were very curious to see him, for they had never met a black child before in their lives. Wilson left school at fourteen and he went to France to learn the French language. When he came back, he went to work in his grandfather's business and soon he had to manage it when his grandfather fell ill. "I'll make a fortune by the time I'm twenty-five years old," Wilson promised himself.

Wilson worked hard at his business. Instead of riding the five miles to London in the horse-bus he used to run there and back again in the evening so as to keep fit. When the first wooden bicycles were invented, he rode his 'velocipede' to work, trying to beat the horse-bus. He was too busy making money to think much about God though he went to Chapel every Sunday. He had always loved music. He played the piano and the organ and the cornet too. Later on, he learnt to play the trombone. In the year 1870 Germany and France

312

went to war, and Wilson Carlile's business overseas ended. Within three years his fortune was gone. He fell ill with worry and while he lay in bed he had plenty of time to read and to think. It was then that his life was changed. "Jesus captured me," he said. For the rest of his life he worked for God instead of money.

Wilson Carlile was married now and he settled at Richmond in Surrey. There he joined the Church of England and soon he was busy running a boys' club, teaching in Sunday School, and teaching boys to read at night-school. In the year 1875 two famous Americans came to London to lead a religious campaign. Wilson Carlile went to help them with the music, but before long he, too, was calling people to God. He knew now that he must give his whole life to God. He went to college to study and in the year 1880 he became a minister in the Church of England. His church at Kensington was famous and important. But he wanted to get out into the streets and win people to Jesus. His open-air services became so popular that the police asked for them to stop. They were blocking roads and holding up traffic! Wilson Carlile gave up his fine church and went to lead missions in the slums of Westminster. There in the year 1882 he started his 'Church Army'. Notices of his meetings said—"The Church Army, under the command of the Reverend W. Carlile, declares war on sin. Come if you dare!" Often the little Army was attacked in the streets and in the newspapers too. But Wilson Carlile never gave in. "Go for the worst" was his motto and he was a fisher of men in the worst slums of London. A wealthy uncle gave him a house for his wife and five sons. He was never paid as leader of the Church Army.

Wilson Carlile led his Cadets through the streets with music. Every one played some instrument, and the 'Chief', as he was called, became famous for his trombone. Training Colleges were set up, first for men and later for women. Then as Captains and Sisters they went out to seek the lost in the parishes of England. But soon the Army found other work besides preaching the Gospel. A Home was set up for drunkards and tramps to bring them back to useful lives. Soon there were Homes in all the big cities. Men who were homeless and unemployed were cared for. Then in the year 1897 the Government at last allowed Wilson Carlile and his Army into the prisons. They were told that they must not let the prisoners laugh. But the Chief's sense

313

of humour was too great to be tied up by rules. Before long his Captains and Sisters were welcomed in prisons up and down the country. They were allowed to visit the prisoners in their cells and to have the keys. The Church Army cared for their families and found work for them when they were set free.

In the year 1892 Wilson Carlile came back from a stay in the country with a new idea. A van was bought to go out to lonely villages and hamlets to help the work of the Church. Within five years there were fifty Mission vans taking the Bible and its message to country folk. So the work grew, caring for both the souls and the bodies of the people. In the year 1914 the First World War broke out and there was new work to be done among the soldiers. By the end of the war the Church Army had set up 2,000 centres wherever there was fighting. In them the troops found a home from home. Every one had the sign over it—"Open to all". 'Bar-cars' took hot food to soldiers in the trenches. Parcels were sent to prisoners of war. Wherever there was a need, the Church Army was there.

Christian work among women and children was part of the Army's life from the beginning and it grew steadily. Today there are Homes for girls, 'Fresh Air Holiday Homes' for mothers and children, and 'Sunset Homes' for elderly women. A thousand houses have been built by the Church Army and they are let at low rents to those most in need.

The Church Army began to spread to other lands. The Chief went to Canada and the United States in 1926 to help its work, even though he was nearly eighty years old and often seriously ill. In 1939 the Second World War brought new work at home and overseas. Church Army vans went wherever there were troops. It was during the war that Wilson Carlile died. He had lived to be ninety-five years old, a valiant soldier of Jesus Christ. His finest memorial is the Church Army which he founded to love and to serve mankind. The work he began goes on throughout the world, taking the Gospel of Jesus to the needy both in word and in deed.

Azariah of India, Apostle of Unity

91

SAMUEL AZARIAH was born in the year 1874. His father, who had been born into the Hindu religion, had run away from home to become a Christian. Now he was a clergyman in a village of Tinnevelly in the south-east corner of India. In the Hindu religion everyone is born into a certain caste. Samuel's family belonged to the low caste of 'Nadars' or 'tree-climbers'. They climbed up the bare trunks of the tall palm trees to gather the sap from which black sugar is made. They were strong and clever people and, like Samuel's father, could become fine men if they were given education. Samuel had a good Christian home. "All my love for the Bible came to me from my mother," he once said.

When he was a boy he was told one day at school how Bishop Hannington had been put to death by the evil King M'wanga of Uganda. At once Samuel gave up his gold bangles, his most treasured possessions, to help the work of the Church in that land. At school Samuel practised his letters in the sand and learnt to read from books made of palm leaves. When he was ten years old he went to boarding school and from there to the Christian College at Madras.

When he left College, Samuel Azariah became secretary to the Young Men's Christian Association for South India. For thirteen years he worked among Indian students, travelling to Christian schools and colleges all over India. They had been founded by white

315

missionaries from abroad. Azariah knew how much India owed to them, but what were Indian Christians doing themselves? Azariah showed his young Christian friends how they must help to spread the Gospel among their own people. In the year 1905 they met in the famous library of William Carey at Serampore. There they formed 'The National Missionary Society of India'. Now Indians would be Christian missionaries to their own people.

Already Azariah and the Christians at Tinnevelly had set up their own missionary society. They had decided to work where no Christian mission had ever been. It was in the Telugu country where the outcastes lived. Two of them had settled at a small railway junction for the collieries named Dornakal. They had turned an old brewery into their mission and they had made out of it a chapel, a school, dormitories for the pupils, and rooms for the missionaries. It was not long before Azariah wanted to join them. He went to see the Bishop of Madras and offered himself for this work. Many of Azariah's friends were horrified. Their splendid leader would be throwing himself away, going to work among drunken outcastes. But the wise Bishop knew better. He was an Englishman and he knew that India must soon have Indian Bishops. He invited Azariah to stay with him and to prepare to become a clergyman. Azariah was ordained in the year 1909 and went at once to Dornakal.

By now Azariah had married a Christian woman who shared his faith and his burning zeal to spread the Good News of Jesus. She made a home for her husband and their six children in the old brewery at Dornakal. The outcastes lived in dirt and filth in their mud huts. They were the lowest caste, despised by everyone. The Hindus called them 'untouchables', and even the shadow of an outcaste defiled a good Hindu. They were always in debt to the money-lenders. They could not read or write. The only escape from their misery was in strong drink. Azariah travelled round their villages in a rough oxcart, bringing them the Gospel of love, teaching them to know the Christian God who loves all alike, high and low, rich and poor. They were too simple even to learn the Lord's Prayer. He taught them to pray in their own simple words. They learnt Bible stories by acting them. They learnt to praise God in songs and dances in their own Telugu tongue. Christian hymns were made into Telugu songs with the Indian music of drums, pipes, tambourines, and cymbals. So the Church grew among the outcastes.

But the fame of Azariah had spread far beyond the outcaste villages. In the year 1910 he was invited to speak at a great World Missionary Conference at Edinburgh in Scotland. Soon the Bishop of Madras made known his great plan. Some church leaders were horrified at the idea of an Indian Bishop. But when they met Azariah their doubts vanished and in 1912 he was made a Bishop in Calcutta Cathedral. The diocese of Dornakal, about the size of Wales, was given into the care of Bishop Azariah.

The new Bishop and his wife were already known and loved as 'Honourable Father and Mother', and the Bishop could speak the Telugu language well. Still he went round the villages in the bullock-cart. Fires were lit round the camp at night to keep away tigers. More and more outcastes were living new lives, giving up their evil ways. Hindus of high caste were astonished at the difference in their despised labourers. "We are better than them in our caste, our wealth and our education," they said to the Bishop. "But we do not have their joy." Bishop Azariah won everyone by his love and his humility. Every morning he rose at half-past four to be alone with God. The three most important things in his daily life were study of the Bible, the Service of the Holy Communion, and loving men for love of God. Dornakal grew into a great centre of the Church. It became even greater when in the year 1939 its new Cathedral of the Epiphany was hallowed to the service of God.

There were other Christian Churches in South India as well as the Church of England. How wrong it seemed to Bishop Azariah that the Church of God should be broken up into different parts—Methodists, Presbyterians, Congregationalists and Anglicans. Ceaselessly he worked to make them one. He died in 1945, but two years later his work was completed when the separate Churches joined together to form the United Church of South India. But Bishop Azariah looked beyond India. At World Missionary Conferences, and at the Lambeth Conference of the Bishops of his own Church, he pleaded for the unity of all Christians. The 'Apostle of the Outcastes' was also the 'Apostle of Unity'.

92 Bishop Fleming, Apostle of the Eskimos

ARCHIBALD FLEMING was born at Greenock in Scotland in the year 1883. He was brought up to love God and on the Lord's Day he and his eight brothers and sisters went to church two by two in their best Sunday clothes. Archibald was as mischievous as all boys. His mother died when he was seven years old and his sister Barbara had a hard task looking after him. One day sister Isa came home with an exciting story. She had seen an Eskimo in Dundee. He had come from Baffin Land on a whaler. She told her brother at bed-time how the Eskimos lived and how there was only one Christian missionary in all the frozen north. When Archibald said his prayers afterwards, he asked God to let him be a missionary to the Eskimos.

Mr. Fleming was a sea-captain and Archibald's ambition was to be a shipbuilder. When he left the Grammar School at Dunoon he went to work in the ship-building yards at Glasgow by the Clyde. For eight years he worked hard by day and studied at the University in the evenings. On Sundays he took a class of rough working-lads in a Glasgow Sunday School. One day in the year 1906 a friend passed him a magazine in the train on the way to work. In it was a letter from a Bishop in Canada asking for a young man to preach the Gospel to the Eskimos in Baffin Land. At once Archibald Fleming remembered his prayer as a boy. He realised now what his real ambition had always been. He offered himself to work for God in the Arctic. In

London he met the Reverend E. J. Peck, who had taken up the work begun by Bishop Bompas. Since 1876 he had lived among the Eskimos of Hudson Bay and in 1894 he had set up the first Christian Mission in Baffin Land. He had made the first grammar book of the Eskimo language which was published by the Government of Canada. He had turned the Book of Common Prayer, some hymns and parts of the Bible into Eskimo. He filled Archibald Fleming with a longing to serve the Eskimo people for love of God.

In the year 1908 Archibald Fleming sailed to Canada. Some of his friends had thought him foolish to give up the fine career in shipbuilding which lay ahead of him. But he knew he could only be truly happy in obeying the call of God. For a year he studied at Wycliffe College, Toronto, to be a clergyman. Then in 1909 he went to do mission work for two years in Baffin Land as part of his training. The sailing-ship *Lorna Doone* took him northwards from Newfoundland, stopping on the way at St. Anthony where Dr. Grenfell did his great work among the fisher folk of Labrador. The ship landed Archibald Fleming and his fellow-missionary at Lake Harbour in the south of Baffin Land. They lived half the year in their own mission hut and the rest with the Eskimos in their igloos. It was so bitterly cold that even ink froze, and their precious coal had to be eked out for two years. Archibald Fleming worked hard learning the Eskimo language. As there was no dictionary, he had to keep asking the names of things. During the winter he lived with the Eskimos in their stuffy, smelly igloos, travelling by sledge from one lonely settlement to another, learning to know and to love his people, teaching both children and their parents, sharing their joys and sorrows.

The Eskimos believed in over fifty different spirits who had to be feared and pleased. The 'angakok' or medicine-man used spells and magic and the Eskimos had charms and amulets to bring them good luck. Archibald Fleming spoke to them of the Great Spirit of Love and the simple, pagan Eskimos slowly turned from magic to worship God. Soon they had given him a new name—'In-nook-tah-kaub', 'One of the family'. It was sad to leave them when in 1911 he went back to Toronto to complete his studies and to be ordained a minister of God.

In 1913 the Reverend Archibald Fleming sailed back to Lake

Harbour to be greeted lovingly by his Eskimo friends. Soon they had built a little church at Lake Harbour. But as he went round the settlements to the west, services had to be held in igloos. Now there were Eskimo Christians, and the Service of bread and wine was held for the first time in an Eskimo snow-house. In the winter Archibald Fleming set off with his sledge and his faithful Eskimo friends, Pudno and Yarley, on a great adventure. He was the first white man to explore the Foxe Peninsula. Through snow-storms and the frozen stillness they plodded on over lakes of ice, sometimes losing their way completely for the maps were often wrong. They made new Eskimo friends, and returned safely, staying with old friends at Cape Dorset and Itinick on the way. For this brave exploration Archibald Fleming was made a Fellow of the Royal Geographical Society. There were other adventures before he left Baffin Land in 1915 for a rest and a holiday. The doctors forbade his return. For a year he had to rest and it was not till 1920 that Archibald Fleming was strong enough to return to the Arctic. Again there was a warm welcome at Lake Harbour, even from his old sledge dog. Now there had to be three services every Sunday because there were so many Eskimos who had come to follow the 'Jesus Way'. For Christian teachers like Pudno had carried on the work of the Church.

For another six years Archibald Fleming had to leave the north because of his health. Then in 1927 he was made Archdeacon of the Arctic to supervise all Christian missions among the Eskimos. Part of the year he spent touring the Arctic and the rest in visiting England to tell about his work and to raise money for it. In 1928 he toured the Western Arctic, where Bishop Bompas had pioneered, travelling 2,500 miles by steamer down the great Mackenzie River, visiting Christian schools, hospitals and missions, and reaching the Arctic Ocean at Atlavik. In 1933 he was made the first Bishop of the Arctic and the 'Flying Bishop' was taken around his diocese by brave flyers, meeting new dangers and adventures. 'Archibald the Arctic' was his new name. "It is the most romantic title in the world," said the Governor-General of Canada when he opened the new hospital at Atlavik in 1937. Bishop Fleming died in 1955 leaving behind him a flourishing Eskimo Church that can never forget the name of this brave adventurer of God.

320

93 Martyrs of Ecuador

NATHANIEL SAINT was born in the year 1923. He had a good Christian home in Philadelphia in the United States of America. Often his sister Rachel read stories to him of missionaries in other lands and Nat grew up with a longing to take the Good News of Jesus to people who had never heard of him. When he was seven years old, his brother took him up in his aeroplane and from that day Nat thought of nothing but flying. As soon as he could, he joined the Air Force. But he was broken-hearted when a weakness in his leg meant that he could not be accepted for flying. When he left the Air Force he went to College to prepare for his life as a missionary. Then one day there came exciting news. Two former pilots had set up the 'Missionary Aviation Fellowship'. They needed other pilots to help in this new and exciting Christian adventure. They planned to use aeroplanes to help missionaries in their work and to link together lonely mission-stations. Nat joined them at once and in 1948 he and his wife flew to Ecuador.

The country of Ecuador lies high up in the mountains of South America. From Quito, the capital city, Nat flew 100 miles south to his new headquarters on the edge of the jungle at the foot of the mountains. It was a place called Shell Mera, from which there is a road to Quito. There he built houses for himself and a second pilot as well as a hangar, making it into a base for their operations and a centre for missionaries throughout the jungle. For seven years he flew between the mission stations, bringing supplies and medicines and letters, and swiftly flying out the sick to hospital. He knew how dangerous it was, landing on the tiny air-strips, but he believed that his life was in the hands of God and he was content to serve him. He became a skilled pilot and he invented a new way of dropping supplies safely. While flying his Piper aeroplane in a spiral, he let out a canvas bucket on a long fishing line. As he circled lower, the bucket hung almost still in the centre of the spiral and he could land it just where he wanted. The bucket contained either supplies or a telephone so that he could find exactly what was wanted without having to land. How grateful lonely missionaries were to have this regular and speedy link with the outside world!

Among them was Ed McCully. He had come out to Ecuador in 1952 with his friends, Jim Elliot and Peter Fleming. Ed had been a good athlete at College and planned to be a lawyer. But God had called him and now he lived at the tiny mission-station of Arajuno with his wife and their little son. Jim Elliot was at Shandia and Peter Fleming at Puyu Pungu. These three fine young Christian men worked among the Quichua Indians. They had learnt the language of the simple, primitive people and they lived among them, healing their bodies, teaching them in their own language, and making known to them the God of love.

South of the Quichua tribes lived the fierce Jivaro tribe of head-hunters. But even more savage were the Aucas, a Stone Age people who lived to the east and were feared by all the tribes. With their sharp wooden spears they killed anyone who went near them. The only white men they had known were the greedy rubber traders who, about sixty years ago, plundered the Indians and treated them like animals. The four missionary friends longed to take the Gospel to the Aucas, ready to give their lives, if need be, in the service of their Master. One day Nat and Ed flew east and found an Auca settlement in a jungle clearing. Excitedly they told their two friends and their wives. They had to make their plans secretly. For even the Government of Ecuador avoided the savage Aucas and no one would go near them without a gun—the only thing the Aucas feared. The four missionaries knew that these suspicious, primitive people could only be won by love, not fear. They made careful plans while they learnt some of the language from an Auca girl who had run away from her tribe. They began to fly regularly over the Auca settlement from Arajuno, which lay close to Auca territory. The native huts were by a stream and once each week they dropped gifts on the beach below, using Nat's dropping bucket with its automatic release. Each time there were more naked Aucas on the beach below. Now they came lower, making signs of friendship with their hands and calling over the loudspeaker in Auca language, "We are your friends!" The Aucas began to send gifts back to them on the line, and to clear the trees round their settlement. So the way was prepared.

On Tuesday, January 3rd, 1956, the four missionaries landed on a sandy beach which they had selected as a landing-strip. It was by the river Curaray, four miles from the Auca huts. They had chosen Roger Youderian to make up their team, and after five plane journeys they set up their base on 'Palm Beach', as they called it, with supplies for two weeks. Each day they flew over the Auca settlement and waited for visitors. On the Friday three Aucas appeared. "Puinani!" "Welcome," shouted the missionaries. They made friends as best they could and took one Auca for a ride in the plane over his village. But the next day no Aucas welcomed them as they flew over. On the Sunday they radioed their wives as usual, saying that they had seen ten Auca men coming towards Palm Beach. The next radio call never came. A search party found their five bodies lying in the river, struck down from behind by the spears and knives of the Aucas.

The President of Ecuador honoured the sacrifice of the five brave martyrs. As the grim news spread in the United States, hundreds of other young Christian men offered to take their place. In Ecuador Christians from among the Quichua and Jivaro Indians prepared to go to the Aucas. The wives of the five martyrs had no bitterness. Today the wife of Jim Elliot and Rachel Saint, who once read missionary stories to her brother Nat, live among the same Aucas who murdered their loved ones, showing them in both word and deed the Christian love for which the five brave martyrs of Ecuador gave their lives.

Brother Douglas, Apostle of the Outcasts

DOUGLAS DOWNES was born in England in the year 1878. His father was a Methodist minister and a writer and Douglas was brought up to love God. He was the youngest in his family and his mother sometimes spoiled him. The headmaster of his school in London told the boys stories of missionaries at school assembly, and even when he was eleven years old Douglas decided that he wanted to be a missionary. Three years later he read the story of St. Francis, the humble disciple of Jesus. Douglas could never forget his life of love and joy and prayer.

In the year 1896 Douglas went to Oxford University. While he was there he decided that he would give his life to the service of God, and in 1903 he became a clergyman in the Church of England. He began his work for God among the poorest people of London. He had good lodgings in his parish at Lambeth but Douglas soon decided to move. He must live with the poor and be one of them. He found two empty rooms at the top of an old house. His furniture was made of orange-boxes painted over. He shared everything he had with his poor friends. He loved best to work among men. At his Men's Club he made friends with tramps and beggars, with drunkards and down-and-outs. "I can't preach for toffee," he said. But he showed them the love of God by the way he lived.

In the year 1908 Douglas was asked to go out to India. His work

325

was to teach at a Christian College. Again, he soon gave up his rooms in the College and lived with his Indian students. In his spare time he travelled round the villages with his lantern and slides. Once he went on a long train journey to the north and saw Mount Everest. "It was like a vision of God," he said, "to see this great white temple." When his six years in India were over Douglas came back to England. Then the First World War broke out and Douglas was asked to be a Chaplain to the British Army. He went out to Egypt to care for soldiers who were convalescing from illness. His camps were near the Pyramids and he took his men round to see the sights. He was full of fun and joy and played the piano for the evening sing-songs in camp. But the men knew that his love and his joy came from his life of prayer with God.

When the war ended Douglas went to work among the students at Oxford University. But he soon found work to do among men who were poor and unemployed. He met Brother Giles who lived like St. Francis among the tramps. When he was offered a farm in Dorset for his work, Douglas persuaded him to accept it. So Flowers Farm, near Cerne Abbas, became the 'Home of St. Francis'. In the year 1922 Brother Giles fell ill and Douglas was asked to take his place. "I'll gladly do it till someone better comes along," he said, cheerfully. He was to follow St. Francis for the rest of his life. The Reverend Douglas Downes became 'Brother Douglas'.

Brother Douglas believed that anything could be done by hard work and trust in God. He was busy all day long, working in the garden, washing clothes in an old copper, even trying to make jam. But his bees were his favourites and he regarded them as his friends. Soon the men at the Home were busy at crafts, weaving, carving and making baskets. Fruit and vegetables from the garden were sold in the market at Dorchester. They were taken there by an old donkey named 'Madam' and then in an old car called 'The Flying Bedstead'. The tramps who came to stay were called 'way-faring folk' by Brother Douglas. The only thing he did not like was laziness. Tramps who would not join in work of some kind were "given their sandwiches"— sent off with food for their journey. But Brother Douglas always hated having to do this. It was a happy life at the Home—work and prayer, games and sing-songs and dances.

Life was hard in England in those days. Many men could find no work. They became beggars or thieves or tramps. They slept on the Embankment in London, in dirty lodging-houses, or in the hard and strict 'work-houses'. Brother Douglas went with them on the roads and slept where they did. He wore the brown 'habit' of the friar, just like St. Francis of old. Soon he was asked to go to the House of Commons to talk about the hard life of the tramps, and new laws were made to care for them. Brother Douglas went round the country speaking and raising money for his work. In the year 1932 five new Homes were opened, to care for men without work or homes. When the wayfarers left after a few months they would be found work in the trades they had learned.

The new Brotherhood of St. Francis needed rules to live by. They lived in poverty, having simply the necessities of life. They did not marry, for their lives were given to God. They lived in obedience to the Brotherhood. When the first Brothers took their vows in the year 1931 they chose Brother Douglas as their Prior or Head. Often he had to be away from the Home, leading missions and pilgrimages and preaching about his work. Then in the year 1939 the Second World War began. Brother Douglas went to London to work among soldiers at a big Hostel opposite Westminster Abbey. He lived in a little room at the top and made a garden on the roof, and kept chickens there. Hundreds of soldiers who stayed at the Hostel on their way through London came to know Brother Douglas as a friend.

In the year 1943 Brother Douglas was asked to go out to Canada to start a Brotherhood there. He was 67 years old now but he found work to do for God among the lumberjacks. When the war ended, he was asked to go to Germany and he settled in the bombed city of Hamburg. At first he worked among British soldiers. But soon he felt the great need of the Germans and he turned to help wounded soldiers. He came back to England where he died in the year 1957. "He was the Apostle of the Outcasts", someone said of this modern Saint Francis.

95 Bishop Berggrav, Hero of Norway

EIVIND BERGGRAV was born in the year 1884 in the city of Stavanger, a seaport in the south-west of Norway. His father was a clergyman and from him Eivind learnt to love the Bible as the word of God. He was a clever boy and he went from school to the University in Oslo, the capital city of Norway. But he was clever with his hands, too, and he wanted to be an engineer. His father hoped that he would be a clergyman but Eivind wanted to make up his own mind. First, in the year 1908, he went to study abroad as many Norwegian students do. For their country is small in population and they all learn English at school. Eivind went to study at universities in England, Germany and Sweden. When he returned to Norway in 1909 he became a teacher at the new National High School. Berggrav was a good teacher and he taught his pupils to know and to live the Christian faith. Then in the year 1919 he was ordained as a clergyman and went to care for the parish of Hurdal, near the city of Oslo.

Pastor Berggrav was a real shepherd to his people. He liked young people best of all for he understood their difficulties in living the Christian life. He had a fine sense of fun and he used to rush about in an old Ford car. When he tore past in a cloud of dust the country folk would say, "That must be the devil—if it isn't Pastor Berggrav." In 1925 he moved into the city of Oslo to care for the men in prison. He showed them the love of God in his life as well as in his words. He could talk simply to them of the things of God. But he had a clever mind and the students crowded to his lectures at the University of Oslo. He was asked to be Chairman of the Student Christian Movement as well, and he led a busy life. Often he had to be away from home, but he set aside special days to spend with his wife Kathrine and their four sons.

In the year 1929 Berggrav was made a Bishop of the Norwegian Church. He left Oslo to become Bishop of Halogoland far away in the north of Norway. Some people thought it wrong that this fine Christian leader should go away from the capital city to work among the lonely mountains of the north. But Bishop Berggrav was happy in the 'land of the midnight sun', where the Lapps wander with their herds of reindeer. Sometimes during the long dark months of winter the Bishop travelled over the snow to lonely villages in a Lapp sledge pulled by reindeer. Often he went by boat to visit the fishing hamlets in the 'fiords' or 'creeks' which cut the coasts of Norway. He won the love of the fishing folk by his ceaseless care for them.

In 1937 a new Bishop of Oslo was needed and Bishop Berggrav was called back to the capital city. Already Bishop Berggrav was famous in his own land. Now he was becoming well-known in other lands, too. He was a leader in the movement to bring the separate Christian Churches together again. At meetings and conferences in different parts of the world the Bishop of Oslo worked with Church leaders from other lands for Christian unity. Plans were made for setting up a 'World Council of Churches'. But before it could meet in the year 1939, the Second World War had been started by Adolf Hitler, the leader of the German people.

Hitler needed to win Norway in order to protect his shipping and to get the Swedish iron ore which was exported through the Norwegian port of Narvik. On the night of April 8th in 1940, German merchant ships lay peacefully in all the chief ports. But their holds were packed with German soldiers and by the next morning Hitler's Nazis and spies had taken over Norway. The King tried to resist but he was forced to leave his land. At first the Nazis promised to respect the laws and customs of Norway. But their evil intentions soon appeared and the people of Norway began to oppose them. Bishop Berggrav united all Christians behind him, and all the bishops gave

329

up their posts under the State. By 1942 the Church aided the people to resist the Germans. A traitor named Major Quisling had been set up as ruler by the Nazis. He sent for Bishop Berggrav. "I ought to have shot you a hundred times!" he shouted. "Well, here I am," said the Bishop calmly. He was forbidden to preach to the people, but he announced that he would preach in Oslo Cathedral on Easter Day. On the Thursday before Easter Bishop Berggrav was arrested and taken to his lonely cottage at Asker, fifteen miles from Oslo, high above the fiord. There he was kept a prisoner for three years till the war ended in 1945.

Bishop Berggrav was ready for this. He could not speak himself that Easter Sunday in 1942. But his words were read in churches all over the land. In Norway clergymen are appointed by the Government to record births and marriages and deaths. "We give up our State appointments," the pastors of Norway said that Sunday. "We will do all our spiritual work but we cannot obey evil rulers. We must obey our conscience. We must be free to speak for God. Parents and teachers must be free to bring up their children in the faith of our fathers." Inspired by the Church, the people united in resisting the Germans. Children were ordered to join the Nazi youth organisation, but their parents kept them at home. Teachers were ordered to teach the German language instead of English, but they refused to do so. Many of them were imprisoned but the schools went on as before. Some of the pastors were thrown out but none of them would obey the Germans.

Bishop Berggrav lived in his lonely cottage. Young Norwegian traitors guarded him but he soon won them over and the Germans had to change them frequently. He kept well by chopping wood. He had his long Norwegian pipe to smoke. Above all, he had his Bible to strengthen him. Messengers came secretly through the woods in the night. From prison he guided his church and inspired his people.

The war ended in 1945 and Bishop Berggrav was free again to carry on his work as leader of the Church of Norway and as a founder of the World Council of Churches. He died in 1959 but the memory of this courageous Christian leader is treasured in many lands and especially in his own land as a great hero of Norway.

Kagawa of Japan, Worker for the Poor

TOYOHIKO KAGAWA ought to have been a very unhappy child. He was born in the year 1888 in the city of Kobe in Japan. When he was four years old he became an orphan and had to go to live in the family village. No one wanted him and he had no friends to play with. He was treated cruelly by his foster-grandmother. He found friends in the animals and birds, and loved to help on the farm. He loved reading too and found out all he could about Buddhism, the religion of his people. When he was twelve he went to live with his uncle in the city. He was a very rich man and planned a fine career for his clever nephew. But Kagawa found a real friend, an American missionary. Soon he was reading the Bible. He loved best the Sermon on the Mount and he prayed, "O God, make me like Jesus Christ." He decided he wanted to become a Christian and to give his life to God. His uncle was furious and turned him out. Kagawa gave up the wealth he would have inherited from his uncle. Without money and without a home he began training to be a Christian minister. He had a long and serious illness, but as soon as he could he went straight back to work.

Kagawa spent part of the day studying and the rest in the dreadful slums of the city of Kobe. Eleven thousand people lived there like animals in tiny rooms like prison cells. They were very poor, many lived by evil and crime, and dreadful diseases spread like fire every

331

year through the dark, crowded slums. Kagawa went among them telling them about 'Yaso', the Japanese word for Jesus. But soon he realised he must live with them if he wanted to teach them the love of God. There was one empty house where no one would live, for a murder had happened in it. Kagawa made it his home. Everyone was welcome there—thieves and beggars, sick people and homeless people. From one of them Kagawa caught a disease which left him nearly blind. Often Kagawa was attacked by thieves and ruffians, but gradually people came to respect him for his courage and his love. "I love men. I can't help loving them," said this saintly Christian.

For fifteen years Kagawa lived in the slums of Kobe helping the poor. But he soon came to realise that there was more to be done. These people needed better conditions of work. Kagawa studied the problems of industry. Soon he began to write books, which told people the dreadful life of the poor and showed how it could be made better. Trade Unions were needed to protect the workers from greedy employers. They were against the law and Kagawa was followed by the police and sometimes he was arrested. But he was a wonderful writer and his books became very famous. Before long he was known throughout Japan. The Government were forced to improve the slums and the conditions of the workers.

In the summer of 1923 a terrible earthquake shook Japan. The capital city of Tokyo lay in ruins. More than a million people lost their homes and many were burned in the fires. Kagawa hurried to the city and was soon leading the work of caring for them. The Government asked him to help them in rebuilding, and he became one of the leaders of his country. He had new opportunities of serving the poor, and the money from his books went to help them.

For some years Kagawa travelled to other countries to find out more about the conditions of workers. When he came back he found a new evil. The military leaders of Japan were planning to go to war. Kagawa loved his country, but he loved God even more. In 1940 he was put into prison for speaking against those who wanted war. When he came out he still preached peace. But in 1941 Japan attacked the American fleet at Pearl Harbour and was at war with America and Great Britain. In Japan a man could be sent to prison even for 'dangerous thoughts'. Twice during the war Kagawa was put in prison. When war ended in 1945 Japan had been beaten and some of its cities were destroyed. There was much to be done for the poor workers.

Kagawa was asked to join the new Government but he refused. He knew that his true work was to care for the poor and to teach them the love of God in both word and deed. Till his death in 1960 he lived and worked among them, preaching the Good News of Jesus, writing his books, seeking justice for everyone. He followed in the steps of Jesus, spreading the Kingdom of God on earth, living a life of peace and goodwill and love.

97 Albert Schweitzer of West Africa

ALBERT SCHWEITZER grew up in a village of Alsace in France. His father was a minister and his home was poor. He had to wear second-hand coats made from the old clothes of his father or his uncle. Once he refused to wear his overcoat. It was not because he thought it was ugly, but because there were boys in his school who had not even old overcoats to keep them warm. He was a good friend to them, but he would not go with them when they went out to shoot birds with their catapults. He knew that God made all living creatures and he believed that it must be wrong to kill them. He always reverenced all living things.

One day he went to the city of Colmar near his home. There was a famous statue in the city put there as a memorial. It was a huge figure of a negro. Its face looked sad and hopeless, and Albert Schweitzer gazed at it for a long time. The negro seemed to be appealing to him, and that statue haunted him long afterwards. He was a clever scholar and went on from school to the university. He became a Doctor of Philosophy and a Doctor of Theology. He could easily have become a famous professor. But when he was twenty-one years old he had decided to give his life to God. He would serve God by serving his fellow-men. He became a minister and worked in the city of Strasbourg. He went on with his studies and wrote books which made him famous. There was something else he could do, too. Ever since he was

334

a boy he had loved music and had become a very good organist. He loved best the organ music of Bach, and he wrote a great book about it which made him even more famous. He was still young and everyone thought what a fine, rich life he would have.

But when he was thirty years old Albert Schweitzer decided how he would serve God. He had never forgotten that statue of the negro at Colmar. He remembered it whenever he heard sad stories of the negroes in Africa. Now he decided he would give his life to them. He began to study again, this time to be a Doctor of Medicine. Many people were astonished. Fancy giving up a wonderful life to go and

live among negroes! But Albert Schweitzer went on with his studies. He often thought of the words of Jesus: "Freely ye have received, freely give." God had given him so much. He must give something in return. He finished his studies and in the year 1913 he sailed to Africa.

He settled at a place called Lambarene by the River Ogowe. It is in West Africa, near the equator. The thick, dark jungle there was full of poisonous insects. The negroes who lived there suffered from many awful diseases such as sleeping-sickness, malaria, and leprosy. They were haunted too by their belief in evil spirits, which terrified them. The fearful witch-doctors had great power and cruel, savage deeds were done at their command.

The news soon spread among the negroes and they came from all round about to see the white doctor. Schweitzer had only a hut for his hospital at first. His 'magic' seemed very powerful to the black people. He gave each patient a small round disc to hang around his neck. On it was written the date, the illness, and the treatment. It was very precious to the natives, for they believed it was a fetish that could work magic. They called the Doctor 'Oganga'—'Medicine Man'. But they soon found he was more than that. He told his patients that the Lord Jesus had sent him and his wife to Lambarene and that many white people had given money for his work of caring for sick negroes. His fame spread quickly and his work grew. Many of his patients suffered from jungle diseases. Others were lumbermen whose limbs had been crushed by giant trees. Others were men and women saved from a cruel death ordered by the witch-doctor. Soon a real hospital was needed and Dr. Schweitzer built it himself, showing his black helpers that there is nothing shameful in hard work.

Every few years Dr. Schweitzer went back to Europe to rest from his work, and to raise money for it by his lectures and organ recitals. He became famous, and he was awarded the great Nobel Peace Prize for his service to mankind. He died at his hospital in 1965, but his name and his example live on. He believed that all men, white and black, are children of God and should live together in peace and brotherhood. He gave up riches and honours to live a humble life in the service of others, and all over the world men honour him as a true disciple of Jesus Christ.

Helen Keller, Worker for the Deaf and Dumb

In the year 1880 a daughter was born to Captain and Mrs. Keller. They lived near the town of Tuscumbia in Alabama, one of the United States of America. Captain Keller had fought for the states of the south in the American Civil War. It had only ended a few years before, and there was still some bad feeling between northerners and southerners. Little Helen knew nothing of this. She was a fine, strong baby with golden hair and bright eyes. Soon she was tottering about, making friends with the farm animals and tumbling among the flowers. She had a lively mind and picked up new words quickly. Then, one day when she was getting on for two years old, she fell ill with a fever. The doctor thought she would die. But Helen was strong and she recovered. But it was not long before her mother made some horrible discoveries. Little Helen did not blink when anything came near her eyes. She did not hear people speaking even when they shouted. So she learnt no more words and soon she had forgotten those she did know. Helen was blind and deaf and soon she was dumb.

Helen lived in a dark and lonely world. She followed her mother everywhere, holding on to her skirts. She knew things by feeling with her hands and by their scent, and she loved the garden best of all. She tried to make sounds and to 'speak' to people by signs. She had so much to say and she could not say it. She was full of life but she was

337

shut up in a lonely prison. So she grew angry and rolled about in her rage, biting and kicking. One doctor after another said there was no hope for her.

Helen's parents let her do what she wanted. Their friends said, "She is becoming an idiot. You ought to put her in an asylum." Life was without hope for the blind and deaf in those days. There were no special schools or homes then where they could be educated. Many of them did become idiots because no one tried to teach them. But in the year 1837 a school for the deaf and blind had been started in the city of Boston by Doctor Howe. He wore bandages over his eyes so that he could feel as his blind pupils did. He taught them by having special books printed, with letters just the same as ours, but 'raised', so that they could be felt on the paper. He used the ancient deaf-and-dumb alphabet too. But it needed two hands and it would not do for blind people who could not see the letter signs. He changed it so that one person 'spoke' by tapping the letter signs on the hand of the 'listener'.

Mrs. Keller sent to Doctor Howe's school as soon as she heard of it, pleading for a teacher for Helen. Anne Sullivan was chosen. She was nineteen years old and had had a sad life. She had been nearly blind and brought up in a grim workhouse. Now she could see quite well but she had learnt to read as a blind girl. In the year 1887 she went to Helen's home to be her teacher.

Anne began at once. She gave Helen a doll and spelt 'd-o-l-l' into her hand. She made Helen behave at the meal-table, too. Often there were tantrums and once Helen knocked out one of Anne's teeth. Captain Keller grew angry and wanted to send Anne back. "She's a a no-good Yankee!" he said. Then one day Anne took Helen to the pump and splashed water over her hand. 'W-a-t-e-r' she spelt on Helen's other hand. At last Helen realised that everything had a name. Now Helen learnt quickly and the doors of her prison slowly opened. Soon she was making friends with animals and flowers once again but now she knew their names and learnt about them. She read books printed in the Braille letters with her fingers. She wrote letters to her relatives and friends. She learnt geography by making islands and lakes down by the river. She learnt to sew and to knit. She had no more rages. Helen was growing into a clever girl. She was kind, too,

and very friendly.

The story of Helen Keller spread and soon she was famous. Teacher Anne took her on journeys. The first place they went to was the Blind School at Boston. When they returned home, Helen began to study languages. Anne still taught her by hand. But when Helen learnt the Morse Code, Anne could 'speak' to her at a distance by tapping dots and dashes with her foot and Helen felt the vibrations on the floor. She was always reading her Braille books and now she had a type-writer for the blind, too. When she was ten years old Helen started trying to speak. She learnt by feeling her teacher's mouth and throat. It was hard work and took many years of patience. There were so many other things to learn. In the year 1896 Helen went to a high school and four years later she entered Radcliffe College at Cambridge in the State of Massachusetts. Teacher Anne was always by her side and they spent four crowded years at College. Helen 'read' her Braille books till her finger tips were often bleeding. Now she began writing

339

books herself, and *The Story of My Life* became very famous. In 1904 Helen passed her examinations. She had taken no longer than any normal girl to win her degree.

Helen and Anne went to live on a farm near Boston City. Anne rested her tired eyes while Helen wrote her books to earn money. Ropes were tied from tree to tree in the grounds so that she could go for a walk when she wanted to. She had her precious dog, too. But often she was.away from home, travelling over the world. She gave talks about the blind and deaf, raising money for them and working for Schools and Homes for them. So the years passed, writing and lecturing. In the year 1936 dear Teacher Anne died, at the age of seventy years. Polly Thompson from Scotland took her place as best she could, living with Helen Keller at her home in America, and answering for her the letters which always poured in from all over the world. For by her courage Helen Keller had brought new life and new hope to the blind and deaf in every land. She died in 1968, but her memory lives on in the special schools for blind children and for deaf children. The care and skill and patience of their teachers prepare them to live happy and useful lives in the world.

A PRAYER FOR THE DEAF AND DUMB

Almighty Father,
Whose blessed Son Jesus Christ
Opened the lips of the dumb
And the ears of the deaf:
Show Thy great compassion,
We beseech Thee,
On all who today
Lack powers of speech and hearing:
That they by faith
May hear plainly Thy voice of love,
And sing Thy praises joyfully in their lives.
Through the same Jesus Christ our Lord.   Amen.

(E. Milner-White)

A PRAYER FOR DEAF AND DUMB CHILDREN

Lord Jesus Christ,
We pray
For children who have never been able to hear.
Help them
To persevere in learning to speak,
And in gaining knowledge.
And to their teachers
Give great patience.
We ask this for Thine own name's sake.   Amen.

(T. H. Sutcliffe)

A POEM BY HELEN KELLER

With alert fingers I listen
To the showers of sound
That the wind shakes from the forest.
I bathe in the liquid shade
Under the pines, where the air hangs cool
After the shower is done.
My saucy little friend the squirrel
Flips my shoulder with his tail,
Leaps from leafy billow to leafy billow,
Returns to eat his breakfast from my hand.
Between us there is glad sympathy;
He gambols; my pulses dance;
I am exultingly full of the joy of life!

From "A Chant of Darkness"

99 Gladys Aylward, Heroine of China

GLADYS AYLWARD was born at Edmonton in London in the year 1901. Her father was a postman and Gladys played in the street with her sister Violet like the other children of the neighbourhood. At school and at Sunday School she learnt to know and to love her Bible and to trust in God. She loved hymn-singing best of all. When the big, frightening Zeppelins sailed over London to drop bombs, in the First World War, Gladys collected her young friends at her house. They sang hymns to drown the noise and to forget their fear.

When Gladys left school she became a parlour-maid. One day she read in a magazine about the China Inland Mission which had been set up by Hudson Taylor. 200 missionaries were needed in China. "That is what God wants me to do," Gladys decided. At once she offered herself to the Mission and she went to train at its College. But after three months the Principal sent for her. "Learning is too hard for you," he said kindly. "Besides, by the time you finished the course here you would be thirty years old. You would find it very hard to learn a new language at that age. There are many other ways to serve God." Gladys Aylward went back sadly to her old work but she could not give up her great ambition. Had not Abraham obeyed God and gone out into a strange land? Did not Moses take up God's call and lead his people out into the wilderness? "They trusted in God. I will, too!" she vowed.

342

Since the Mission would not accept Gladys, she knew she would have to find the money herself to get to China. She went to a new post in the household of a famous explorer in London. When she got there Gladys had 2½d. and her Bible. "O God," she prayed, "here's my Bible and my money and here's me. Please use us!" It cost £90 to go to China by sea. But Gladys found that going by railway right across Europe would cost £47 10s. 0d. "But Russia and China are at war and you might never get to China," she was told. Nothing could put her off and she began to save hard, working even in her free time to earn extra money. One day she heard of Mrs. Lawson, a missionary in China, who was very old and wanted a helper. Gladys wrote to her at once and soon came an exciting letter from China. "If you can get to Tientsin I will send a guide to meet you," Mrs. Lawson wrote. Gladys saved harder than ever.

In October 1930 Gladys Aylward left London by train for China. She had 9d. in her pocket, a traveller's cheque for £2, her passport and her train tickets, her Bible, one suitcase for her clothes and another full of food. A saucepan and a kettle were tied to a suitcase with string. For ten days the train rattled and jolted across Europe and Siberia. Then, near the borders of Manchuria, there came the sound of guns and the train could go no further. Gladys Aylward had to walk back many miles along the railway track to the last station, camping at night on the line in the bitter wind and blinding snow of Siberia. She got another train to Vladivostok and from there went by boat to Japan where missionaries helped her to find a ship sailing to China. At last, after travelling for a month, Gladys Aylward reached Tientsin in China. Then by train and bus and mule she went far inland to Yangcheng where she found Mrs. Lawson living in a tumble-down house.

Gladys Aylward soon found how difficult her work would be. Chinese peasants threw mud at her. "You must not mind," Mrs. Lawson said. "We are 'Lao-yang-kwei'—'foreign devils' to them. We must get to know them. Let's turn this house into an Inn for the Muleteers. Yang, my old cook, will give them good food. We will tell them Bible stories. Then they will carry the Good News of Jesus wherever they go." Soon the Inn was repaired and opened. 'The Inn of Eight Happinesses' it was named. At first none of the muleteers

343

would come. Then Gladys dragged the first mule of a train into the Inn. The other mules followed and the muleteers had to come too. Before long good food and fine stories filled the Inn every night. Yang taught Gladys the Chinese language and so she too could tell stories of Jesus.

When Mrs. Lawson died, Gladys Aylward was left alone. One day the Mandarin of Yangcheng came to the Inn with all his servants. "The Government has made a new law," he said. "Women must not bind their feet any more. We need a woman to see this law is carried out. You can have wages, a mule and two soldiers. Will you do it?" "Yes," said Gladys, "so long as you realise that I shall teach my Christian religion wherever I go." "That is your own affair," replied the Mandarin. Gladys went round the villages, seeing that the new law was obeyed, and making friends with the women and children. Eagerly they listened to stories of Jesus, the peasant of Galilee who came from God and died to win their love.

Gladys Aylward lived a busy life. One day she was summoned urgently to the prison where thieves and cut-throats were rioting. Boldly she went in, while frightened soldiers stayed safely outside, and stopped the killing. The fame of 'Ai-weh-deh', 'The Virtuous One', spread wider than ever. Another day she met a dirty child-dealer and bought the poor little girl she had for sale out of pity. Before long Gladys Aylward had adopted four other orphan children.

In 1938 war came to Yangcheng. Japanese bombers came over, killing and maiming, and soon they were followed by soldiers. Gladys Aylward was beaten unconscious with rifle butts and kicks. Later, the Japanese offered 100 dollars reward for her capture. Gladys had 100 orphan children to care for. She took them across the mountain and the great Yellow River to safety at Sian in the south. Then after a long illness she came back to England. Gladys Aylward had been 20 years in China. But in 1957, with her health restored, she went back to the East. There, on the island of Formosa, Gladys Aylward, the London parlour-maid, went on with her great work for God, spreading the Gospel of Jesus among the Chinese people, until her death in 1970.

Martin Luther King, Leader of Black Americans

100

WHEN the Pilgrim Fathers landed in America, in the year 1620, they found the land where they settled inhabited by Red Indians. But in the far south, in the islands of the West Indies, there were people of another race already living in the New World of America. They were black-skinned negroes from Africa. They had been taken to America from their African homeland to work as slaves.

John Hawkins, a famous English seaman in the reign of Queen Elizabeth I, first took negro slaves to the Spanish colonies in America and traded them for fine cargoes. Many English seamen followed him in the slave trade. So did adventurers from the other seafaring countries of Europe. These countries set up colonies in the New World, where land was plentiful, and great wealth could be made. But they all needed workers to develop their colonies—to work on the plantations and down the mines. Negro slaves, snatched from their homes in Africa, and brought across the sea, were used to the hot climate. They were cheap, too, and the slave-traders kept up the supply.

More and more settlers came to the New World. There grew up thirteen British colonies, ruled from England. But they rebelled, and their war against England ended in 1783 when the colonies won their freedom. They formed themselves into The United States of America by their Declaration of Independence. Its most famous words were—"All men are created equal. All men have the right to Life, Liberty, and the pursuit of Happiness".

But the negroes from Africa had no liberty—they were slaves, not free men. By 1850 there were more than three million negro slaves in the United States. Most of them were in the South, toiling on the plantations, producing cotton and tobacco and sugar for their rich owners. Slavery there was one of the causes of the terrible Civil War between the States of the North and the States of the South. It was during the war, in 1862, that President Abraham Lincoln set free all the slaves in the United States of America.

The negroes were now *free* citizens of the United States. They were black Americans. But they were still not *equal* with white Americans. They did not have the same rights as citizens—that is, *civil rights*. Many laws and customs separated black citizens from white citizens —in schools and colleges, in cinemas and hotels, in buses, and even in some churches. Black Americans could not hope for better jobs, with more pay, because of their poor education. In any case, many jobs were closed to them. They were second-class citizens, lower than white citizens. They badly needed a leader to help them to win their civil rights.

It was in 1955 that a leader rose up—Martin Luther King. He was a negro minister in Montgomery, a town in the State of Alabama in the deep South. A law of the town ordered that a negro, sitting in a bus, must give up the seat to any white person who was standing. A certain black woman refused to do this, and she was arrested. The negro ministers of Montgomery asked the black people in their churches not to travel by bus on the day of her trial. Their appeal was very successful, for nearly three-quarters of all bus passengers in the town were negroes. The black citizens decided to go on with their ban, refusing to travel on the town's buses. They chose Martin Luther King as their leader. Their ban lasted for 382 days. Then the judges of the Supreme Court of the whole United States ordered that all citizens, black and white, must have equal rights on the buses in the town of Montgomery.

This was the first victory of black Americans in seeking their civil rights as equal citizens. It made Dr. King famous throughout the country. But it brought him bitter enemies among white people, too.

When a bomb exploded outside his house a crowd of angry negroes quickly gathered.

"Now let's not get panicky", Dr. King said to them. "If you have weapons take them home. We cannot solve this problem through violence. We must love our white brothers no matter what they do to us. We must make them know that we love them. Jesus still cries out—'Love your enemies'. That is what we must live by. We must meet hate with love".

In other towns, too, black citizens began to claim their rights as equal citizens. But Dr. King always taught his followers to seek them peacefully—not by force and violence. In 1960 four students from a University in North Carolina decided to see if this way would work. They started a "sit-in" at a lunch counter, in a Woolworth's store, which was for white people only. Other students joined them, newspapers spread the story, and soon there were negro "sit-ins" throughout the United States. These negroes were often attacked, but they would not use violence and fight back. Shopkeepers and businessmen lost trade, and in more and more places they ended the separation of white and black citizens.

During the next year the followers of Dr. King held "freedom rides". They drove in buses down to the States in the South where negroes were most despised. They organised "sit-ins" wherever local laws separated black people from white people. The "freedom-riders" were attacked and ill-treated, too, but they refused to hit back. Many people admired them for this and supported them.

But the campaign was not always successful. It was hard for negroes not to seek revenge when they were hated and attacked by bitter white people. Dr. King taught them that hate is always bad—it hurts the person who hates, as well as those he hates. But would his way of peace and love really work?

In 1963 Dr. King went to the city of Birmingham, in the State of Alabama, where negroes were despised and often treated unjustly. "We are heading for freedom land and nothing is going to stop us", he told the black people of the town. But nine days later Dr. King was in prison, with many of his followers, and the news spread round the world.

Some people said that this campaign for the rights of black

citizens was foolish—they should wait patiently, and not cause public disorder. Dr. King replied to them from prison, reminding them how many long years negroes had already waited for their rights as equal citizens. How hard it is to wait, he said, "When you try to explain to your six-year-old daughter why she can't go to the public amusement park that has just been advertised on television, and see tears welling up when she is told that Funtown is closed to coloured children. . . . When you have to make up an answer for a five-year-old son asking, 'Daddy, why do white people treat coloured people so mean?' . . . When you have to sleep night after night in your car because no motel will accept you. . . . When you are humbled day in and day out by nagging signs reading 'white' men and 'coloured'. . . . When your first name becomes 'nigger', and your middle name becomes 'boy', however old you are, and your last name becomes 'John'. . . . When your wife and mother are never given the respected title 'Mrs.'. . . . When you are always fighting the feeling of being a 'nobody' ".

Dr. King was released from prison on bail, and the campaign went on in the town. A children's march to the City Hall was planned. They gathered in church, and sang the famous hymn of the campaign—*We Shall Overcome*. But when they set out the police were waiting for them, and nearly a thousand children were imprisoned. Again, next day, children gathered at the church. But when they tried to set out on their freedom-march the police turned water hoses and police dogs upon them.

By now the prisons were full, soldiers had been brought in to help the police, and angry negroes were fighting them in the streets. Television and newspapers showed the whole country what was happening. When Dr. King made an agreement with the police and businessmen of the town it was called "fair and just" by the President of the United States. Separation of white and black citizens in public places was to end, more jobs were to be open to negroes, prisoners were to be freed, and a council of white and coloured citizens was to meet regularly. The agreement was kept. But bitter white people kept up their attacks—and angry negroes fought back.

In 1963 a vast crowd of over 100,000 black citizens gathered in Washington, the capital of the United States. Dr. King spoke to them from the steps of the Memorial to Abraham Lincoln, the President who had freed the black slaves.

"I have a dream that one day this nation will rise up and live out its belief that 'all men are created equal'.

"I have a dream that my four little children will one day live in a nation where they will not be judged by the colour of their skin but by their character.

"I have a dream that one day, right down to Alabama, little black boys and black girls will be able to join hands with little white boys and white girls as sisters and brothers. . . .

"With this faith we will be able to work together, to pray together, to struggle together, to go to jail together, to stand up for freedom together, knowing that we will be free one day".

By now the fame of Dr. King had spread through the world. He was honoured in many lands, and in 1964 he was given the Nobel Peace Prize—the great, international honour awarded to those who have striven for peace and goodwill among men.

In the United States more and more laws and customs which separated black and white citizens were ended. But some States refused to change their laws. There were other negro leaders, too, who said that Dr. King's way would never work—that black citizens would only win their rights by fighting and being violent, not by peace and love. During the long, hot summers from 1963 to 1967 there were riots of violent negroes in many towns. But still Dr. King taught the way of peace and love.

In 1968 he went to the city of Memphis, in the State of Tennessee, to help negroes there. People had warned him not to go, for many threats had been made against him. He planned to lead a great, peaceful march through the town. At a rally, before the march, Dr. King spoke of the threats against his life—

"And then I got to Memphis. And some began to talk of what would happen to me from some of our sick white brothers. . . . We've got some difficult days ahead. But it really doesn't matter with me now. . . . Like anybody, I would like to live a long life, but I'm not concerned about that now. I just want to do God's will. . . ."

The next day, Dr. King was busy planning his campaign. In the early evening, he came out on to the balcony of the motel where he was staying and talked with friends in the street below. He had just finished talking with them when a bullet struck him in the face. He died in hospital, shortly after, 39 years old.

In his last sermon Dr. King had said—
"If any of you are around when I have to meet my day, I don't want a long funeral. I'd like somebody to mention that day that Martin Luther King tried to give his life serving others, and I want you to say I tried to love and serve humanity".

The news that Dr. King had been assassinated flashed through his country and around the world. Violent riots broke out in more than twenty cities in the United States. The worst of all was in Washington, the capital, where two-thirds of the people were coloured. Bitter, angry negroes wanted revenge for the murder of their leader. New leaders encouraged them, preaching hate and violence against white Americans. They formed the Black Power movement, urging their people to be proud of their race and colour, and to fight for their rights.

It might seem that Dr. King's life and work had been a failure—that his way of peace and love does not work. But men cannot live together in freedom and happiness if they are slaves to hatred and violence. Martin Luther King did not live and die in vain. His name and his message will be remembered as long as people believe that "all men have the right to Life, Liberty, and the pursuit of Happiness" because all men are created equal.